Reformation in the Low Countries, 1500–1620

This accessible general history of the Reformation in the Netherlands traces the key developments in the process of reformation – both Protestant and Catholic – across the whole of the Low Countries during the sixteenth century. Synthesizing fifty years' worth of scholarly literature, Christine Kooi focuses particularly on the political context of the era: how religious change took place against the integration and disintegration of the Habsburg composite state in the Netherlands. Special attention is given to the Reformation's role in both fomenting and fuelling the Revolt against the Habsburg regime in the later sixteenth century, as well as how it contributed to the formation of the region's two successor states, the Dutch Republic and the Southern Netherlands. *Reformation in the Low Countries, 1500–1620* is essential reading for scholars and students of early modern European history, bringing together specialized, contemporary research on the Low Countries in one volume.

Christine Kooi is the Lewis, Katheryn and Benjamin Price Professor of History at Louisiana State University. She writes on the religious history of the early modern Low Countries and is the author of *Liberty and Religion: Church and State in Leiden's Reformation* (2000) and *Calvinists and Catholics during Holland's Golden Age: Heretics and Idolaters* (Cambridge University Press, 2012), as well as numerous essays and articles.

Reformation in the Low Countries, 1500–1620

Christine Kooi

Louisiana State University

CAMBRIDGE
UNIVERSITY PRESS

CAMBRIDGE
UNIVERSITY PRESS

University Printing House, Cambridge CB2 8BS, United Kingdom

One Liberty Plaza, 20th Floor, New York, NY 10006, USA

477 Williamstown Road, Port Melbourne, VIC 3207, Australia

314–321, 3rd Floor, Plot 3, Splendor Forum, Jasola District Centre,
New Delhi – 110025, India

103 Penang Road, #05–06/07, Visioncrest Commercial, Singapore 238467

Cambridge University Press is part of the University of Cambridge.

It furthers the University's mission by disseminating knowledge in the pursuit of
education, learning, and research at the highest international levels of excellence.

www.cambridge.org
Information on this title: www.cambridge.org/9781316513521
DOI: 10.1017/9781009072793

© Christine Kooi 2022

First published 2022

A catalogue record for this publication is available from the British Library.

ISBN 978-1-316-51352-1 Hardback
ISBN 978-1-009-07395-0 Paperback

In fond memory of my grandparents,
Reformed Netherlanders all

Contents

Illustrations

Maps

Acknowledgments

I think that I have always wanted to write this book. I have wanted to write it at least since the days I roamed the stacks of Sterling Memorial Library at Yale University as a graduate student, fingering dusty volumes on the history of the Reformation in the Low Countries. A work of synthesis, however, is best done later in one's career, and so after thirty or so years of seasoning I offer this volume as an attempt to fill a lacuna in the historiography. It has been a labor of love in all the senses of those words.

First I would like to offer some institutional thanks: I am grateful to the College of Humanities and Social Sciences of Louisiana State University (LSU) for providing me with both grants and leave time to research and write this book. My particular thanks go to the Inter-library Loan Office of LSU Library for its heroic work in securing for me books on obscure topics from faraway libraries, especially during the COVID-19 pandemic. On the other side of the Atlantic I spent many happy hours working on this project in the Royal Library in The Hague, a congenial venue for scholarship of all varieties. Since 2013 I have presented portions of this work at an array of conferences and meetings in such far-flung places as San Juan, Leuven, Wittenberg, Bologna, Ghent, Dordrecht, Kampen and Grand Rapids. I warmly thank my hosts at each of these occasions for their invitations to talk about this project.

At the Free University of Amsterdam's Centre for the History and Heritage of Protestantism I finished a preliminary draft of the manuscript. My appreciation goes to my hosts, Mirjam van Veen and August den Hollander, for providing time and space for the project and for doing it so collegially. Likewise the H. H. Meeter Center for Calvin Studies at Calvin University offered me a month to complete the last touches on the manuscript before submission to Cambridge University Press. I thank Karin Maag, Paul Fields and Deborah Snider for their help during my visit. And, as ever, my heartfelt gratitude goes to René Vanhaelen for continually providing me with a home during my stays in the Netherlands.

This manuscript found a home with Cambridge University Press, a storied publishing house with which I am proud to be affiliated. My thanks go to Liz Friend-Smith of the Press for her interest in the manuscript and for her work in bringing it to fruition.

My LSU colleague Leslie Tuttle and Mirjam van Veen of the Free University of Amsterdam kindly read, from very different perspectives, an early iteration of the manuscript. Bits and pieces of it have also been read by Lee Wandel, Jesse Spohnholz and the members of the online workgroup affectionately known as "Paapse Stoutigheden." All of their comments have improved the manuscript substantially, and I appreciate their taking the time to read my work. My thanks also to the Winter Writing Group of Ray Ball, Kathleen Comerford and Liz Lehfeldt for the occasional and much-needed cheerleading as I slogged through the writing process.

This book rests on the work of many fine scholars on both sides of the Atlantic, some of whom I have known personally. My special thanks go to Alastair Duke for encouraging me in this endeavor from the beginning; he appreciates better than most how complicated an undertaking this has been. The time I have spent working on this book was punctuated by the presidency of the Sixteenth Century Studies Conference in 2017; it was a privilege to shepherd, briefly, such a vital and convivial community of scholars of all things early modern.

Over the course of thirty years working in the field of Netherlandish history, I have had many colleagues in early modern European history ask me to recommend a good overview on the Reformation in the Low Countries. It took some time, but I hope this work will provide them with at least some of the insight they sought.

A Note on Nomenclature

This book is about a place that has historically been difficult to name. It uses the terms "Low Countries," "Netherlands" and "Netherlandish" interchangeably to describe the collection of territories that in sixteenth-century Europe was tucked in between the western border of the Holy Roman Empire and the northern border of the kingdom of France. This region corresponds roughly to the present-day Netherlands, Belgium and Luxemburg, as well as to northern parts of the French Republic. Today these are of course all sovereign states, but back then they were mostly gathered under the composite monarchy of the Habsburg dynasty and so here they are referred to as the "Habsburg Netherlands." The adjective "Dutch" is limited to those parts and peoples of the region that were either Dutch-speaking or that came under the control of insurgents starting in the 1570s, provinces that formed the nucleus of the eventual Dutch Republic. Those parts of the region that remained under or were restored to Habsburg control in the later 1500s are referred to as the "Southern" or "archducal" Netherlands. "Reformation" is used as a shorthand, nonsectarian term for the many momentous and enduring religious changes that took place during this period: the rebellion against the established church and the concomitant emergence of new types of Christianity, as well as the reinvigoration of Catholicism.

Abbreviations

AGKKN	*Archief voor de Geschiedenis van de Katholieke Kerk in Nederland*
AGN	*Algemene Geschiedenis der Nederlanden*
AHN	*Acta Historiae Neerlandica*
ARG	*Archiv für Reformationsgeschichte*
BMGN	*Bijdragen en Mededelingen betreffende de Geschiedenis der Nederlanden*
BRN	*Bibliotheca Reformatoria Neerlandica*
NAGN	*Nieuwe Algemene Geschiedenis der Nederlanden*
NAKG	*Nederlands Archief voor Kerkgeschiedenis*
SCJ	*Sixteenth Century Journal*
TvG	*Tijdschrift voor Geschiedenis*

Introduction

On the morning of the first day of July in the year 1523, the Grand Place of Brussels was scene to an unusual event. Before the city's resplendent late Gothic town hall, as crowds gathered, a procession of mendicant monks bearing banners and crosses solemnly entered the square. They were followed by theologians from the University of Leuven, mitered abbots and other high dignitaries of church and state, who assembled on a platform constructed in front of the town hall. Shortly thereafter a young Augustinian monk, dressed in full priestly vestments, was brought out to the platform and made to kneel before an altar placed there. Behind him a Franciscan friar preached a sermon to the assembled onlookers. At the same time a bishop slowly and methodically stripped the Augustinian of his clerical regalia in a solemn act of degradation. Two more Augustinians were brought out to the square to receive the same treatment; all of them underwent their ordeal calmly and without resistance. Having been publicly defrocked, they were then asked by an inquisitor to renounce the errors of which they had been convicted, but they refused. The inquisitor then handed them over to the custody of the worldly authorities in the city hall, who not long afterward brought two of them out again to a pyre erected in the middle of the square and tied them to a stake. Once more they were asked to repudiate their heresies and again they refused, declaring that they wished to die as true Christians. To some observers they almost seemed cheerful. As the flames slowly consumed them, they were heard singing the *Te Deum* and the *Credo*.[1] Their executions were the climax of a powerful moment of high ceremony that symbolically united church, city and state in the purgation of heresy from the Christian community.

What beliefs had brought these two Antwerp Augustinians, Hendrick Vos and Johannes van den Esschen, to their deaths? According to their accusers, the monks were guilty of erroneous thinking on at least sixty-two points of Christian doctrine. The men had declared, among other things,

---

[1] Cramer and Pijper, *BRN*, pp. 35–36.

1

that Holy Scripture was the only true authority for Christian faith, that any ecclesiastical institution not resting on scriptural foundations was improper, that there were only three legitimate sacraments (baptism, communion and confession), that salvation came through the grace of Jesus Christ alone, that the Eucharist should be served to the laity in both kinds, and that purgatory probably did not exist. They had even reportedly told their confessors, "We believe in God and in one Christian church. We do not believe in your church."[2] From these assertions the inquisitors had concluded that the men were guilty of Lutheran heresy.[3]

The executions made a deep impression on contemporary observers. Reading of their deaths in Basel, the humanist scholar Desiderius Erasmus commented in a letter to the reformer Huldrych Zwingli in Zurich on the friars' "exemplary and unheard-of determination," and even six years after the event he still wrote with evident feeling about it, admiring the composure with which the men reportedly went to their deaths.[4] The Saxon reformer Martin Luther, upon hearing of the executions of his fellow Augustinians Vos and Van den Esschen, immediately claimed them as martyrs to the cause of reformation, writing a letter of encouragement to Netherlandish evangelicals extolling "those two precious jewels of Christ, Henry and John, [who] have held their lives of no account in Brussels in order that Christ and his Word might be glorified," and even composing a hymn commemorating their deaths.[5] The Antwerp monastic house to which Vos and Van den Esschen belonged was part of the Saxon province of the Augustinian Eremite order, Luther's own province, and it had close ties to Wittenberg.[6]

Between 1518 and 1522 the Antwerp cloister's prior had been Jacob Praepositus, a sympathizer with Luther, whose evangelical preaching was so deeply felt that he won the admiration of Erasmus and the hostility of inquisitorial authorities.[7] It was thanks to dissenters like Praepositus, Vos and Van den Esschen that Lutheran and Zwinglian notions of church reform had spread in the early 1520s within the bustling city of Antwerp, the foremost commercial metropolis of the Netherlands. To their sympathizers who witnessed their execution in Brussels it was immediately apparent that Vos and Van den Esschen had died for their faith.[8] For their

---

[2] Cramer and Pijper, *BRN*, pp. 16–17.   [3] Cramer and Pijper, *BRN*, pp. 39–43.
[4] Estes, *The Correspondence of Erasmus*, no. 1384, p. 81; Allen, *Opus Epistolarum Des Erasmi Roterodami*, no. 2188, pp. 211–212.
[5] Tappert, *Luther*, p. 193; Akerboom and Gielis, "'A New Song Shall Begin Here . . . .'"
[6] Vercruysse, "De Antwerpse augustijnen en de lutherse Reformatie."
[7] Vercruysse, "De Antwerpse augustijnen en de lutherse Reformatie," p. 199.
[8] Decavele, "Vroege Reformatorische Bedrijvigheid in de Grote Nederlandse Steden," p. 16.

pains the latter two monks ended up becoming the Netherlands' first Protestant martyrs.

And not only the Netherlands. As a tradition of martyrology developed across Protestant Europe by the mid-sixteenth century, its authors and compilers claimed Hendrick Vos and Johannes van den Esschen as the Reformation's protomartyrs, the first people in Europe to be put to death for espousing identifiably Protestant beliefs.[9] Almost six years after Martin Luther's initial protest in Wittenberg, two years after his condemnation as a heretic and a rebel at the Diet of Worms, these two Antwerp friars were celebrated by evangelical dissenters as the first Christians to give up their lives for the sake of the movement calling for church reform that he had first ignited.[10]

The fact that the two men who were later deemed the Reformation's first martyrs were killed in the Netherlands was not mere chance. The Netherlands were the patrimonial lands of the powerful Holy Roman Emperor Charles V, scion of the house of Habsburg, and here he had a freer political and legal hand to fight heresy than in the German-speaking territories of the Empire where dissident reformers were first active. With great determination Charles mobilized all the considerable juridical apparatus at his disposal to suppress what he and most people regarded as Luther's dangerously heretical ideas in his family lands. Already in 1520 he issued an edict banning the publication of heretical books in the Netherlands, and the University of Leuven had responded by publicly burning some of Luther's writings. More such decrees followed, and in 1522 Charles further authorized the formation of an inquisition to root out and exterminate heresy in the Low Countries. This inquisitorial regime, supported and abetted by the Catholic Church, claimed the lives of Vos and Van den Esschen and approximately two thousand others by the end of the sixteenth century.

The executions of Hendrick Vos and Johannes van den Esschen thus highlight one of the distinctive features of the Reformation in the Low Countries, the very well-organized and sustained judicial persecution it provoked. For at least the first fifty years of their existence the various Protestant movements in the Netherlands were harassed, hounded, pursued and persecuted by a strict government campaign against heresy. More than thirteen hundred people would be executed for heresy in the Netherlands between 1523 and 1566. During the same time in France, a kingdom with nine times the population and equally roiled by religious

---

[9] On the evolution of a martyrological tradition in the Protestant Reformation, see Gregory, *Salvation at Stake*, pp. 139–196.

[10] Christman, "Early Modern German Historians Confront the Reformation's First Executions," pp. 245–250.

dissent, about five hundred people would be killed.[11] That early and prolonged history of illegality, danger and oppression influenced the character of the various Protestant churches that later won legitimacy in what became the Dutch Republic. In the immediate post-Reformation era Mennonite and Reformed churches continued to harbor ambivalent attitudes toward the society and polity in which they found themselves, and they spent the better part of the seventeenth century slowly settling into the republican regime. Likewise Catholics in the Low Countries found themselves subject to persecution in those regions where Protestants gained ascendancy, suffering banishment, exile, violence and imprisonment. The memory of persecution, suffering and violence remained a long one for all parties involved and deeply colored the various confessions' relationships with each other and with political authority.

Another notable feature of the Netherlandish Reformation this incident reveals was how these religious protests were very much reformations from below.[12] The Habsburg government's reaction to religious dissent was so harsh in part because there was popular sympathy to evangelical ideas evident among the Low Countries' inhabitants; calls for church reform had been echoing in the Netherlands since the beginning of the century, if not earlier, at all levels of society. Vos and Van den Esschen were ordinary monks who harbored and taught risky ideas; they were not men of power or authority. The Netherlandish Reformation was in many respects an oppositional movement, not one imposed by princely or magisterial authority, as was the case in many imperial territories, the Scandinavian monarchies or the kingdom of England. There was deep sympathy within significant sectors of the population for serious religious change and church reform, and it was from those wellsprings of sentiment that reformation first arose. Very few Netherlanders advocated heresy, but many of them saw in the established church considerable room for improvement.

This vignette also underscores another characteristic of the Netherlandish Reformation – its deeply international character. The two friars burned in Brussels had ties to evangelical movements flourishing in the European hinterland far from the Netherlands. Perhaps more so than any other region of northern Europe, the sixteenth-century Low Countries, by virtue of both geography and economy, were broadly open to foreign influence. That the first stirrings of religious dissent were found in Antwerp, the region's commercial hub into which virtually all European commodities (including books and ideas) flowed, made

[11] Benedict, *Christ's Churches Purely Reformed*, p. 177.   [12] Israel, *Dutch Republic*, p. 74.

perfect sense. That outside influence remained a factor in the evolution of religious reform in this region. Throughout its history the Netherlandish Reformation would be in constant conversation with religious influences, Protestant and Catholic alike, from abroad, be they from the Empire, the Swiss cities, France or Rome.

A final peculiarity of the Reformation in the Low Countries is that it led, unexpectedly, to the creation of an entirely new state, the Dutch Republic or United Provinces. Nowhere else in Europe did the religiously charged wars of the sixteenth century result, however haphazardly and unintentionally, in such a redrawing of the political map. To be sure, initially the separation of the seven northern Netherlandish provinces from the Habsburg *imperium* starting in the 1570s was nothing more than the consequence of military happenstance; there was no expectation that permanent independence for some provinces would be the final outcome. That this ultimately proved to be the case was due at least in part to the fierceness of the confessional passions and discord the Reformation had unleashed – for many decades neither side was willing to concede either ground or principle. Those passions were greatly fueled by spectacles such as occurred on the Grand Place of Brussels on the first day of July in 1523.

The history written about the sixteenth-century Low Countries has been dominated by two themes: religion and war. In the historiographical literature of the past half-century the Netherlandish Reformation (religion) and the Netherlandish Revolt (war) have developed a peculiar relationship with each other. When it comes to surveys, broad overviews and general treatments, the Reformation in the Low Countries is almost invariably eclipsed by the wars (only half-accurately called the "Dutch" Revolt) it helped in part to incur. In the predominant narrative arc the Reformation happens until about 1566 and then the Revolt entirely takes over the story. In this scheme religious dissent and protest serve principally as prologues to conflict and then somewhere around 1566 elide with hardly a trace into political and military accounts of the wars (despite the fact that religious questions continued to plague the politics of the period well after 1566). In 1977 Geoffrey Parker first published his pathbreaking *The Dutch Revolt*, which novelly (and controversially) placed the Netherlandish wars squarely in a larger Spanish geopolitical context; while his narrative explains the role religious discontent played in the origins and the course of the Revolt, it is primarily focused on political and military questions.[13]The most recent

---

[13] Parker, *Dutch Revolt*.

synthetic accounts of Netherlandish history have tended to follow this pattern. W. P. Blockmans's treatment of the "Habsburg century" of Netherlandish history in Blom and Lambert's *History of the Low Countries*, for example, devotes a scant three pages to the subject of the Reformation before moving on to an account of the Revolt three times as long.[14] Jonathan Israel's magisterial *The Dutch Republic* devotes only one chapter to the "early Dutch" Reformation up to 1565 but four to the subsequent Revolt (which themselves contain occasional discussions of religious issues).[15] Paul Arblaster's *A History of the Low Countries* narrates the Reformation up to 1566 and then with the iconoclastic riots of that year turns to a largely political-military description of the wars.[16] Most even-handed is Groenveld and Schutte's textbook *Delta 2: Nederlands verleden in vogelvlucht. De nieuwe tijd: 1500–1813 (A Bird's-Eye View of the Dutch Past)*, which dedicates a chapter each to the Reformation and the Revolt, though here again the former is treated up to roughly 1570 and then the latter takes over the story.[17] The second edition of the *General History of the Netherlands* published around 1980 does address the Netherlandish Reformation, but only in chapters devoted to six-teenth- and seventeenth-century religious history more generally.[18] James C. Kennedy's more recent survey *A Concise History of the Netherlands* largely subsumes the story of sixteenth-century religious change within chapters about Habsburg centralization and the revolt against it.[19] Juliaan Woltjer's *Op weg naar tachtig jaar oorlog (The Path to the Eighty Years' War)* can be summarized by its subtitle: "The Story of the Century in which Our Land Began."[20] More than most treat-ments of the Netherlandish sixteenth century, it pays a great deal of attention to religious developments, but in the end its chief interest, the creation of an independent Dutch state, remains political. It remains the case that in most of the recent literature on the Netherlands in the 1500s religion is quickly superseded by war.

Synthetic works dealing with the general religious history of the Netherlands treat the Reformation era more directly and extensively, of course, but still not in ways that are fully comprehensive. Even in these

---

[14] Blom and Lambert, *History of the Low Countries*, pp. 129–140.
[15] Israel, *Dutch Republic*, chaps. 5, 7–10.
[16] Arblaster, *History of the Low Countries*, pp. 113–131.
[17] Groenveld and Schutte, *Delta 2: Nederlands verleden in vogelvlucht*, chaps. 5 and 8.
[18] Blok et al., *AGN*, vols. 5, 6.
[19] Kennedy, *Concise History of the Netherlands*, pp. 112–135.
[20] Woltjer, *Op weg aar tachtig jaar oorlog*.

accounts a more holistic narrative is still lacking. Otto de Jong's 1972 institutional history *Nederlandse Kerkgeschiedenis* devotes several chapters to the period, primarily concentrating on the various Protestant movements, and the southern Netherlands effectively disappears from this account after the Habsburg reconquests of 1585.[21] Two more recent overviews, one focused on church history, stressing institutions and doctrines, and the other on religious history, with a more broadly cultural and social perspective, also give the Reformation a distinctly Protestant and northern-Netherlandish cast.[22] Both overviews describe sixteenth-century reformation primarily as a reaction to (or against) the Catholic Church, even though it was a phenomenon that also took place within that church, and both confine their narratives to the boundaries of the modern Dutch nation-state.

Recent syntheses that are more specifically devoted to the history of the sixteenth-century Netherlands have been exclusively about the Revolt.[23] The Reformation in the Netherlands per se, related to but distinct from the Netherlandish wars, has not been the subject of a general, book-length survey since the distinguished University of Liège historian Léon-Ernest Halkin published *La Réforme en Belgique sous Charles-Quint* in 1957.[24] Halkin's account, brief in both length and chronology, extends no further than the end of the reign of Charles V in 1555. The English historian Alastair Duke's seminal *Reformation and Revolt in the Low Countries*, published in 1990, makes a nod in the direction of a survey but is a collection of essays chronologically arranged rather than a true synthesis.[25] The closest we have to a modern general account of the Netherlandish Reformation is the collection of essays in the catalogue accompanying the exhibition *Ketters en papen onder Filips II* (*Heretics and Papists under Philip II*), which was organized by the Catharijneconvent Museum in Utrecht in 1986.[26] Its individual essays are insightful, but as a collection it lacks the narrative cohesion of a single account. Likewise the essays assembled in the 2017 volume *De Reformatie*, commemorating the five hundredth anniversary of Luther's initial protest, treat a variety of topics about the Reformation and the Netherlands, but not as a unified synthesis.[27] In 2012 Huib Noordzij published *Handbook van de*

---

[21] De Jong, *Nederlandse Kerkgeschiedenis*.
[22] Selderhuis, *Handboek Nederlandse kerkgeschiedenis*; Van Eijnatten and Van Lieburg, *Nederlandse religiegeschiedenis*.
[23] See, for example, Darby, *Origins and Development of the Dutch Revolt*; Limm, *Dutch Revolt*; Van der Lem, *Revolt in the Netherlands*; Arnade, *Beggars, Iconoclasts and Civic Patriots*; Woltjer, *Op weg naar tachtig jaar oorlog*.
[24] Halkin, *La Réforme en Belgique sous Charles-Quint*.
[25] Duke, *Reformation and Revolt in the Low Countries*.
[26] Dirkse, *Ketters en papen onder Filips II*.   [27] Van Leeuwenberg et al., *De Reformatie*.

*Reformatie: De Nederlandse kerkhervorming in de zestiende en zeventiende
eeuw (Handbook of the Reformation: Dutch Church Reform in the Sixteenth
and Seventeenth Centuries)*; the work's expansive title belies the fact that it
is not really about the Reformation itself but instead is mostly
a confessionally tinted history of the early modern Dutch Reformed
church.[28] In the past two decades a number of important essays and
book chapters have appeared briefly relating the general history of the
Netherlandish Reformation, but no extended monographic treatments.[29]

That this should be the case is perhaps not surprising, for as a historical
phenomenon the Netherlandish Reformation was decidedly inchoate,
fragmented, eclectic and chaotic, certainly more a congeries of reformations than a single process. This was due to the nature of the Low
Countries themselves. For such a small region, with a population of at
most three million at the mid-sixteenth century, the Low Countries
proved surprisingly diverse, linguistically, socially, culturally, economically and legally. The Burgundian dukes who in the later Middle Ages
labored to fashion a coherent union out of these lands could not come up
with a more comprehensive name for the region than "the lands over
here."[30] Those lands comprised a host of discrete and prickly sovereignties, powers, privileges and customs that the Burgundian and later
Habsburg lords who nominally ruled them interfered with at their
own risk; it was a composite state with a minimal central government. One might say that the Netherlanders of the sixteenth century
enjoyed too much liberty for us to generalize about them easily.[31] Or,
to paraphrase the British historian J. S. Bromley, Netherlandish
history is very much the sum of its local histories.[32] The diffused
nature of the Low Countries' polity made their reformations equally
fissiparous; religious upheavals that afflicted urban Flanders, for
example, were barely felt in rural Luxemburg. As Alastair Duke has
aptly noted, "One cannot write an adequate account of the
Reformation in the Low Countries from the standpoint of
Brussels."[33] The history of religious change in this region is therefore
exceedingly complicated because it is highly variegated.

---

[28] Noordzij, *Handboek van de Reformatie*.
[29] Marnef, "The Netherlands"; Leeuwenberg, "De religie omstreeks 1559"; Bergsma,
"The Low Countries"; Spaans, "Reform in the Low Countries"; Woltjer and Mout,
"Settlements."
[30] Blockmans and Prevenier, *Burgundian Netherlands*, p. 9.
[31] My thanks to Thomas A. Brady Jr., who shared this observation with me in conversation.
[32] The original quote is: "Dutch history, more than any other, is the sum of local histories."
Bromley, "Rise and Fall of the Dutch Republic," p. 987.
[33] Duke, *Reformation and Revolt*, p. x.

National sentiment has been another hindrance to a fashioning a cohesive account of the Netherlandish Reformation. The region's wars of the late sixteenth and early seventeenth centuries, fueled in part by religious discord, resulted eventually in the emergence of two distinct states whose present-day descendants are the kingdoms of Belgium and the Netherlands. This in turn has resulted in the development of two separate sets of national historiography.[34] Later historians looked through a presentist lens to explain the religious upheavals of the period. In the nineteenth century especially, historians in both states were at pains to portray the events of the sixteenth-century Low Countries in a national light, trying to discern in them the origin of their national identity, be it Dutch or Belgian. Thus Dutch historians, for example, tried hard to demonstrate what was distinctively and natively "Dutch" about the Reformation in the Low Countries, particularly in its early stages, while Belgian historians used sixteenth-century religious history as fodder in contemporary political debates between liberals and Catholics.[35]Many of these accounts confined themselves to the geographic parameters of the two modern states, as if a north–south divide existed before the Revolt. They were attempts to uncover a national past out of a time when neither of those two nation-states existed. As Nicolette Mout has pointed out, national history is an anachronistic framework upon which to construct a history of the sixteenth-century Netherlands.[36] Until rebellion and civil war permanently split the region into two polities toward the very end of the sixteenth century, the Low Countries were of a piece, a fractious collection of discrete sovereignties tenuously gathered under a single ambitious dynasty, and should be understood in that way.[37]

Further confounding the historiographic picture, besides nationalism, was of course religious conviction. The sectarian writing of Reformation history, whether Catholic or Protestant, colored its historiography well into the first half of the twentieth century.[38] For a long time, depending on the confessional allegiance of the historian, the Reformation tended to be portrayed as either triumph or disaster. Belgian and Dutch historians were not immune from this trend. Catholic Church historians writing in Belgium in the nineteenth century highlighted the perseverance and eventual triumph of the traditional church against the onslaught of heresy

[34] Soen, "Which Religious History?" pp. 764–769.
[35] Nauta, "De reformatie in Nederland in de historiografie," p. 214; Vercauteren, *Cent ans d'histoire nationale en Belgique*, pp. 178–179; Tollebeek, "Enthousiasme en evidentie."
[36] Mout, "Reformation, Revolt and Civil Wars," p. 23; De Schepper, *Belgium Nostrum*, p. 2.
[37] A point underscored recently by Beyen, Pollmann and Te Velde, *De Lage Landen*, pp. 7–13.
[38] Dickens and Tonkin, *The Reformation in Historical Thought*, especially chaps. 5–8.

and celebrated the role the Habsburg government played in bringing about Catholic restoration.[39] Meanwhile in the kingdom of the Netherlands the neo-Calvinist revival of the nineteenth century ushered in a wave of confessional histories written by Reformed scholars celebrating the triumph of the Reformed Church and underscoring the "naturally" Calvinist character of the Dutch people.[40] Not to be outdone, non-Reformed Dutch historians in turn argued instead that the native religious character of the Dutch was spiritualist, Erasmian and tolerant and that Calvinism was a foreign theology imposed by a state-supported religious minority (on this latter point they were joined by Dutch Catholic historians).[41] This kind of sectarian historiography, in both kingdoms, was at least as much about contemporary confessional competition and identity as it was about religious turmoil in the sixteenth century.

The secularized, post-confessional history writing that started emerging in the post–World War Two era largely left these kinds of essentialist arguments behind in favor of more neutral and more specialized approaches. The gradual secularization of Dutch and Belgian society was accompanied by a parallel historiographical secularization, one that considered social, economic, cultural and political factors and not just doctrine as determinants of religious change. This new perspective drove historians to concentrate on particular circumstances to explain the nature of religious transformation in the sixteenth-century Low Countries, and that in turn caused them to narrow their analytic lenses down to the level of locality. The general character of contemporary historical research on the early modern Low Countries has thus also discouraged the construction of any kind of general, synthetic history of the Netherlandish Reformation. Grand narratives, so beloved of nineteenth- and early twentieth-century historians, have long ago been eschewed for painstaking archival research in the rich repositories of the contemporary kingdoms of Belgium and the Netherlands.[42] Specialization prevails, driven along by its motor the local study. The themes of locality and diversity predominate and current research favors the particular over the general.[43] Depth has been favored over breadth and this has enriched our knowledge of the Netherlandish Reformation

[39] Soen, "Which Religious History?" pp. 767–768.
[40] Van Veen, "Tegen 'papery en slaverny'"; Van Rooden, *Religieuze Regimes*, pp. 147–168.
[41] Soen, "Which Religious History?" pp. 765–767.
[42] Janse, "The Protestant Reformation in the Low Countries"; Decavele, "Historiografie van het zestiende-eeuws Protestantisme in Belgie."
[43] Pollmann, "The Low Countries"; Cloet, "Een kwarteeuw historische produktie in België betreffende de religieuze geschiedenis van de Nieuwe Tijd."

considerably. Many important and groundbreaking local studies have appeared in the past fifty years, often focusing on a particular city or region or even an individual. The sheer variety of stories and experiences these case studies have brought to the fore has been dizzying, if not intimidating. They have also been absolutely critical in bringing nuance and subtlety to our understanding of religious dissent and reform in the Netherlands.[44] They have revealed that those earlier grand narratives, for all their sweep and brio, were very problematic indeed when it came to accuracy and interpretation. The very abundance of such specialized studies has also made it that much more difficult to step back from the archival trees and survey the whole historical forest.

Given all these caveats, it is small wonder that few historians since the redoubtable Léon-Ernst Halkin have attempted to take stock of the Netherlandish Reformation in all its bewildering and vertiginous complexity. Nevertheless a survey of the Reformation in the Low Countries, synthesizing the extraordinarily rich research published since the 1960s, is long past due.[45] What this book proposes to offer is not so much a grand narrative as a useful one, one that digests and interprets what a half-century of hard work by many fine scholars has to tell us about the field of early modern European religion more generally. Like all narratives, it is constructed and thus to that degree artificial, but it also provides a wider perspective that will perhaps enliven our understanding of the tangled events of this particular time and place. It makes a break with current historiographic practice by disentangling, at least to some extent, the Reformation in the Netherlands from the Revolt in the Netherlands. Politics will not disappear; in fact the central contention of this book is that the political environment of the sixteenth-century Low Countries determined the course and outcomes of reformation there. It also argues, however, that the opposite was true: religious events, questions and developments in turn affected the political outcomes of the Netherlandish wars. This book's primary concern, however, is with religion; the Revolt was first and foremost political in nature, a contest over political control, though religious dissent would certainly fuel both its direction and intensity. The wars will of course be considered in their context, but the focus of this book is on the trajectory of religious change that began with the first dissensions from the established church in the early sixteenth century and ended with the emergence of two separate

[44] Kooi, "The Netherlands"; Marnef, "Belgian and Dutch Postwar Historiography"; Soen and Knevel, "Slingerbewegingen."
[45] Duke, *Reformation and Revolt*, p. x. For an overview of the recent literature focusing primarily on the later sixteenth century and the Dutch Republic, see the introduction to Kaplan, *Reformation and the Practice of Religious Toleration*, pp. 1–26.

states with distinct confessional identities by about 1620. It will also, in keeping with sixteenth-century understandings, span the whole of the Low Countries, roughly the present-day states of the Netherlands, Belgium and Luxemburg, rather than focus on merely one or the other of the region's successor states, the Dutch Republic or the Southern Netherlands. It thus gives the Netherlandish Reformation its own distinct story, one that certainly includes the turbulent politics of the era but opts to focus specifically on religious developments. Returning to the Netherlandish Reformation its own narrative offers a fresh perspective, one that is mindful of local differences yet also presents a broader tableau of religious transformation. It also follows the wider current of contemporary early modern European historiography as understanding "Reformation" not so much as an exclusively Protestant phenomenon, but as an umbrella category for the host of challenges, transformations, upheavals and conflicts that afflicted sixteenth-century Latin Christendom more generally and that led to its permanent fragmentation. Reformation in this sense is about religious change more broadly rather than just its Protestant outcomes.

The book starts by setting the context, the Low Countries at the beginning of the sixteenth century, in Chapter 1. Like the rest of early modern Europe this was a world of composites and contrasts: at once urban and rural, French and Dutch, prosperous and struggling, proudly self-governing yet subject to powerful princes. Its many sovereignties, some of them splendidly rich, chafed against the ambitions of a dynamic and ambitious princely dynasty. It was a world where late medieval Christian religious devotion flourished in all its dazzling variety, yet that also harbored among its literate elites some of the traditional church's sharpest critics. There was certainly a lot of criticism of the church in the air, but not much in the way of heresy. In this environment, however, the sustained evangelical protest that arose out of the German-speaking lands to the east and southeast by 1520 found so much resonance and soon grew so radical that in reaction a powerful judicial regime was constructed to suppress it, as described in Chapter 2. These early reformation movements were inchoate, eclectic and disorganized, picking and choosing what they liked among the various evangelical notions that spread across central Europe in the 1520s and 1530s. Some of them wanted to break with the church, but many preferred to hope for reform from within. To the established church and the central authorities, however, they were all dangerously heretical and needed to be curbed before they grew out of hand. When indeed one stream within these groups, fired up by the prevailing apocalyptic mood, opted for an alarmingly militant and millenarian set of ideas and tried violently to act on them, anxious political authorities nearly persecuted Netherlandish religious dissenters out of existence by late 1530s and 1540s.

By mid-century, however, as described in Chapter 3, underground reforming movements, both within and without the Catholic Church, persisted in the region despite the ongoing suppression. They retained their eclectic and protean quality, but among some of them we see the beginnings of a kind of confessional turn, as more and more of them published and articulated their beliefs in confessions or statements of doctrine, thereby highlighting more of the differences among them. Among the dissenters the two most significant, distinctive streams to emerge were the Mennonites/Doopgezinden and the Reformed; at the same time, the Tridentine reforms of the Catholic Church were making themselves felt locally as new religious orders were introduced and local bishoprics were rearranged. In this ongoing search for identity three broad Christian reforming movements thus began to distinguish themselves – Mennonite, Reformed and Catholic. To be sure, boundaries among these three movements could still be quite porous, but the lines between them were becoming more visible. Despite the efforts of "middle groups" and religiously neutral parties to bridge common ground among reform-minded Netherlanders, the confessional turn exacerbated religious confusion and difference precisely at a time when political discontent with the Habsburg overlordship was also growing. As the Reformed movement in particular grew more aggressive and garnered more support it converged with the expanding political opposition to King Philip II's centralizing policies. As Chapter 4 relates, the late 1560s saw a turning point – during the "wonder year" of 1566 the Reformed understanding of the gospel was for the first time openly preached, and Catholic churches were attacked in an iconoclastic rage. Protest turned to violence, and opposition turned to revolt. The government's harsh and persecutory backlash against this brief and heady eruption of religious freedom drove its evangelical and political opponents into a ongoing if sometimes bumpy alliance with each other against the Habsburg regime – reformation yoked itself to revolt. With religious rebellion now came war.

The Revolt of the Netherlands, by the time it broke out in earnest in the late 1560s, was by turns (and sometimes at once) a rebellion, a civil war, a religious war and a great power conflict. Bloodshed, destruction and displacement were widespread, regardless of confession. Both Catholic and Protestant Netherlanders found themselves forced to flee to foreign safe havens during various periods during the wars, and for some of them this proved a formative experience in that they found spaces in which they could worship without fear of persecution. In exile the most militant among the Reformed Protestants imagined various schemes for godly reformation should they ever be allowed to return to their homelands. The wars were to these most zealous Protestants fought for the sake of religion, which often led to uneasy relationships with their noble patrons and magisterial allies in the political opposition, who saw the conflict primarily as a struggle for liberty against Habsburg overreach. When the political rebels gained control of large parts of the northern Netherlands in the 1570s and 1580s, the Reformed parlayed their support for the rebellion into a guarantee of a monopoly on religious expression there. Reformed Protestants were a distinct minority, but their activism and organization won them ecclesiastical domination in the areas under rebel control, areas in which most inhabitants were still Catholic. Abortive attempts at brokering religious peace among different confessional groups failed in this highly charged atmosphere, and the Catholic leaders within the political opposition grew increasingly alienated from Reformed zealotry. By 1579 the rebel coalition, for a few brief years united in its distrust of the Habsburgs, faltered over the question of religion.

With the opposition in disarray, the Spanish reconquest of lands once held by rebels took on steam in the 1580s and by the beginning of the seventeenth century the war had stalemated along a rough north–south frontier just south of the river Rhine. Chapter 5 explains how out of this military circumstance gradually grew more fixed political and religious boundaries, even though the wars would go on in fits and starts until the middle of the century. The lands held or reclaimed by the Habsburgs – roughly the ten southern provinces of the Low Countries – were also re-Catholicized along Tridentine models and became a bulwark of Catholic Europe. The lands that threw off Habsburg control – the seven northern Netherlandish provinces – developed into what became known as the Dutch Republic and adopted an officially Reformed Protestant religious identity. In effect, two new confessional states, one Catholic and the other Reformed, emerged out of the chaos of revolt and reformation; the consequence of dissent and war was, ultimately, schism. In the course of a hundred years the Reformation in the Low Countries led, however unintentionally, to a redrawing of the European political map. One polity would restore a vibrant and reformed Catholicism to its population; the other privileged the Reformed Church while allowing a wide variety of other faiths to flourish within it unofficially. Both states would forge distinct religious identities that would mark their history for centuries afterward. By 1620 the story of one Netherlandish reformation became two, and religious developments in both countries subsequently followed very different trajectories.

1 The Netherlands in the Early Sixteenth Century

"The Lands Over Here"

Nestled in the far western corner of the vast plain that stretches across northern Europe lie the Netherlands, or Low Countries. In the early sixteenth century these lands comprised, very roughly, the modern-day states of Belgium, Luxemburg and the Netherlands, as well as north-ern bits of the French Republic. The dominant geographic feature of this region is water, both maritime and riverine. The North Sea laps the region's coast from the southwest tip of Flanders to the eastern reaches of Groningen, while the great rivers Rhine, Maas (Meuse) and Scheldt flow through its central sections, forming a broad estuarial landscape that gradually rises southeastward from the sea toward the highlands of the Ardennes. The Low Countries therefore comprise three major geographic zones: the coastal plains, the river valleys of the center and the uplands of the southeast.[1] Water and land wrested from water form indelible marks on the region's topography; large portions of the coastal zone lie below sea level and were only made inhabitable in the Middle Ages thanks to large-scale and long-term drainage, dredging and diking. "The sea," wrote the Italian observer Lodovico Guicciardini, a long-time resident of the region in the six-teenth century, "may well be termed not only a neighbor but also a member of these Low Countries."[2]

In this diverse and watery geography lived approximately three million people by the middle of the sixteenth century.[3] Three million people inhabiting such a relatively small space, about the same geographic area as Scotland, made the Low Countries one of the most crowded regions of Europe, rivaling northern Italy in the density of its inhabitants. Two-thirds of this population lived in the western provinces of Flanders, Brabant, Holland, Zeeland and Hainaut; at the beginning of the sixteenth

[1] Blom and Lamberts, *History of the Low Countries*, p. 2.
[2] Guicciardini, *The Description of the Low Countreys*, fol. 9r.
[3] Van Houtte, *Economic History of the Low Countries*, p. 126.

15

Map 1.1 The Low Countries in 1566

century more than a quarter of it lived in Flanders alone.[4] These regions had population densities of as much as thirty-five people per square kilometer.[5] Urbanization rates, as a consequence, were very high in the western provinces: nearly a third of the populations of Flanders, Brabant, the Tournaisis and Hainaut and almost half of the population of Holland lived in towns and cities.[6] The metropolis of Antwerp, the Netherlands' biggest city, ballooned to nearly one hundred thousand inhabitants by midcentury.

The inhabitants of these lands comprised the full range of early modern social categories: from grandee nobles of vast lands and privilege, to middling folk engaged in trade or artisanship, to farmers and hardscrabble day laborers, to the marginalized poor and vagabonds. Tucked between France and the Empire, this population followed the general European pattern of comprising a variety of ethnicities and languages. Across the southernmost tier of provinces, Artois, Hainaut, Namur, Luxemburg and southwest Flanders, regional variants of Walloon French were spoken, while in the western and central provinces, from Flanders east to Guelders and Brabant north to Holland, dialects of Dutch predominated. In the far north and east, Frisian, Gronings, Oosters and variations of Low German were the common spoken languages.[7] A farmer in Groningen would likely have had great difficulty understanding a seamstress in Artois. There was thus little to unify the Netherlands linguistically, though French served as the language of administration for the Burgundian and later Habsburg central governments, as well as the lingua franca of the nobility. In language as in nearly all other things Netherlandish, localism prevailed, though linguistic difference appeared not to have been much of a hindrance to commerce or exchange of any kind.

As with all preindustrial European societies most Netherlanders made their livings in agriculture, but a considerable portion, as much as a third to a half, of the population lived in towns and cities and thus found work in the urban economy as merchants, shopkeepers, craftsmen, lawyers, notaries, scholars, teachers, domestic servants, printers, innkeepers, prostitutes and day laborers. Thanks to its aqueous geography the Netherlands enjoyed one of the most prosperous and diversified economies of sixteenth-century Europe, outshone in size and affluence perhaps only by the city-states of Renaissance Italy. Agriculture and fisheries were of course staples of economic activity, but the transportation routes that the region's coast and rivers provided also fostered the growth of both

---

[4] Blom and Lamberts, *History of the Low Countries*, p. 103; De Schepper, "Burgundian–Habsburg Netherlands," p. 511.

[5] Parker, *Dutch Revolt*, p. 23.

[6] Blom and Lamberts, *History of the Low Countries*, p. 104.

[7] Donaldson, *Dutch*, pp. 21–24.

commerce and manufacturing. Towns in Flanders and Brabant had been centers of wool production since the High Middle Ages, and in the sixteenth century the cloth industry further expanded into the manufacture of lighter textiles such as baizes, serges, silks and linens. Raw materials were imported from other regions of Europe, such as wool from England that was processed in the Netherlands and then exported in the form of finished products to markets as far away as the lands around the Mediterranean Sea. Local municipal governments actively supported this industry and commerce through favorable economic policies and regulations. Aside from textiles, brewing, shipbuilding and printing were also industries of central importance to the Netherlandish economy.

Indeed in the sixteenth century, thanks to its Spanish Habsburg connections, the Netherlands became the hub of a worldwide commercial system, as Iberian explorations and subjugations of lands in Africa, Asia and the Americas expanded Europe's economic reach overseas. At the pinnacle of this global commercial system stood the proud and bustling Brabantine city of Antwerp on the river Scheldt, which served as an emporium for virtually all of the goods the global economy produced, and in particular served as the entrepôt for the transcontinental European trade between the Mediterranean and Baltic regions.[8] This position made Antwerp conspicuously prosperous. When the German painter Albrecht Dürer visited the city in 1520 he marveled at its wealth, including that of its ornate churches: "In Antwerp they spare no cost on such things, for there is money enough."[9] The city government welcomed all who wanted to do business. Iberian, Italian and German agents and factors in particular flocked to this metropolis to facilitate trade and to export goods further into Europe. The mercantile population also included a small community of Portuguese New Christian merchants, descendants of forcibly converted Iberian Jews, who for a time enjoyed relative safety within the city's commercial cosmopolitanism until Habsburg policy forced them out of the city at midcentury.[10] American sugar, Asian spices, English wool, German metals, French salt and countless other commodities all made their way through the markets of the Netherlands' largest city. The business of Antwerp was decidedly business. The Bourse, one of the world's oldest commodities exchanges, was set up there in 1531. To be sure, the Netherlandish commercial economy that Antwerp dominated was sensitive to disruptions – for example, the Habsburgs' ongoing wars

[8] Limberger, "'No Town in the World Provides More Advantages'"; Van der Wee, "Handel in de Zuidelijke Nederlanden"; Van Houtte, *Economic History of the Low Countries*, pp. 175–187.
[9] Dürer, *Diary of His Journey to the Netherlands*, p. 60.
[10] Christman, *Pragmatic Toleration*, pp. 107–130.

with France – but in general it would prove resilient for at least the first two-thirds of the sixteenth century, until it succumbed for a time to the tumult of the Netherlandish wars. For most of the sixteenth century this was a very rich part of the world, and despite military disruption it would become so again in the seventeenth century. Along with this economic expansion came demographic increase. Precise figures are spotty, but we can get a sense of the scale of growth. The population of the central province of Brabant, for example, rose by 29 percent between 1480 and 1565, while that of Holland increased by 30 percent between 1496 and 1514.[11] The strongly urbanized character of Netherlandish society (or at least of its western, maritime core), with its extensive economic and social networks, would play an important role in the reception and spread of ideas of reformation.

It was thanks to this urbanization that high rates of literacy were found among Netherlanders. Statistics are lacking, but there are many indications that literacy was widespread. Foreign visitors remarked upon how many people, especially women, seemed able to read. Book production, thanks to a flourishing print industry, was substantial. Religious texts in particular, the Bible in vernacular translation chief among them, found an avid readership. The region enjoyed a large number of schools. Virtually every village had a schoolmaster who gave lessons in basic reading, writing and figuring, and most larger towns had a municipal Latin school to educate older boys whose parents could afford the tuition. By 1500 Amsterdam had two Latin schools and Antwerp had five. In addition, private schools proliferated, and they tutored boys and girls alike. Indeed, one prominent historian asserts that the Habsburg Netherlands were "the educational leaders of Europe."[12] The growth in trade also demanded at least some basic literacy and numeracy from merchants. A dense network of towns, especially in the core provinces, as well as the impetus of an economy driven by trade and industry, ensured that literacy was a highly valued skill.

Because economic and demographic growth were so heavily concentrated in the western regions, the Low Countries in the early sixteenth century had something of a split personality. Long before the Netherlandish Revolt severed the region into two distinct northern and southern states, there already existed a more fundamental socioeconomic divide between its western and eastern lands. The highly urbanized and populous west contrasted sharply with the rural, more sparsely populated east. The lion's share of the manufacturing and commercial economy was

---

[11] Soly and Thys, "Nijverheid in de Zuidelijke Nederlanden," p. 30; Van Houtte, *Economic History of the Low Countries*, p. 125.

[12] De Ridder-Symoens, "Education and Literacy in the Burgundian–Habsburg Netherlands," pp. 16–21.

concentrated in the west, while agriculture predominated in the east.
Flanders, Brabant, the Tournaisis, Hainaut, Utrecht, Zeeland and
Holland comprised the region's core provinces while eastern, landward
regions such as Groningen, Overijssel, Limburg, Luxemburg and Namur
formed a distinct periphery of secondary provinces in the Netherlands'
economic, demographic and political landscape.[13] Several of the rural
northeastern provinces were not acquired by the Habsburgs until well
into the 1500s and were therefore on the region's political periphery as
well. Though it has been periodically fashionable among some historians to
argue for an inherent Netherlandish south–north divide (thereby projecting
modern-day state boundaries back into the past), in fact during the sixteenth
century the region's more obvious fissure could be found between east and
west.[14] The sparsely populated eastern provinces, stretching from
Groningen south to Luxemburg, would always take a back seat, economically and politically, to the more dynamic western lands.

Taken as a whole, however, the Low Countries comprised one of the
most prosperous parts of Europe in the early sixteenth century. This
prosperity, based as it was principally on trade, manufacture and
exchange, made the region unusually open to influences and developments from abroad; its economy was conspicuously modern. At the same
time the Netherlands remained distinctively early modern in its political
culture. The careful guarding of rights, liberties and privileges by local
authorities protected and to some extent nourished the region's ethnic,
cultural and economic diversity. Most Netherlanders preferred to live in
the extremely diffused political constellation that characterized the
region's medieval tangle of fiefdoms, bishoprics, castleries, towns and
domains. Power, they had long believed, worked best in local hands.
This combination of contradictory qualities – economic modernity and
political traditionalism – would have a direct effect on how the eruptions
triggered by the Reformation would play themselves out in the region.

The Habsburg Composite State

The Reformation in the Netherlands took place against a very specific
political backdrop: the integration and disintegration of the Low
Countries as a unitary composite state under the control of the Habsburg
dynasty.[15] Cradled between the kingdom of France and the Holy Roman
Empire, the territories of the Netherlands had theoretically always been

[13] De Schepper, *Belgium Nostrum*, p. 7.
[14] The most recent historian to argue for a natural north–south Netherlandish divide has
been Jonathan Israel in his *The Dutch Republic*.
[15] De Schepper, *Belgium Nostrum*, p. 17.

subject to one of these two crowns, though by the High Middle Ages this meant very little in practice as the region's local powers grew accustomed to governing their own affairs. Starting in the fourteenth century, however, a new political actor began to make itself felt in the region.

Through inheritance, marriage, diplomacy and war the dukes of Burgundy, a cadet branch of the French Valois dynasty, tortuously forged a personal union of various Netherlandish territories in the course of the later Middle Ages.[16] Between 1384 and 1477 the house of Burgundy gained control of Flanders, Brabant, Holland, Zeeland, Namur, Artois, Limburg, Luxemburg and Hainaut. In 1477 Duchess Mary of Burgundy inherited these lands and married Archduke Maximilian, scion of the house of Habsburg. In 1506 their grandson Charles of Ghent (1500–1558) inherited these lands in turn, as well as the kingdom of Spain from his mother, and in 1519, continuing centuries of Habsburg political ambition, he was elected the King of the Romans and thus became the de facto Holy Roman Emperor as Charles V, though he was not formally crowned until 1530. Joined with his Spanish and Italian dominions, the imperial office made Charles, at least on the map, the most powerful ruler in Europe.

Under Charles V the Habsburg dominion of the Netherlands was extended further still when he acquired, principally through warfare, lands in the northeast, including Utrecht, Guelders, Friesland, Drenthe, Groningen and Overijssel. Like his Burgundian ancestors Charles was principally interested in the expansion of princely power in order to extract an optimal amount of revenue from these wealthy possessions; state-building was a natural if secondary consequence of this ambition. In effect he created the sixteenth-century Netherlandish composite state, a region with a distinct – if still fluid and imprecise – identity separate from both France and Germany.[17] He expanded his Netherlandish territory to its limits in the 1540s, with his conquest of the duchy of Guelders and his securing of the formal recognition of a separate Netherlandish "Burgundian Circle" (*Burgundischer Kreis*) by the Imperial Diet of the Holy Roman Empire.[18] Under Charles V the Habsburg Netherlandish composite state grew as big as it was ever going to get. It also became part of the larger Habsburg *imperium* that included Austria, Spain and its overseas dominions, the Empire and southern Italy. Charles's political success in integrating the Low Countries would later come undone under his son and successor, Philip II (r. 1555–1598),

[16] Blockmans and Prevenier, *Promised Lands*.
[17] Duke, "Elusive Netherlands," in *Dissident Identities*.
[18] Arndt, *Das Heilige Römische Reich und die Niederlande 1566 bis 1648*, pp. 32–38.

when the Netherlands split apart under the pressures of rebellion and civil war, conflicts fueled in no small part by religious discord. The integration and disintegration of the Habsburg Netherlands thus took place fairly rapidly within the space of two generations.

This Burgundian and later Habsburg Netherlandish political union, it should be stressed, was almost purely dynastic and artificial, very much dependent on the cooperation and collaboration of local powers. It was, at least formally, a collection of titles – duke of Brabant, count of Zeeland and the like. There were no ethnic, geographic or topographical boundaries that would have allowed for or encouraged the creation of a natural Netherlandish state.[19] Even within the boundaries of the lands controlled by the Habsburgs there were independent sovereignties, most notably the prince-bishopric of Liège (though this latter domain fell well within the Habsburg sphere of influence). As the venerable Dutch historian Johan Huizinga put it, the Netherlandish composite state of the first half of the sixteenth century was achieved only by "the enterprising policy of a high-minded dynasty."[20] Insofar as the Low Countries had an identity, it was exceedingly amorphous, as was true for most early modern European countries. Indeed, the muddled nomenclature of this corner of Europe offers a good illustration of how diffused its identity was. The medieval dukes of Burgundy, who forged this state in part as a strategic counter-weight to their French royal cousins, routinely referred to the region as the "lands over here" (les pays de par deçà) to distinguish them from the "lands over there" (les pays de par delà), their ancestral holdings in French Burgundy proper.[21] Local humanist scholars tried to invent a classical pedigree for the region by referring to it as "Belgica" or "Gallia Belgica" or "Germania inferior" after the fashion of ancient Roman authors such as Julius Caesar and Tacitus, though this conceit never really spread beyond learned circles.[22] Ordinary Netherlanders tended to identify their patria by locality – that is, whichever town or region they came from or inhabited. Still, it was clear that by the middle of the century the Habsburgs were forging a state, if not quite a nation. By this time there began to appear in official documents regular references to the "seventeen" provinces of the Netherlands, although the origin of this number was never clear.[23]

Certainly there were far more than seventeen identities in these lands surrounding Europe's northwest river deltas. The Netherlands embraced

[19] Woltjer, Op weg naar tachtig jaar oorlog, p. 35.
[20] Huizinga, "How Holland Became a Nation," p. 271.
[21] Duke, "Elusive Netherlands," pp. 26–27; Poelhekke, "The Nameless Homeland of Erasmus."
[22] Duke, "Elusive Netherlands," pp. 15–16.   [23] Stein, "Seventeen."

a vast patchwork of sovereignties: bishoprics, counties, duchies, baronies, marquisates, cities and towns, most of which jealously guarded their own prickly sets of legal and political rights and privileges, and had been doing so for hundreds of years. This amalgamation of diverse languages, cultures and privileges also comprised, as noted earlier, a dynamic, well-integrated network of urban commerce and communication, so that the region's hallmarks were both prosperity and localism.[24] For all the region's economic integration, however, local interests could diverge considerably, and the various territories had an intermittent history of internecine rivalry, suspicion and conflict. In times past these sovereignties had fought one another, such as Holland and Flanders's long wars for control of the Zeeland islands in the 1200s. Even during the sixteenth century, the Guelders Wars of 1502–1543, a protracted but ultimately unsuccessful struggle by the duchy of Guelders to resist Habsburg control, included brutal military attacks on Holland and Brabant.[25] Conflict could also be internal; the county of Holland suffered from fierce factional wars in the late 1300s and early 1400s. More Habsburg overlordship, however, largely brought such intra-regional strife to an end by the early sixteenth century. Still this tradition of political particularism was deeply ingrained, as the Habsburgs would discover to their cost. The wars that afflicted the region in the second half of the sixteenth century were fought precisely over the question of sovereignty, of local versus dynastic power. Noble grandees, municipal patricians and ordinary burghers who had long cherished their autonomies objected, ultimately violently, to Habsburg encroachments on what they saw as their traditional rights. Ironically this resistance would be the one thing that briefly united all of them: the Pacification of Ghent, which in 1576 gathered nearly the entire region in opposition to the Habsburg government's military policies, explicitly demanded the return of "old privileges, customs and freedoms."[26] The desire to preserve and defend local privilege against a centralizing monarchy would, at least for a few brief years, unite the Low Countries as nothing had before.

The people of the sixteenth-century Low Countries, therefore, were accustomed to sources of authority that were local; the further up the power structure they went from the bottom, the more abstract and unreal it became to them. They believed strongly in their privileges or "liberties," as they sometimes called them, even if they might have been hard-pressed to explain precisely what those were. Broadly speaking, the privileges fell

[24] Soen, "Which Religious History?" p. 764.
[25] Tracy, *Holland under Habsburg Rule*, pp. 64–89; Noordzij, "Against Burgundy."
[26] Kossmann and Mellink, *Texts concerning the Revolt of the Netherlands*, p. 127.

under the rubric of self-government; most provinces and towns had their own forms of administration made up of prominent men chosen from local elite families, while nobles of course had the customary, feudal right to govern their own lands. By far the most important of these powers of local self-government, aside from levying certain types of taxes, was the administration of justice. Local gentry, sheriffs, bailiffs and aldermen had the power and the responsibility to secure law and order in their communities, and citizens accused of crimes had the right to be tried in local courts.[27] Law, both its expression and enforcement, was therefore a local affair. It was this legal tradition that Habsburg religious policy would ultimately run most afoul of. In particular, the unprecedented inquisitorial mechanisms Charles V established to extirpate religious dissent created an extra-local, alien judicial entity whose powers, justified by the war against heresy, overrode all local justice. The sweep of this inquisition made Habsburg sovereignty anything but abstract or remote to ordinary burghers. Instead many of them came to see it as a grievous intrusion into local autonomy, a violation of the common customs of the particular community, so much so that vigorous protest and opposition seemed the only possible recourse. It was this confrontation between particularism and central government, between medieval privileges and modern monarchy, that sparked the revolt of the Netherlands.

In the countryside nobles, squires, monasteries and gentry made up the principal political authorities to whom local folk were expected to defer. In the towns, the typical Netherlander encountered political authority in the person of sheriffs, bailiffs, burgomasters, aldermen and city councilors. These officials superintended civic life – from law and order to sanitation to regulating trade – and they usually came from the prominent families of the community. These were men who deeply believed the paramount social virtue was civic harmony; insofar as they had an ideology, at its core was a fierce commitment to using rules and norms to protect that harmony by managing conflict and overseeing all manner of economic, judicial and social activity.[28] They did so in cooperation with long-standing and deeply integrated civic associations, such as guilds and civic militias, that facilitated the economic and political motors of municipal life. Guilds of merchants and skilled artisans tightly regulated civic economies, while civic militias maintained municipal order. These associative networks were tightly interwoven with the public life of cities, as they contributed to municipal charity and participated in corporate

---

[27] Woltjer, "Dutch Privileges, Real and Imaginary."
[28] Boone and Haemers, "'The Common Good.'"

religious devotion. Some of the early supporters of religious reform would
be found among their ranks.[29]

Together local elites from town and country, representatives of civic
and noble governments, joined by the clergy, met in powerful provincial
assemblies or estates. These provincial states had been meeting regularly
since the High Middle Ages, and they had considerable powers, including
levying taxes and raising troops. It was the provincial states in particular
that assiduously defended local privileges against any centralizing
encroachments by the Burgundian–Habsburgs. By the fifteenth century
the Burgundian dukes had started meeting joint delegations from these
provincial assemblies, and this practice slowly led to the evolution of
a permanent parliamentary institution, the States-General, which gathered
twice per year; the Habsburgs' financial dependence on the region (they
always had expensive wars with France to pay for) gave the States-General
potentially powerful leverage over the sovereign.[30] In its deliberative capac-
ity, however, the States-General was completely captive to the provincial
assemblies, to whom its delegates had to refer back for instruction before
making any major decision. Additionally, each province had its own high
court that served as a court of appeal for its judicial affairs. The most
important non-dynastic political force in the Low Countries, therefore,
could be found at the provincial level, and it formed the principal counterbalance to the centralizing ambitions of the Burgundian-Habsburg
dynasty.

As a consequence of these centuries-old traditions of diffused sovereignty, Burgundian–Habsburg control of the often fractious Low
Countries was frequently contested and seldom complete. Local powers
proved very reluctant to give up their authority to a central, dynastic court
in Mechelen or Brussels intent on extracting as much revenue as possible
from these prosperous lands. The effort to impose central authority was
often halting and tortuous. The proud cities of Flanders, particularly
Ghent, rose in rebellion against Burgundian centralization a number of
times in the course of the fifteenth century. Flanders, Holland, Brabant,
Guelders and Zeeland rebelled against the regime of Maximilian I and
Mary of Burgundy between 1477 and 1492, a conflict that presaged many
of the particularist themes of the revolt against their great-grandson Philip
II a century later.[31] Always fractious Ghent would rise up in protest once
more against Charles's taxation efforts in 1539. Princely centralization

[29] Blondé, Buylaert, Dumolyn, Hanus, and Stabel, "Living Together in the City," in *City and Society in the Low Countries*, pp. 93–127; Knevel, *Burgers in het geweer*, pp. 18–61; Israel, *Dutch Republic*, pp. 119–122.
[30] Koenigsberger, *Monarchies, States Generals and Parliaments*, pp. 16–41.
[31] Israel, *Dutch Republic*, pp. 29–30.

was a slow, haphazard process that went on for centuries and was never completed. Both Charles V and his son Philip II, who had expensive wars to pay for, would find that Netherlandish particularism made the exploitation of Netherlandish wealth a fraught and complicated enterprise.

Nevertheless, by the 1530s the Habsburgs had put several organs of central government firmly in place. At the central court in Brussels the sovereign, Charles V, was represented by a regent, initially his aunt Margaret of Austria (r. 1517–1530) and later his sister Mary of Hungary (r. 1531–1555). These regents governed with the aid and advice of several grand councils: a council of state for policy, a council of finance for revenues and expenditures and a secret or privy council for the administration of justice. As recent innovations these councils were sometimes sources of concern to wary local authorities. The council of state comprised a dozen or so Netherlandish grand nobles, but Charles appointed to his privy council a number of non-noble professional jurists and bureaucrats, some of them foreigners, upon whom he relied more and more to execute actual state policy, much to the grandees' resentment.[32] In the Brabantine town of Mechelen, the central government's supreme court (*Grote Raad*) acted as a final arbiter of judgments handed down by each province's own central court. Together these bodies would function as the Habsburg Low Countries' organs of national government, overseeing foreign policy, finance and justice, through the end of the sixteenth century. By the 1530s the Habsburgs had successfully transformed the Netherlands from a confederate to a federal state; in the core western provinces especially a careful balance between central power and particularist interests was achieved.[33] It was, however, an exceedingly delicate balance requiring continuous negotiation, if not to say argument. The regent Mary of Hungary noted with exasperation at the end of her tenure in 1555 that "here in the Netherlands one has to gain everyone's good will, nobles as well as commons, for this country does not render the obedience which is due to a monarchy."[34] The Habsburgs were monarchs in Spain, but they were learning that they were not kings of the Low Countries. Just as the integration of the Habsburg princely polity over this fractious region seemed possible, religious dissent would break out in earnest and would severely test its viability. In particular the central government's reaction to this religious protest would exacerbate the fissures and tensions already present between Brussels and the provinces.

---

[32] Israel, *Dutch Republic*, pp. 35–37.
[33] De Schepper, "Burgundian–Habsburg Netherlands," pp. 509, 526.
[34] Quoted in Koenigsberger, "Prince and States-General," p. 128.

The Church

Over the three million souls who lived in this crowded, diverse corner of
Europe the Catholic Church universal presided as spiritual guide and as
the sole conduit of God's grace. It prayed for every soul, preached the
gospel, taught morals, regulated the calendar, served as a link between the
quick and the dead, presided over life's milestones, performed important
charitable and educational functions, and, most importantly, offered
eternal salvation through the sacraments. The Low Countries had been
co-opted into the orbit of Western Latin Christendom starting in late
antiquity, and by the early Middle Ages the region's Christianization was
complete; one of the few things that formally united sixteenth-century
Netherlanders was their baptism. With the later Middle Ages came
a blossoming of religious activity that spread throughout Europe, particularly by the laity, and the Catholic Church in the Netherlands in the early
1500s gave every impression of strength and vitality.[35] All the trappings of
late medieval religion flourished here as they did in the rest of Europe,
especially in the north, where the laicization of piety and practice proceeded at a rapid pace. In a society that thought corporately, collective
participation in church ritual and worship was an important mechanism
for fostering a sense of solidarity and community. Even the landscape
became more ecclesiastical; the later Middle Ages was a great era of
church building, and nearly every Netherlandish town of any consequence proudly boasted a splendid late Gothic church, sometimes funded
by the enthusiastic purchase of popular papal indulgences, as was the case
of the massive, foursquare tower of St. Rumbold's church in the
Brabantine town of Mechelen, completed in 1520 (Illustration 1.1).[36]
The enthusiasm for construction spread across Netherlandish parishes far
and wide. Several of the parish churches in Lille underwent elaborate
renovations and redecoration in the 1400s and 1500s, including the earliest introduction of Renaissance-style sculpture in that city.[37] Hundreds
of monastic houses, abbeys and convents dotted both cityscape and
countryside, and the growth of monastic communities was particularly
marked in the region's prosperous towns in the later Middle Ages.[38]
Clergy, recognizable by their distinctive vestments, were a visible part of
every community. The sheer physical presence of the church, with its
manifold sacred spaces and objects, was palpable everywhere; as an
institution it was at once universal and local.

[35] Pollmann, *Catholic Identity and the Revolt of the Netherlands*, pp. 20–25.
[36] Caspers, "Indulgences in the Low Countries," pp. 72–76.
[37] DuPlessis, *Lille and the Dutch Revolt*, pp. 158–159.
[38] Nissen, "De gevolgen van de Reformatie," p. 180.

Illustration 1.1 Tower of the Church of Saint Rumbold, Mechelen. Photo courtesy City of Mechelen

By all accounts lay Netherlanders participated fully and enthusiastically in the associative and ceremonial aspects of late medieval Western Christianity: sacraments, processions, pilgrimages, confraternities, sermons, feast days, the veneration of saints. Communities rallied around religious activity of all kinds and a kind of "civic religion," intermingling the spiritual with the material, developed among tightly knit town populations.[39] Superintended by clergy and encouraged by magistrates, ordinary Christians took avid part in the economy of salvation. In particular devotions dedicated to the Eucharist expanded considerably in popularity; the late medieval feast day of Corpus Christi had its origins among devout religious women in the bishopric of Liège in the early thirteenth century.[40] Likewise devotion to the Virgin Mary grew considerably. In 1503, for example, the cult of Our Lady of Seven Sorrows, which emphasized Mary's suffering during her son's Passion, was set up in the Old Church in Delft. With the help of high political patronage and the adept circulation of printed publicity, it soon became a popular devotional site for pilgrims from all over the Low Countries; within two decades of its founding no fewer than 178 miracles were reported there.[41] Similarly, an image of the Virgin in Amersfoort reported nearly 400 miracle stories in 1444.[42] In Lille the cult of Notre-Dame de la Treille, an old thirteenth-century devotion, was revived with great success in the 1450s.[43] Devotion could also be individual in addition to collective; in 1506 the Mouscron merchant family of Bruges paid the Florentine sculptor Michelangelo thousands of florins to sculpt a luminous marble Madonna and Child to ornament their family chapel.[44] The cult of the saints proved immensely popular, and manifestations of it could be found everywhere.

In general Netherlanders came across as very reverent. "No one walks about in the churches or makes merry there as in Italy," wrote the Italian traveler Antonio de Beatis with some wonderment in 1517.[45] In his otherwise terse diary of his journey to the Netherlands in 1520, the German artist Albrecht Dürer described at length a two-hour procession in honor of the Assumption of the Virgin he witnessed in Antwerp, "when the whole town of every craft and rank was assembled, each dressed in his best according to his rank." As Dürer watched, rows of militiamen, guildsmen, merchants, magistrates, pipers and drummers, widows, scholars and clerics walked by, followed by wagons outfitted with *tableaux vivants* from the life of the Virgin, such as the Annunciation and the flight to Egypt, and the parade was rounded out by portrayals of St. Margaret and St. George, the latter accompanied by a large dragon.[46] In churches layfolk of means endowed chapels and commissioned devotional art, as did many civic guilds, confraternities and magistracies. Religious devotion

[39] Marnef and Van Bruaene, "Civic Religion," in *City and Society*.
[40] Rubin, *Corpus Christi*, pp. 164–176.   [41] Verhoeven, *Devotie en negotie*, pp. 58–60.
[42] Van Herwaarden and De Keyser, "Het gelovige volk," p. 407.
[43] DuPlessis, *Lille and the Dutch Revolt*, p. 161.
[44] Mancusi-Ungaro, *Michelangelo*, pp. 35–46.
[45] De Beatis, *Travel Journal of Antonio de Beatis*, p. 103.   [46] Dürer, *Diary*, pp. 60–61.

and civic pride were often yoked. Cities conducted lavish festivals and processions in honor of patron saints. The dukes of Burgundy and the Habsburgs recognized the value of such common ceremonial and carefully tailored their political ritual to complement local religious devotion; Habsburg overlordship of the Netherlands was heavily sacralized.[47] The Habsburg "theater state" was closely attuned to the population's desire for religious spectacle.[48] Local and national political concerns intersected in myriad ways with the divine; the city of Amsterdam, for example, organized seventeen general processions between 1481 and 1511, the majority of which were responses to specific political crises in Burgundian–Habsburg rulership.[49] In Bruges no fewer than twenty-two religious processions were staged in the single year 1475.[50] Lay participation in all these kinds of rituals and events, which were integral components of civic and social life, was keen and widespread, as was reading the Bible in the vernacular. Devotional life in the Low Countries in the early sixteenth century was anything but stagnant.

Lay movements in religion were indeed a significant feature of late medieval Netherlandish Christianity; devotion and worship were not left merely to the religious professionals, as more and more layfolk explored mechanisms to help them express their religious conviction. For some of the most ardent faithful among the laity, the traditional outlets for devotion offered by the church were not enough, and they sought out other ways to exercise their piety. The most famous example of this phenomenon was the Modern Devotion, founded in the 1370s by the Deventer-born deacon and preacher Geert Groote. The *Devotio Moderna* began as a movement of laity and clergy in the late fourteenth century in the IJssel river valley in the northeastern Netherlands; it focused on inner piety, the conversion of the self to a Christlike life of devotional medita-tion, prayer and good works. Its laic arm would come to be known as the Sisters and Brothers of the Common Life, while its monastic counterpart centered on the Augustinian monastery of Windesheim near the Overijssel town of Zwolle. What began as informal gatherings among devout souls eventually grew into more institutionalized networks of brother- and sister-houses across the northern Netherlands. The Modern-Day Devout, whose membership reached a peak in the 1490s, lived together in communal households, studied scripture and practiced spiritual exercises designed to increase piety.[51] They took no vows and

---

[47] Arnade, *Beggars, Iconoclasts and Civic Patriots*, pp. 12–49.
[48] Van Bruaene, "The Habsburg Theatre State."
[49] Caspers, *De eucharistische vroomheid*, pp. 121–122.
[50] Van Herwaarden and De Keyser, "Het gelovige volk," p. 413.
[51] Van Engen, *Sisters and Brothers of the Common Life*, p. 308.

were not part of any recognized religious order and yet lived as if they did, which led some contemporaries to look upon them with suspicion as neither laic fish nor clerical fowl, neither entirely in the world nor entirely separated from it. The houses supported themselves with various kinds of work, including textile production, copying manuscripts and schooling, and they produced a large corpus of spiritual literature that both sustained and defended them, the most famous and influential of which was the handbook *The Imitation of Christ*, composed around 1420 and attributed to the Windesheim canon Thomas à Kempis. This work, with its stress on self-examination, intense meditation and prayer, became one of the most widely read and reprinted books of the fifteenth and sixteenth centuries. At the movement's height houses of the Modern-Day Devout stretched across the Low Countries and into the northern reaches of the Holy Roman Empire. An older generation of historiography saw in the Modern Devotion a direct forerunner of the Reformation, but currently it is understood less tendentiously as an expression of late medieval piety, as part of a broader European effort to appropriate aspects of religious life for the laity, distant echoes of which would later be found in the lives and ideas of sixteenth-century religious reformers, both Protestant and Catholic.[52] It is an error to see the Modern Devotion as a harbinger of the Reformation; the former remained safely orthodox and never challenged the power or doctrine of the established church in the way the latter did. It is more useful to think of the Modern Devotion as an example of the depths of devotion among lay Netherlanders that late medieval Christianity could inspire.

Another important example of lay devotion that emerged in the Netherlands, as well as other parts of northern Europe, were the Beguines. These were communities of laywomen who lived together as if in a religious order. In order to control their property, however, they took only vows of chastity and obedience, not poverty. Such communities first started appearing in the Low Countries in the prince-bishopric of Liège and the duchy of Brabant in the early thirteenth century; by the mid-1500s there were nearly three hundred Beguine groups in the southern Low Countries alone, and they became the single most popular means for devout laywomen to pursue a religious vocation.[53] Most major Netherlandish towns in the sixteenth century were home to a beguinage, a courtyard with small homes arranged around it where the sisters, mostly of middling or lower social status, lived together as if

[52] Van Engen, *Sisters and Brothers of the Common Life*, pp. 315–320; Weiler, "Recent Historiography on the Modern Devotion."
[53] Simons, *Cities of Ladies*, p. 48.

in a religious community. Some towns had multiple beguinages, such as Arras in the county of Artois, which housed no fewer than twenty-four. The residents of these communities could range in number from the dozens to the hundreds; the largest of the beguinages, in Mechelen, boasted a membership of more than fifteen hundred women.[54] In the beguinages the sisters lived both contemplative and active lives, the latter of which they spent in charitable work, teaching young children and supporting themselves through textile work such as lace-making. Although church authorities occasionally looked on with suspicion at the women's activities, the Beguines largely kept themselves confined within the bounds of orthodoxy, dutifully worshipped in their parish churches, and by the early sixteenth century were regarded as a simple and innocent form of female devotion.[55] Like the Modern Devout, the Beguines represented a kind of *via media* between the laity and clergy that was widespread in late medieval Netherlandish religious culture.[56]

Confraternities were still another popular form of lay devotion in the Netherlands, as they were all over Latin Christendom. These were local voluntary associations that gathered men and women together in common prayer and ritual. They worshipped and participated together in acts of communal devotion such as processions and provided opportunities for lay leadership in local parishes.[57] They endowed chapels in parish churches; the church of Saint John in Gouda boasted no fewer than thirteen altars financed by confraternities, where chaplains were paid to say masses for the dead.[58] The Flemish city of Ghent had twenty-two such organizations in 1500, while Antwerp counted thirty-one of them by the end the century.[59] In the city of Utrecht some 90 percent of the citizens (i.e., adult men who had obtained the legal right of citizenship) belonged to a confraternity, whose memberships typically numbered in the dozens and even hundreds.[60]

Often these associations were dedicated to a particular saint. In the 1490s, for example, the Flemish priest Jan van Coudenberghe received papal approval to establish a confraternity specifically devoted to the Seven Sorrows of the Virgin, a veneration whose popularity had only recently spread across the Low Countries (see Illustration 1.2).[61] This

---

[54] Simons, *Cities of Ladies*, pp. 54–55.   [55] Simons, *Cities of Ladies*, pp. 136–137.
[56] Marnef and Van Bruaene, "Civic Religion," p. 137.
[57] Dieterich, "Confraternities and Lay Leadership in Sixteenth-Century Liège."
[58] Marnef and Van Bruaene, "Civic Religion," p. 143.
[59] Trio, *Volksreligie als spiegel van een stedelijke samenleving*, p. 83.
[60] Bogaers, *Aards, betrokken en zelfbewust*, pp. 431–432, 453–454.
[61] Van Herwaarden and De Keyser, "Het gelovige volk," p. 406; Thelen, *Seven Sorrows Confraternity of Brussels*.

Illustration 1.2 Anonymous, *Lamentation with the Seven Sorrows of the Virgin*, 1507. This print depicts a popular devotion that spread across the late medieval Low Countries. The Virgin Mary, center, is seen suffering along with her son during various episodes of Christ's Passion. Courtesy Rijksmuseum Amsterdam

kind of corporative religiosity ensured that the laity played a leading and even influential role in the sacral community.

One distinctive type of confraternity, the chamber of rhetoric, first emerged in the towns of Flanders during the middle of the fifteenth century. The chambers were urban literary societies, dedicated to the art of "rhetoric" – that is, public presentations of literature, mostly plays and poetry. Their growth and popularity reflected both the increasing prosperity and the increasing literacy among urban populations. The chambers resembled confraternities and guilds in that as associations they had a patron saint (most frequently the Virgin Mary), maintained an altar in the local church, and sometimes engaged in collective religious observance such as processions. Their membership came overwhelmingly from the middling strata of urban society, mostly skilled artisans and merchants, teachers and occasional priests, and the chambers served as a kind of boisterous cultural outlet for increasingly assertive and self-confident civic populations in which they were deeply embedded.[62] They put on pageants, plays and *tableaux vivants*, and local chambers often entered friendly literary competitions with each other at the provincial level. The subjects of their literary performances were often (though not always) religious and sometimes didactic in nature, and they frequently staged productions at municipal religious occasions such as processions and festivals. In doing so they provided a kind of basic religious and moral instruction to the wider population. For example, the 1531 play *The Farce of the Fisherman* by the Bruges rhetorician Cornelis Everaert describes a husband and wife confessing their sins to each other while trapped by a storm at sea; the play turns into a lesson about forgiveness and conjugal harmony: "You ought to be content and not peer/ Into each misdeed, great or small./ Live with peace in accord together/ And guard each other's honor, whenever you can."[63] The literature produced by the chambers of rhetoric was full of this kind of virtuous instruction, and it appealed tremendously to urban audiences, who appreciated its sometimes irreverent depictions of clergy as well as its sympathy for more genuine forms of devotion.[64] As such the chambers were very much expressions of and vehicles for the distinctively urban religious culture of the late medieval Netherlands.[65] All these manifold forms of lay piety, from chambers of rhetoric to confraternities to Beguines to processions and saint veneration, formed part and parcel of

---

[62] Waite, *Reformers on Stage*, pp. 26–41.
[63] See "The Farce of the Fisherman," in Parsons and Jongenelen, *Comic Drama in the Low Countries*, p. 205.
[64] Marnef, "Chambers of Rhetoric."   [65] Van Bruaene, *Om beters wille*, p. 206.

the boisterous and colorful popular religious landscape in the Netherlands at the beginning of the sixteenth century.

Given their high level of participation in collective religious life, the Netherlandish laity could and did take their religion seriously, and their expectations of religious professionals could therefore be high; on one Sunday in 1501 in the Ghent parish of Saint Nicholas, for example, the collection plate came up empty because of congregational dissatisfaction with that day's sermon.[66] Still, however ardent their devotion, layfolk could not do without priests. A large corps of clergy, both secular and regular, superintended and aided in the execution of this popular religiosity at every ecclesiastical level. The Netherlandish first estate, those who pray, reflected the general hierarchies of early modern society, from powerful prelates (the bishop of Utrecht, for example) who wielded considerable spiritual and political influence to rural parish priests as poverty-stricken as their flocks. An ordained caste apart, priests were the only persons authorized by the church to celebrate the sacraments through which God's grace was obtained; they were indispensable to the effective operation of the economy of salvation. The diocese of Utrecht alone had roughly five thousand secular clergy serving it, and it was home to nearly five hundred cloistered institutions where some thirteen thousand women and men in regular orders lived.[67] The northern Brabant city of 's-Hertogenbosch boasted more than twelve hundred clergy inside its walls; one out of every eighteen inhabitants was a member of the first estate.[68] In Antwerp in 1539 the church of Our Dear Lady, the major parish of the city, had ninety-six chantry priests alone to read masses each week.[69] The traveling Italian cleric Antonio de Beatis noted with approval the sedulousness of the Netherlandish clergy he encountered: "in every parish church there are two sung masses a day at least, one for the dead and another for that day's saint."[70] The 506 parishes of the bishopric of Tournai boasted no fewer than twenty-five hundred chaplaincies charged with reading weekly masses in the mid-fifteenth century.[71] At virtually all manifestations of the worship of God the clergy were present, and they were a familiar and integral part of the social fabric and landscape, even though their ordained status formally and legally set them apart from lay Christians.

[66] Decavele, "Kerk en geloofsbeleving onder druk aan de vooravond van de Reformatietijd," p. 8.
[67] Post, *Kerkelijke Verhoudingen in Nederland vóór de Reformatie*, pp. 149, 165; Bogaers, *Aards, betrokken en zelfbewust*, p. 40.
[68] Van Gurp, *Reformatie in Brabant*, p. 23.
[69] Marnef, *Antwerp in the Age of Reformation*, p. 50.
[70] De Beatis, *Travel Journal of Antonio de Beatis*, p. 103.
[71] Van Herwaarden and De Keyser, "Het gelovige volk," p. 414.

The clergy represented a diverse group of religious professionals who performed a wide array of functions, not only the pastoral but also the legal, the educational, the bureaucratic, the fiscal and the political. At the basic level stood the parish priest or pastor; these men, out of all the clergy, were perhaps the most closely integrated into the lay community around them. Many of them were named to their posts by local authorities such as nobles or gentry. A prosopographical study of parish priests in the north Brabantine regions of the bishopric of Liège reveals that they generally came from the middling to upper echelons of society, and the vast majority of them had strong familial and regional ties to their parishes.[72] Contrary to popular anticlerical stereotypes that later gained currency in the Reformation, research suggests that most Netherlandish priests had received at least some formal schooling, even in an era before seminaries were common. At least a fifth of the clergy in the diocese of Utrecht had some university education, while in north Brabant about one half did, mostly at the universities of Cologne or Leuven.[73] In other respects, however, the behavior of the clergy often did conform to stereotypes: in the fifteenth century nearly two-thirds of beneficed priests in north Brabant were absent from their parishes.[74] About one fourth of the priests in Utrecht reportedly lived with a common-law wife or concubine, while in north Brabant the majority of priests appear not to have bothered to adhere to the rules of celibacy much at all.[75] Yet in the early sixteenth century this kind of flouting of the discipline of celibacy did not cause much consternation or scandal among ordinary parishioners, so long as the priests did their jobs and paid nominal fines to their superiors. The West Frisian priest and deacon Jan Graaf, for example, lived with his concubine and had two children, but it was only when he was accused of greed and handling in false documents that parishioners' complaints about his relationship with her actually arose.[76] In this case sensuality was clearly a more tolerable sin to the flock than venality. The moral health of the clergy in the Netherlands was probably no worse and no better than anywhere else in Europe. Only later in the sixteenth century would Catholic reform efforts attempt to discipline more systemically the morals and behavior of clergy, particularly with regard to such problems as absenteeism and celibacy.

---

[72] Bijsterveld, *Laveren tussen kerk en wereld*, pp. 89–90, 122.
[73] Post, *Kerkelijke Verhoudingen in Nederland vóór de Reformatie*, p. 55; Bijsterveld, *Laveren tussen kerk en wereld*, pp. 209–212.
[74] Bijsterveld, *Laveren tussen kerk en wereld*, p. 378.
[75] Post, *Kerkelijke Verhoudingen in Nederland vóór de Reformatie*, p. 125; Bijsterveld, *Laveren tussen kerk en wereld*, pp. 340–348.
[76] Post, *Kerkelijke Verhoudingen in Nederland vóór de Reformatie*, p. 107.

In 1500 the highest church authority in the Netherlands was the bishop; the region's ecclesiastical polity was even more tangled than its secular counterpart and was very much a relic of the area's early medieval past. Its diocesan boundaries in no way matched its political ones, and in the Middle Ages the church had enjoyed considerable economic and judicial autonomy. Many of the people employed by the church, its ecclesiastical bureaucrats, were charged to manage the church's wealth, which was considerable, especially in terms of land.

The region's parishes, chapters and deaneries fell variously under the jurisdiction of eight large bishoprics (Arras, Cambrai, Liège, Münster, Osnabrück, Thérouanne, Tournai and Utrecht), which in turn were answerable to the archbishops of Cologne, Trier and Reims, all three of them sees that fell well outside Habsburg authority.[77] The church had its own legal system; cases involving clergy or marriage could only be tried in ecclesiastical courts. An important goal of the Burgundian–Habsburg centralization policy of the 1400s and 1500s was to reduce this ecclesiastical autonomy. In theory bishops were freely elected by local canons, but in practice the Habsburgs intervened actively in these elections to make sure that their candidates were named to the region's sees, especially along the strategically critical southern border with the kingdom of France.[78] Through their capacities as count of Holland, duke of Brabant and the like the Habsburgs had the influence and clout to ensure that their favored officials were appointed to a large number of beneficed clerical posts, the most lucrative of which spared the central government the cost of their salaries. Since bishops were also administrators of their sees in addition to being spiritual leaders, in effect the Habsburgs used the church to defray some of the costs of governing their lands.[79] Controlling bishoprics was therefore critical to Habsburg policy in the region. By the mid-sixteenth century under Charles V the central government was able to exercise considerable authority over the church in fiscal and juridical matters; the church had long lost much of the independence it had once enjoyed in the early and High Middle Ages.[80] Episcopal authority grew more and more limited under Habsburg rule. Ecclesiastical appointments were more political than spiritual; the twenty-two men who served as Netherlandish bishops between 1515 and 1559 all came from reliable princely or aristocratic families.[81] A fairly typical example of the kind of

[77] Dierickx, L'Erection des Nouveaux Diocèses aux Pay-Bas, p. 8.
[78] Cools, "Bishops in the Habsburg Netherlands," pp. 49–50.
[79] Woltjer, Op weg naar tachtig jaar oorlog, p. 94.
[80] Fühner, Die Kirchen- und antireformatorische Religionspolitik, pp. 89–165.
[81] Cools, "Bishops in the Habsburg Netherlands," p. 51.

figure whom the Habsburgs named to the prelacy in the early sixteenth century was Philip of Burgundy (r. 1517–1524), illegitimate son of the Duke Philip the Good, a knight who was hastily ordained upon his elevation to bishop of Utrecht, but who preferred to leave his episcopal duties to his underlings while he enjoyed more leisurely noble pursuits such as romance, horses and artistic patronage.[82] Cut from similarly aristocratic cloth was the bishop of Tournai Charles de Croÿ (1525–1564), who was mostly absent from his diocese and who concerned himself chiefly with his castles and his income.[83] Indeed, the high nobility of the Netherlands expected to be tapped for such lucrative ecclesiastical posts as bishoprics and abbacies; they considered such positions of leadership their natural due. In this regard the Netherlands was no different than the rest of sixteenth-century Europe; the church, as a universal institution, was completely enmeshed in local political and social arrangements, and bishops were at least as much politicians as shepherds. Still, not all aristocratic bishops were neglectful or disinterested in their vocations; Charles de Croÿ's cousin Robert, who served as bishop of Cambrai in the same period, was inspired by Leuven theologians and his attendance at the Council of Trent to implement administrative reforms in his diocese.[84] Another reform-minded Netherlandish prelate, Adriaan Boeyens of Utrecht, onetime rector of the University of Leuven and tutor to Charles V, even reached the summit of ecclesiastical authority by serving as Pope Adrian VI in the years 1522–1523, a tenure too brief to permit him to make much headway against what he saw as Christendom's twin challenges – the Luther question and an expanding Ottoman empire.[85]

As a group the clergy, from priest to prelate, were decidedly mixed in their competence and devotion, and they were therefore regarded with concomitantly mixed feelings by the laity. Anticlerical feeling is sometimes cited as a factor in the coming of the Reformation to the Low Countries, though whether criticism of clergy was any stronger here than elsewhere remains a question.[86] The first estate was a privileged caste throughout Europe, and that privilege was subject to envy and suspicion everywhere. Resentment of the benefit of clergy, which included such perquisites as exemption from local taxation and justice, and complaints about clerical abuses of power were common enough in most communities, especially in the urban world that made up such an important part of Netherlandish society. City governments in the

---

[82] Sterk, *Philips van Bourgondië.*   [83] DuPlessis, *Lille and the Dutch Revolt*, p. 167.
[84] Van de Meulebroucke, Soen and François, "Robrecht van Croÿ."
[85] Verweij, *Adrianus VI.*   [86] Tracy, "Elements of Anticlerical Sentiment."

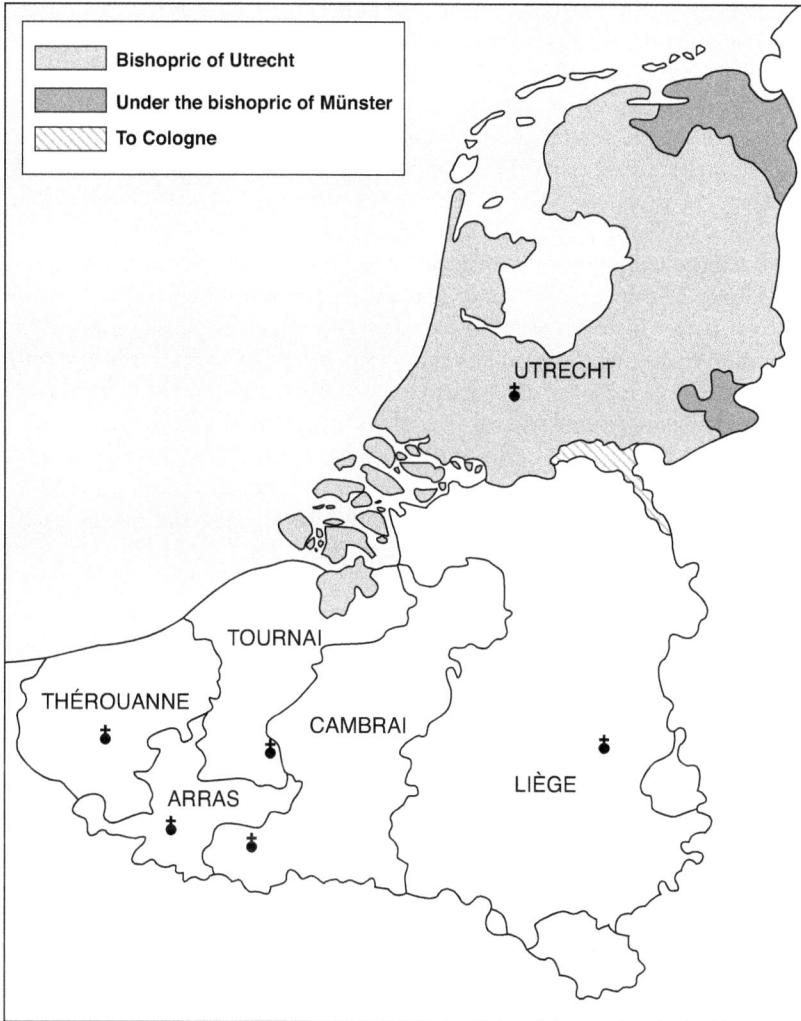

Map 1.2 Diocesan boundaries in the Low Countries before 1559

fifteenth century tried hard to restrict the growth of monastic property within their walls for fear of losing sources of tax revenue.[87] During the 1520s popular disturbances about clerical tax exemptions were reported

---

[87] Parker, *Reformation of Community*, pp. 46–48; Nissen, "De gevolgen van de Reformatie," pp. 183–184.

in The Hague, Antwerp, Roermond and Utrecht.[88] In 's-Hertogenbosch, where a third of the city's land was in church hands, a mob of weavers attacked local cloisters in 1525 to protest the clergy's unwillingness to contribute to the city's tax burden.[89] Even the brethren among the Modern Devout, for all their orthodoxy, kept an ambivalent distance from the traditional clerical estate and did not encourage their members to aspire to priestly status.[90] The literary culture of the chambers of rhetoric also tapped into this anticlerical feeling among urban populations. Clergy were perennially popular targets of the chambers' mockery and satire. The fifteenth-century carnivalesque monologue *The Guild of the Blue Barge*, for example, invited sinners of all stripes to join its merry company, including "you priests and you clerks,/ Who yearn to work with your loins/ And long to fulfill your desires/ With maidens or with housewives,/ Or desire to drink wine/ ... And at night and by day/ Frolic, play, gamble and drink."[91] These kinds of jibes against lazy, lascivious and licentious priests were common currency in late medieval popular culture across Europe, and there is little evidence to suggest they were more prevalent in the Low Countries than anywhere else.

That the church was in need of improvement no one doubted, but that had been the case since its inception. In the later Middle Ages, particularly after the debacles of the Avignon papacy and the Western Schism, the calls for reform were loud, persistent and widespread from both within the church and without. It was perhaps inevitable that as popular religious participation grew more notice would be taken of the church's shortcomings; the by-product of increased lay religiosity, including a heightened desire for spiritual *reformatio*, was a sharper eye for where clergy fell short. *Reformatio* and *renovatio* in all areas of the individual and corporate Christian life (not just the church or clergy) was a common theme running through much of the learned commentary of the time. Building heavily upon biblical and classical inspiration, advocacy for reform and renewal came from such disparate quarters as the monastic orders and the conciliar movement.[92] By the sixteenth century the loudest voices calling for reform were found among the devotees of the new learning of the Renaissance, the humanists.

Renaissance humanism and its revival of antiquity, its reassessment and reevaluation of Roman and Greek literature and philosophy, began in

---

[88] Tracy, "Elements of Anticlerical Sentiment," p. 261.
[89] Van Gurp, *Reformatie in Brabant*, pp. 23–24.
[90] Van Engen, "Late Medieval Anticlericalism."
[91] "The Guild of the Blue Barge," in Parsons and Jongenelen, *Comic Drama in the Low Countries*, p. 47; see also Pleij, *Het gilde van de Blauwe Schuit*.
[92] Strauss, "Ideas of *Reformatio* and *Renovatio*."

Italy but by the second half of the fifteenth century had spread to all of
Europe to become an international intellectual movement. The humanists called for a revival and renewal of culture and society based on their
reading of classical models. They dismissed the Latin of the medieval
church as barbaric and insisted instead on Latin instruction in classical
Roman primary sources. Perhaps inevitably, any such intellectual fashion
dedicated to the notion of rebirth would join in the ongoing chorus for
reformatio. Across Europe men of deep learning and high moral seriousness, who became known as the Christian humanists, would cast
a discerning and censorious eye over their own era, compare it to antique
models, and find it grievously wanting. The Christian church especially
seemed to have strayed far from its earlier, classical history as the humanists understood it from their readings of scripture and the church fathers.
The church of the first century struck them as far more authentic and
admirable than the church of their own era. More and more the humanists demanded a renewal of personal piety and a reform of ecclesiastical
malpractice so that Christendom might conform more to what they
imagined was its purer and more spiritual apostolic age.[93]

The humanist movement first appeared in the Low Countries in the
fifteenth century, when its program for the renewal of study in classical
language and literature came to the region's monasteries, towns and
schools, and eventually to the University of Leuven, the only one in the
Netherlands, which had been founded in 1425. Antonius Haneron
(1400–1499), professor of Latin there in the 1430s, did much to bring
the "new Latin" to Netherlandish higher education, including the Italian
fashion of Latin-language instruction based on classical rather than medieval sources. The scholar Rudolf Agricola (1443–1485), secretary of the
city government of Groningen, traveled extensively in Italy and brought
the new learning back with him, fostering enthusiasm for Latin and Greek
studies among like-minded intellectuals. His contemporary Wessel
Gansfort (1419–1489), also a son of Groningen, likewise pursued and
promoted the *studia humanitatis* and was primarily interested in it as an
aid in biblical studies.[94] Gansfort had educational connections to the
Modern Devotion, which, like humanism, was dedicated to the goal of
religious renewal, though the Devout advocated a study of scripture that
was far more spiritual than scholarly. By the later fifteenth century local
school rectors and teachers began to take a greater interest in the renewed
Latin studies, and by 1500 municipal schools across the Netherlands

---

[93] Rummel, "Voices of Reform from Hus to Erasmus."
[94] IJsewijn, "The Coming of Humanism to the Low Countries"; Strietman, "The Low
Countries."

were following the new modes of instruction.[95] Works by Italian humanists from Petrarch to Alberti spilled from Netherlandish printshops.
Humanism's linguistic agenda was firmly entrenched in the Netherlandish
educational establishment by the turn of the sixteenth century, and its
attendant calls for reform and renewal would find a wider and wider hearing
in the region's urban landscape. The Spanish scholar Juan Luis Vives
(1493–1540), for example, found a Netherlandish home first in Leuven
and later in Bruges, writing learned treatises on the need to modernize many
social institutions: education should be wrested from the hands of hidebound scholastic theologians, and public charity should be secularized
and thus rationalized to meet civic needs.[96] Pieter Gillis (1486–1533),
a printer and later town secretary of Antwerp, was such an avid supporter
of the new learning that Thomas More dedicated his masterpiece *Utopia*
to him. Humanism penetrated Habsburg circles as well; Hieronymus van
Busleyden (1470–1517) served as a diplomat for regent Margaret of
Austria and enthusiastically patronized the arts and letters at her court
in Mechelen, as well as working to establish instruction in ancient
languages at the University of Leuven. By the early 1500s Leuven
became a center for published philological scholarship on Greek and
Latin.[97]

The introduction and consolidation of humanism in the Low
Countries was the work of many hands: scholars, teachers, rhetoricians,
printers, courtiers and learned patricians. But it would of course find its
most famous personification in the scholar Desiderius Erasmus of
Rotterdam (1466–1536). The illegitimate son of a Holland priest,
Erasmus was in many ways an emblematic product of late medieval
Christianity, particularly its Netherlandish version. In a quite literal manner, he was, much to his embarrassment, an embodiment of the relaxed
observance of the rules of clerical celibacy common among clergy in the
Low Countries. In his youth he attended schools that had some association with the Modern Devout, entered holy orders at an Augustinian
monastery in Gouda founded by the Brethren of Common Life, and
then later escaped it by becoming the secretary to the bishop of
Cambrai.[98] Much of his intellectual formation thereafter took place outside the Low Countries, yet he maintained ties to his homeland and lived
in the duchy of Brabant for various periods in his life. His most tangible
contribution to the study of "good letters" in the Netherlands was his
work in helping establish the Collegium Trilingue at the University of

[95] Cameron, "Humanism in the Low Countries," pp. 138–139.
[96] Noreña, *Juan Luis Vives*, pp. 176–227.
[97] IJsewijn, "The Coming of Humanism to the Low Countries," p. 278.
[98] Augustijn, *Erasmus*, pp. 21–30.

Leuven, dedicated to the study of the three most important ancient languages: Hebrew, Greek and Latin.[99] Though he never taught there himself, its educational mission mirrored his own scholarly interest in the texts of antiquity, which included the publication of a new edition of the Greek New Testament.

Erasmus's greatest fame, however, was the eloquence and wit with which he called for the *reformatio* of the Christian life. From the *Enchiridion* to *The Praise of Folly* he directed his sharp and satirical pen at what he considered the corruptions, abuses and foibles of contemporary Christendom: ignorant priests, greedy monks, pompous theologians, power-hungry bishops and credulous layfolk. He saw religious and moral hypocrisy everywhere and gleefully pointed it out in widely printed and publicized texts. A Christian life, he argued, demanded a high degree of personal piety and spiritual sincerity. One of his biographers, James D. Tracy, has plausibly argued that this vision of the spiritual life was very much a reaction to Erasmus's upbringing in the Low Countries, a crowded, corporatist world where the civil and social functions of religion tended to prevail over interior belief and personal morals. The body of Christ was, in Erasmus's mind, made up of individual believers rather than communities; faith should be individual rather than corporate.[100] Much of the popular religious devotion in which Netherlanders avidly partook, such as papal indulgences, he sneered at: "What's to be said of those who happily delude themselves with forged pardons for real sins, measuring out time to be spent in purgatory as if on a chronometer, calculating the centuries, years, months, days and hours, as if on a mathematical table, so as not to make the slightest error?"[101] He had very little use for much of the common religious practice of his day, most of which he dismissed as superstition, or worse still, as clerical chicanery. His stinging criticisms of the religious professionals of the day, from priests to theologians to friars, were probably among his most popular in a time and place where the social, economic and legal privileges of the first estate were sometimes resented.

And yet at the same time he was much more than a gadfly; his writings also presented a vision of a better Christianity, one that artfully combined the teachings of the gospels with the best virtues of classical antiquity. His idealization of the Christian life, the *philosophia Christi* or philosophy of Christ, found at least as much resonance as his criticisms of the church. He urged Christians to read the Bible, a call that resonated in a region where scriptural lecture was already comparatively widespread. His

---

[99] Augustijn, *Erasmus*, pp. 115–116.   [100] Tracy, *Erasmus of the Low Countries*, p. 38.
[101] Erasmus, "The Praise of Folly," p. 42.

educated, urban compatriots found his vision of a spiritual common-wealth, a community of faith where ritual, dogma and hierarchy took distinctly second place to a life of personal devotion and charity, very attractive. The same region that could produce a movement as earnestly pious as the Modern Devout would, perhaps not surprisingly, also react favorably to the great humanist's call for inner transformation (*reformatio*) to a more Christlike life. Erasmus the author developed a following among many educated Netherlandish Christians, both clerical and lay.[102] He enjoyed substantial intellectual influence in his homeland. All of this is not to say that there was anything particularly "Erasmian" about the Low Countries, but rather that there was perhaps something distinctly Netherlandish about Erasmus. Both what he embraced as the core prin-ciples of the Christian faith, and what he rejected as adiaphoral about it, he had experienced quite personally in his homeland. His calls for *refor-matio* were not unique, except perhaps in their eloquence and range, but they sprang directly from the environment in which he came of age, an environment in which laity demanded their fair share of participation in the worship of God, in which the Christian church exhibited both vitality and decay, in which local loyalties and divisions had powerful political resonance, and in which new wealth and expanding urban populations would create an audience receptive to the notion of renovation and reform. Erasmus's books were widely read in the Netherlands, and some of the works put on by the chambers of rhetoric in the 1500s were clearly inspired by him.[103] By 1520 Christian humanism, most famously but not exclusively personified by Erasmus, had become firmly entrenched in many educational and scholarly circles in the Low Countries; it became very much, as historian Gérard Moreau wrote specifically of the city of Tournai, "*à la mode.*"[104]

Such was the Netherlands at the turn of the sixteenth century: urbane, crowded, wealthy, politically diffused, culturally advanced, yet also feu-dal, agricultural and traditional. In many ways it was a microcosm of all of Europe in that era.[105] The Netherlanders of the first quarter of this century, the generation of Erasmus, had of course no inkling how much their lands would be swept up in and transformed by the movement of religious change. For now, all seemed as it always had been: the Habsburgs plotted and machinated in the faraway Brussels court, but politics was preeminently local, wars were fought abroad, discontents waxed and waned at home, livings had to be made, there was plenty to

---

[102] Trapman, "'Erasmianism' in the Early Reformation in the Netherlands."
[103] Marnef, "Erasmus of Rotterdam."
[104] Moreau, *Histoire du Protestantisme à Tournai*, p. 57.
[105] Tracy, *The Low Countries in the Sixteenth Century*, p. vii.

complain about and perhaps a few things to be grateful for. New ideas and new information, about the past and about the rest of the world, and new commodities, from all corners of the globe, circulated about Netherlandish cities and provided the era with its own particular intellectual and commercial excitement. To some, it may well have seemed a time of great possibility as the Netherlands teemed with economic and cultural accomplishment. Christendom, the community of the baptized, continued to comprise both the sacred and the profane. The church was an imperfect institution that could be grumbled about and mocked, but it continued to function as well as it ever had and still tended to the spiritual needs of most of its people. There was no reason to think it would not keep on doing so into the foreseeable future.

2   Inchoate Reformation

For the majority of Christians living in the Low Countries in the sixteenth century, the Reformation was like an unwanted houseguest: it came early and stayed long. That is, most Christians in the Netherlands remained loyal to the traditional church and saw little attraction in or advantage to joining any of the movements calling for drastic religious change that swept through the region during the 1500s. The various strains and sects of what eventually came to be collectively labeled Protestantism, for all their effects and influence and for all the upheaval they caused, remained a demographic minority by the time Reformed Protestants won their own state, the Dutch Republic, at the century's end. In the eyes of many Netherlandish Christians, to say nothing of the established church, Protestantism in all its manifestations amounted to little more than heresy. It is important to keep this fact in mind while considering the history of the Netherlandish Reformation; there was nothing inevitable or ineluctable about it. Its beginnings were disorganized and unpromising; in the 1520s dissent against the Catholic Church was scattered, eclectic and inchoate, more a sentiment than a movement. In the 1530s religious protest took a more militant and disruptive turn, attracting some Christians but alarming many more. The Habsburg government, meanwhile, would react swiftly and sharply against dissident groups, attempting to suppress heresy as thoroughly as possible.

The Catholic Church had dealt successfully with heresy in the past, and there was no evident reason to think that things would be any different this time around; manifestations of Hussite heresy in Tournai were effectively quelled in the 1420s, for example.[1] Indeed the desire to reform Christianity was nearly as old as Christianity itself; that some were calling for change was nothing new. Movements for religious reform had proliferated in Europe throughout the Middle Ages; by 1500 the call for *reformatio*, both institutional and personal, was widespread and urgent, most eloquently articulated by the Christian humanists. That change and

---

[1] Fudge, "Heresy and the Question of Hussites," pp. 81–84.

improvement were needed few disputed. In the 1520s and 1530s new and more politically charged notions of reformation, arising originally from central Europe, made their way into the Low Countries. Mediated through the young technology of print, these ideas spread rapidly and electrified their readers because of their eloquence and relevance; in a sense what happened in the Low Countries starting in the 1520s was *reformatio* amplified.

Evangelicals

As it turned out, the first potent demand for reformation of the new century arose far from the Netherlands in an undistinguished corner of the Holy Roman Empire, with the Saxon monk Martin Luther's public denunciation of papal indulgences in Wittenberg in the fall of 1517. Using the Bible as his sole standard, Luther rejected the church's teachings on salvation and instead argued that justification came by faith in God's grace and not through human effort. And, perhaps more powerfully, he dismissed much of the church's sacerdotal and sacramental trappings, claiming a priesthood of all believers and offering a ringing defense of Christian freedom, thereby calling for the end of the first estate's special status. Supported by powerful German princes, Luther's defiance turned into open rebellion by 1521. At roughly the same time, to the south in the Swiss city-state of Zurich, the priest Huldrych Zwingli also advocated, from the pulpit and in print, for a more bibliocentric Christianity, but unlike Luther insisted on an even stricter adherence to scriptural standards. This approach led Zwingli to, among other things, reject the notions of the real or corporeal presence of Christ in the Eucharist, clerical celibacy and privilege, most feast days and fasting during Lent, and the use of imagery in churches. Supported by the Zurich magistracy, he implemented reform in the city, a development that soon spread to other cities in the Swiss Confederation. By the early 1520s German-speaking Europe was in the grip of a movement for wholesale evangelical (i.e., gospel-based) reformation. To many Christians the reformers' exaltation of *sola fide* (by faith alone) and *sola scriptura* (by scripture alone) seemed to promise that longed-for reform that would bring the Christian soul closer to God, as well as reduce the powers and privileges of the clergy. To many others, of course, Luther's and Zwingli's message was the rankest heresy and rebellion.

Thanks to printing technology, the German reformers' writings, principally in pamphlet form, circulated widely and found a sympathetic audience, especially in the cities of the Empire. One of the places beyond the Empire to which they also found their way early on was the urbanized, densely populated, literate society of the Netherlands, whose inhabitants were already preoccupied with the juggling of central and local power, with the dislocations caused by an expanding economy and with the unsettling moral and religious questions posed by scholars of the new learning. The Netherlands' highly developed commercial infrastructure – its extensive network of ports, roads and waterways – made the traffic in Luther's trenchant pamphlets in particular quite fluid. There already was in place, in other words, both an economic and an intellectual market in the Netherlands open to the German reformer's ideas, which he articulated with vividness and verve in his writings. As an eminent historian has put it, "Luther was no less the author of the Reformation in the Low Countries than in Germany."[2]

By 1520 translations of the German evangelicals, especially Luther, were being printed in Antwerp.[3] To many of the Christian humanists among the region's school rectors, jurists, priests, civil servants, intellectuals and burghers the Saxon monk's call for a restoration of the Christian church to biblical norms, his criticisms of the failures of the institutional church, his advocacy of Christian freedom and his stress on the centrality of scripture to Christian life were decidedly congenial. Luther's focus on the Gospel and faith in Christ echoed their own preoccupation with both text and devotion. It sounded very much to them like their hero Erasmus's project for the *philosophia Christi*. To them Erasmus and Luther, whose own relationship was at best ambivalent in these years, seemed allied in the cause of restoring Christianity.[4] A Liège correspondent of Erasmus commended Luther to him in 1518 as "the liberator of the spirit."[5] "Everywhere good letters arise again," exulted the Antwerp town secretary and erudite Cornelius Grapheus in 1521, "the Gospel of Christ has been reborn and Paul has come to life once more."[6] The enthusiasts for *reformatio* believed that perhaps their moment had come.

The writings of Luther and Zwingli stirred up enthusiasm, or at least interest, among a small but significant group of Christians in the Netherlands; by the mid-1520s these enthusiasts were being called, among other things, "evangelicals," for their stress on the centrality of

---

[2] Duke, "The Origins of Evangelical Dissent in the Low Countries," in *Reformation and Revolt*, p. 15.
[3] Visser, *Luther's Geschriften in de Nederlanden tot 1546*, pp. 1–5, 28–49.
[4] Trapman, "'Erasmianism' in the Early Reformation in the Netherlands," p. 173.
[5] Halkin, *La Réforme en Belgique sous Charles-Quint*, p. 27.
[6] Quoted in Duke, "Moulded by Repression: The Early Netherlands Reformation 1520–55," in *Dissident Identities in the Early Modern Low Countries*, p. 77.

the gospel message.[7] Not a great deal is known about these earliest evangelical dissenters. A principal source about them is inquisitorial records, which were of course invariably hostile and therefore colored in their descriptions of what precisely they may have believed. And recent scholarship has in fact determined that many of what were once thought to be their writings are of a later date, from the 1540s and 1550s.[8] One of the most important scholars of the Netherlandish Reformation, Alastair Duke, has called this early period "inchoate, derivative and protean."[9] There was little to unite these evangelicals beyond like-mindedness; they had no native Luther or Zwingli who could confidently and charismatically point them in a particular theological direction, nor did they share a common theological vision. They picked and sampled from among the many evangelical ideas and books now circulating not only from their own native traditions but also from Wittenberg and the Swiss cities. They came from all corners of society, clerical and lay, and met in small conventicles to read and listen to and discuss Bible verses together. Priests caught up in the zeal for reform preached in small groups in private spaces. They circulated among themselves the latest evangelical works coming from Germany and Switzerland; Erasmus, Luther and Zwingli appear to have been their principal sources, but some also read native theologians such as the fifteenth-century Groningen humanist Wessel Gansfort. They criticized indulgences and purgatory, questioned whether Christ was really in the Eucharist, exulted in the notion of Christian freedom, wondered if the veneration of saints, including the Virgin Mary, was idolatrous, mocked the privileges and pretensions of the clergy, and suspected that the Bible was a more reliable authority on all matters religious than the pronouncements of the church.[10] Most of them had no interest in separating from the church and certainly did not regard themselves as heretics, but hoped instead for a rebirth of Christendom. Similar to the imperial lands in the 1520s, the Reformation in the Netherlands at this early stage was what German historians have called a *Wildwuchs*, a wildfire proliferation of ideas, preaching, pamphlets, gatherings, exchanges and protests that made up in excitement what it lacked in coherence.[11]

---

[7] Duke, "The Face of Popular Religious Dissent in the Low Countries, 1520–1530," in *Reformation and Revolt*, p. 54.
[8] Woltjer, *Op Weg naar tachtig jaar oorlog*, pp. 137–138.
[9] Duke, "Dissident Voices in a Conformist Town: The Early Reformation at Gouda," in *Reformation and Revolt*, p. 63.
[10] Duke, "Face of Popular Religious Dissent," pp. 40–53.
[11] Lau and Bizer, *Reformationsgeschichte Deutschlands bis 1555*, pp. 40–41.

Who were these evangelicals? They were not a large group, but they seem to have come from nearly every stratum of the Netherlands' urban society and could be found in greater or lesser numbers in virtually every major town. They were especially concentrated in the cities of the western provinces of Brabant, Flanders, Holland, Zeeland and the southern Walloon (French-speaking) towns of Tournai, Valenciennes and Mons. Foremost among these evangelicals were members of the clergy, the religious professionals, many of whom had firsthand knowledge of the church's shortcomings and the dissatisfactions of the laity. Some priests, monks and scholars, attracted by these new ideas, began to preach them publicly, quite a number of them directly from the pulpit. A parish priest in a village outside Ghent gained such a following in 1525 with his evangelical ideas that he had to move his preaching outside to accommodate his growing number of listeners.[12] An analysis of persons who came under suspicion of heresy between 1518 and 1528 reveals that nearly a third of them were clerics.[13] The house of the Augustinian order in Antwerp, affiliated with Luther's own monastery in Wittenberg, was one of the early hotbeds of evangelical activity in the Low Countries. Its priors Jacob Praepositus and Hendrik van Zutphen admired Luther and preached on the Gospels according to Lutheran themes, including the denunciation of indulgences. The first martyrs of the Reformation, as we have seen, were two young Augustinian monks from that same Antwerp house.[14] In cloister-rich Friesland Luther's attack on monastic vows seem to have stirred up some unrest among the religious houses there.[15] Inquisitorial records show that a number of priests came to the attention of ecclesiastical authorities for sermonizing on suspect doctrines. The Antwerp priest Claes van der Elst was stripped of his office for his evangelical opinions, but continued to preach privately to interested groups against the real presence of Christ in the Eucharist, the mediation of the Virgin and the practice of fasting in various private venues in Brussels, Antwerp, Amsterdam and Leiden in the later 1520s.[16] In the Zeeland town of Veere in the late 1520s there were reports of local priests even using catechisms to instruct their listeners about the new theology.[17] In Ypres the earliest spreaders of the reforming message were monks.[18] Tournai's first evangelicals were likewise monks from the city's

---

[12] Decavele, *De dageraad van de Reformatie in Vlaanderen*, pp. 265–266.
[13] Duke, "Origins of Evangelical Dissent," p. 15.
[14] Vercruysse, "De Antwerpse augustijnen en de lutherse Reformatie," pp. 193–216.
[15] Woltjer, *Friesland in Hervormingstijd*, p. 79.
[16] Decavele, "Vroege reformatorische bedrijvigheid," pp. 13–29.
[17] Rooze-Stouthamer, *Hervorming in Zeeland*, pp. 65–67.
[18] Decavele, *De dageraad van de Reformatie in Vlaanderen*, p. 292.

Augustinian cloister, but they also included secular priests.[19] Clerical networks allowed for the spread of evangelical ideas. Evangelical sympathizer Hinne Rode, the rector of an Utrecht friary affiliated with the Modern Devout, personally brought Dutch reformist writings to the attention of Luther, Zwingli and the Strasbourg reformer Martin Bucer as early as 1521.[20] Questioning priests and monks appear to have been the vanguard of the spread of evangelical and reformist ideas in the Netherlands in these decades; in the early 1530s evangelicals in the town of Dinant in the county of Namur were found to have been meeting secretly in a Franciscan cloister.[21] It was clergy who first circulated these new notions among a receptive laity.

It became increasingly clear that there was in fact considerable interest among some Netherlandish layfolk for these new ideas as well. In the early years this interest seemed confined largely to the urban intelligentsia. The Christian humanists among the region's teachers, scholars, officeholders and jurists of course eagerly consumed evangelical teachings, and they believed that the German-speaking reformers had joined Erasmus in helping to usher in a new era of restoration of Christian faith and practice. The defrocked priest Claes van der Elst lectured to small circles of elite lawyers and artists in Brussels, some of them affiliated with the Habsburg court.[22] The learned Hague jurist and councilor Cornelis Hoen wrote a treatise on the Eucharist in 1521, bringing to light writings of the fifteenth-century Groningen scholar Wessel Gansfort that seemed to call into question the real presence of Christ in the eucharistic elements; Zwingli was impressed enough with Hoen's treatise to have it published in Zurich four years later.[23] Among educated, urban elites the interest in reforming ideas grew considerably in the 1520s, and they read and discussed them eagerly across the region.

Some printers, already involved in the business of publishing and selling evangelical works, started joining dissenting groups as well. The medium of print proved to be an effective means to spread new ideas through both text and image. Some 170 evangelical titles saw publication in the Netherlands between 1520 and 1540.[24] It was during this decade that the first native works of evangelical theology, products of the educated elite, started to be published. The *Summa der godlicker schrifturen*, first printed in Leiden in 1523, was an anonymous compilation of

[19] Moreau, *Histoire du Protestantisme*, pp. 63–67.
[20] Mellink, "Preformatie en vroege reformatie," p. 148.
[21] Dupont-Bouchat, "La Repression de l'hérésie," p. 191.
[22] Decavele, "Vroege reformatorische bedrijvigheid," pp. 16–17.
[23] Spruyt, *Cornelius Henrici Hoen*, pp. 59–84.
[24] Johnston, "The Eclectic Reformation," p. 4.

Erasmian theology and translations of Luther. It strenuously defended the idea of justification by faith, as well as Erasmus's understanding of baptism as a vow sufficient to render all others (e.g., those required for holy orders) unnecessary. It also echoed Luther in its emphasis on Christian liberty.[25] Translations of the complete Bible into Dutch and French, some of them based on Erasmus's 1516 edition of the Greek New Testament, were published as early as the 1520s, responding to evangelical desires to make Holy Writ more accessible in the languages of ordinary Christians.[26] The demand for vernacular Bibles and evangelical texts within a population already primed to devotional reading grew considerably. Roughly forty different printers of evangelical literature in the Netherlands worked in the period before 1566, approximately one-fifth of the total number of printers active at the time.[27]

The interest in the new religious ideas soon moved well beyond educated elites to broader populations of ordinary Netherlanders. Those listening to what dissenting priests had to say soon comprised members of the middling artisanal and commercial classes living in the region's many towns. Nearly every town in the Low Countries had its conventicle of dissenters by the mid-1520s, especially in the western provinces.[28] Erasmus wrote to a correspondent in 1525 that the largest part of the populations of Holland, Zeeland and Flanders knew about Luther's teachings.[29] A conventicle discovered in Antwerp in 1524 revealed attendees who were mostly skilled textile workers, metalworkers, grocers and the like.[30] In Maastricht they met in the house of a shoemaker.[31] Even in a village on the far northern island of Texel conventicles of barbers, laborers and their wives met to hear preachers criticize the clergy and reject the real presence of Christ in the mass.[32] A deacon in rural West Friesland reported that local farmers were saying that people had turned to "lutherizing" (*luteriseren*) because greedy priests and prelates were too busy selling church goods among themselves.[33] The overall impression church and state authorities had of such evangelical gatherings was that they were largely made up of ordinary, sometimes unlettered, humble folk, people who might be led astray by smooth-talking preachers. Exact

---

[25] *De Summa der godliker scrifturen.*
[26] Den Hollander, *De Nederlandse Bijbelvertaling*, pp. 15–18.
[27] Johnston, "The Eclectic Reformation," p. 11.
[28] Duke, "Building Heaven in Hell's Despite: The Early History of the Reformation in the Towns of the Low Countries," in *Reformation and Revolt*, p. 77.
[29] Rooze-Stouthamer, *Hervorming in Zeeland*, p. 51.
[30] Duke, "Face of Popular Religious Dissent," p. 33.
[31] Alastair Duke, "The Netherlands," in *Early Reformation in Europe*, p. 149.
[32] Waardt, "I Beg Your Pardon," pp. 334–338.
[33] Post, *Kerkelijke Verhoudingen in Nederland vóór de Reformatie*, p. 518.

numbers or social profiles are not available from sources, but it seems clear that a fairly wide spectrum of urban skilled workers and tradesmen were interested in or at least curious about the new ideas. One of the earliest individuals to be accused of heresy in Ghent, for example, was a baker who had boasted of owning some of Luther's books.[34] The number of dissenters from these middling social groups grew as more militant reformers appeared on the scene by decade's end. At this early stage in the 1520s, however, the notion of a break from the church did not appear to occur to most evangelicals; they seem to have been more concerned initially with reform within the church rather than separation from it. Indeed some saw their attendance at evangelical gatherings as supplemental to their regular sacramental worship in their parish church.[35] Certainly they did not believe themselves to be heretics, and there is little evidence of any efforts to form distinct churches before 1530.[36] Despite this lack of organization, many dissenters were bound together via familial and professional networks.[37] Early on, for example, there emerged a small, informal and specifically Lutheran community in Antwerp, principally comprising German merchants, but it deliberately laid low and did not organize into an official congregation until the 1560s.[38] Conventicles of evangelicals were deliberately small and private, popping up here and there and disappearing just as quickly. The gatherings could number anywhere from a few individuals to several dozen. Usually a portion of scripture was read and discussed either by a single leader or by the group, and then hymns were sung. The meetings usually closed with prayers and care for the poor members, including the collection of alms. This was not a church or even a protest movement but a scattering of intermittent, irregular, private gatherings of like-minded souls, in homes, in taverns and even outdoors.[39]

What did these dissenters believe? Identification of what ideas Netherlandish evangelicals may have espoused at this early stage remains inconclusive at best, but they all point to what Duke has called a "profound transformation" in religious attitudes in the third decade of the sixteenth century.[40] The writings of the Christian humanists and the German and Swiss reformers had spurred a general questioning and reconsidering of traditional religion among a significant number of

---

[34] Decavele, *De dageraad van de Reformatie in Vlaanderen*, pp. 236–237.
[35] Duke, "The Netherlands," p. 152.   [36] Duke, "Moulded by Repression," p. 89.
[37] Duke, "The Netherlands," p. 150.
[38] Marnef, *Antwerp in the Age of Reformation*, pp. 80–82; Van Maanen, *Lutheranen in de Lage Landen*, pp. 47–66.
[39] Augustijn, "De opmars van de calvinistische beweging in de Nederlanden," pp. 425–426.
[40] Duke, "Origins of Evangelical Dissent," p. 8.

Netherlandish Christians. Their interest in reformation was eclectic and largely unoriginal, borrowing heavily from Erasmus, Zwingli and Luther. For at least a generation humanist scholars had been calling for various types of *reformatio*, moral and institutional, which was certainly an attractive idea to many, at least in the abstract. There was enough everyday anticlericalism in the air that those demanding a reform of the behavior and privileges of the clergy met with a favorable response. The failings of some clergy and the occasional worldliness of the church were there for all to see. Beyond mere criticism of priestly malfeasance various theological points of Christian doctrine were circulated and debated, though to be sure not in any systematic fashion. Certainly there was no uniformity of belief among them. What the evangelicals can be said to have in common was a desire to be closer to God, in part by questioning the mediating function of the church and in part by seeking God more directly through scripture. For these very serious Christians, the established church as they knew it seemed more and more an obstacle, or at least an inadequate medium, in their quest for that spiritual communion.[41] Disappointment or dissatisfaction in the church and its practices was a key sentiment that animated them.

Another important component of early Netherlandish evangelical pre-occupations was biblicism. The Germanophone reformers' central tenet of *sola scriptura*, arguing for the Bible as the Word of God and therefore the supreme authority in all matters religious, as well as the Christian humanists' stress on scriptural study to increase devotion, found resonance among an urban population with relatively high rates of literacy. Bible lecture, which was already widespread in the region, thus became the predominant activity within Netherlandish evangelical conventicles; not all could read, to be sure, but many listened to what was read. Gathering together privately to hear and discuss scriptural passages was the principal means by which evangelicals learned, communicated and exchanged new ideas. A hatmaker named Hector van Dommele, for example, developed a following among his artisanal colleagues in Bruges in the mid-1520s for sharing his biblical knowledge, reciting chapter and verse to them by heart.[42] Evangelicals adopted the reformers' privileging of scripture, the Word of God, over all other Christian authority; a tailor in Gouda argued that more merit was to be gained from reading biblical accounts of the Passion than consulting a book of hours or praying the rosary.[43] The Bible was thus seen by some as at least as

[41] Augustijn, "Anabaptism in the Netherlands," pp. 207–208.
[42] Decavele, *De dageraad van de Reformatie in Vlaanderen*, p. 251.
[43] Duke, "Dissident Voices," p. 68.

important an intermediary between God and the individual Christian soul as the church. A popular preacher in Tournai insisted that one day the Gospel would be preached by everyone, even little children.[44] A Ghent evangelical complained loudly and angrily of a monk's sermon that he found to be "outside the Gospel."[45] Likewise the reformers' denial of the biblical justification for such beliefs as indulgences, purgatory and saintly mediation found echoes in Netherlandish evangelical circles.[46] Purgatory was nothing more than "the inside of the priest's purse," as one Zeeland evangelical tartly put it.[47] "Injurious and blasphemous words" impugning the honor of the Virgin and the saints was a common accusation against those charged with heresy in this period.[48] Physical attacks on images of saints were reported as early as 1525 in Antwerp and Delft.[49] Demand that more priests preach directly from the Bible spread through parishes across the region. There was clearly a hunger, fueled by both reformers and the humanists, among many Netherlandish Christians in the 1520s to hear and know more from scripture. And what they heard from it often seemed to them to be at odds with what they saw the institutional church teaching and practicing.

Another theological question that came up among some reform-minded Netherlanders was that of the real presence of Christ's body in the Eucharist. On this they parted ways with Luther, who was adamant that Christ was corporeally present in the elements of communion, and they leaned more toward Zwingli, who interpreted the Eucharist instead as a sign of Christ's presence. The rejection of the real presence also appears to have stemmed from more native traditions of theological dissent. The Hague lawyer Cornelius Hoen concluded as early as 1520 that the scriptural verse "This is my body" (Luke 22:19) should be interpreted figuratively rather than literally; the sacrament, he argued, was a symbol of divine grace in the same way that a ring was a token of marital fidelity.[50] The sacrament of the mass, then, became in some questioning minds a symbol rather than a sacrifice, and, by implication, priests had no power to translate the elements into the body and blood of Christ. This was a major denial of one of the central sacramental tenets of medieval Christianity, the doctrine of transubstantiation, as well as a powerful negation of the authority of the priesthood. Small wonder

[44] Moreau, *Histoire du Protestantisme*, p. 76.
[45] Decavele, *De dageraad van de Reformatie in Vlaanderen*, p. 245.
[46] Duke, "Face of Popular Religious Dissent," pp. 40–43.
[47] Rooze-Stouthamer, *Hervorming in Zeeland*, p. 66.
[48] Moreau, *Histoire du Protestantisme*, p. 70.
[49] Duke, "Face of Popular Religious Dissent," p. 42.
[50] Spruyt, *Cornelius Henrici Hoen*, pp. 86–91.

church authorities reacted with alarm. Evangelicals all over the Netherlands appear to have denied or at least questioned the physical presence of Christ in the Eucharist. Wendelmoet Claesdr, a Holland evangelical who was the first woman in the Netherlands executed for Protestant heresy in 1527, dismissed the host as mere "bread and flour."[51] A tailor in Middelburg, in a drunken moment, claimed he too could be a priest and consecrate the sacrament.[52] A Tournai evangelical dismissively asserted that if you consecrated one piece of bread but not the other and then presented both to "the wisest men" of the city, they would not be able to tell any difference between them.[53] Many dissenters appeared to have shared this skepticism about the real presence, at least insofar as inquisitorial records tell us, and their doubts earned them the epithet "sacramentarians" from their opponents. Earlier generations of Dutch historians tried to hold up this handful of Eucharist questioners as evidence of a uniquely native or "national" strain within the Reformation in the Low Countries, but this perhaps overstates the case.[54] Questions about the metaphysics of the mass arose nearly everywhere in early Reformation Europe, starting with Zwingli in Zurich; it was not a uniquely Netherlandish phenomenon. Sacramentarianism was but one piece of the farrago of ideas, notions, propositions and questions posed by early evangelicals in the Low Countries.

Given this eclecticism and incoherence, it is perhaps safer to agree with the distinguished historian of the early Netherlandish Reformation, Cornelis Augustijn, that what made this first decade, the 1520s, distinctive was its combining of two major strains of reform, the Christian humanism as exemplified by Erasmus and the German theologies coming from the Empire and Switzerland. Coupled with already high levels of lay religious participation and literacy, this early confluence predisposed questioning Netherlanders to be open to other, later influences such as Anabaptism and the Reformed movement.[55] The broad evangelical search for greater fellowship with God in the 1520s and 1530s would pick and choose, like a thieving magpie, from among a wide variety of reforming notions, not just anticlericalism or biblicism or sacramentarianism. Enthused by this array of new ideas, dissenting Netherlanders would ask questions about the practices of the church, the meaning of scripture and their relationship to God, but at this initial stage they did

---

[51] Duke, "Face of Popular Religious Dissent," p. 45.
[52] Rooze-Stouthamer, *Hervorming in Zeeland*, p. 57.
[53] Moreau, *Histoire du Protestantisme*, p. 71.
[54] Trapman, "Le role des 'sacramentaires' des origines de la Réforme."
[55] Augustijn, "Niederlande," p. 478.

not arrive at any uniform or systematic answers. The Reformation in the Low Countries started as a hybrid, and it would remain that way for the rest of the sixteenth century.

Anabaptists

As the decade of the 1520s came to a close, other strains of dissent from further east made their way into the Low Countries to add to the already simmering mix of religious discontent and protest. The *Wildwuchs* grew, as it were, even wilder. In the German-speaking lands, as the ramifications of the Lutheran and Zwinglian reformations played themselves out, some Christians called for even more sweeping church reform than either Luther or Zwingli, who were careful to cultivate government support for their programs, could tolerate. The biblicism inherent in the doctrine of *sola scriptura* led some of them to the notion's logical extreme: they came to the conclusion that anything not found in or sanctioned by scripture was ungodly and therefore to be rejected. This radically reductionist stance naturally provided them with a wide array of targets, doctrinal and institutional, to attack in the traditional church. These dissenters drew the most extreme conclusions from their understanding of scripture, and this made them appear quite radical in the eyes of contemporaries, particularly in their challenge to political as well as religious authority. Among other things, their biblical literalism led them to conclude that scripture provided no warrant for infant baptism, and therefore true Christians should be baptized as voluntary adult believers. This tenet was not their only one, but it was their most conspicuous and most shocking to contemporaries, for centuries of Christian tradition and social practice had made the baptism of infants not long after birth normative; in addition to conveying God's grace, the sacrament signaled the entry of a newborn soul into the community of Christ. Adherence to the doctrine of believer's baptism also led their enemies to call them Anabaptists, or "rebaptizers." (The Dutch name for them, *Doopsgezinden* – literally "baptism-minded" – reflects that association.) The epithet "Anabaptist" has since become an umbrella term for a wide variety of movements, beliefs and practices, but all of their adherents shared a belief in immediate, extreme and direct personal and ecclesiastical *reformatio*. The Anabaptists took literally biblical injunctions to avoid the temptations of the flesh and exalt the spirit instead, which meant in practice that unlike earlier evangelicals they espoused an immediate deliberate separation from the established church. Their conspicuous nonconformity distinguished them from other evangelicals. Many of them also rejected bearing arms, taking oaths, and owning property because of scriptural dictates. This eschewing of some very commonplace early modern European social practices also scandalized outsiders. This radical biblicism, spiritualism and separatism emerged in central Europe in the 1520s in a profusion of small but vocal movements, and their proliferation contributed mightily to an increasingly apocalyptic mood in Europe as it entered the ensuing decade. Nearly all of these groups demanded a much more thoroughgoing reformation of the Christian church than any authority (Catholic or evangelical) was comfortable with, and their literal reading of scripture, including the book of Revelation, made them open to chiliastic and millenarian ideas. In the Holy Roman Empire, the turbulent violence of the Peasants War (1524–1525), whose leaders borrowed much of the protest rhetoric of the evangelicals, contributed to this general mood of heightened polarization and expectation. A diverse number of figures among the radicals took on prophetic roles and preached about the coming of the final judgment and the need for a root-and-branch reordering of church and society. For many such visionaries the end of history seemed at hand.[56]

For the Netherlands the German lands were once again the wellspring for these new religious ideas, whose most important messenger was the peripatetic Franconian furrier Melchior Hoffman (1495–1543). Hoffman started out as a follower of Luther but became radicalized in the 1520s and began to style himself a prophet. He traveled throughout northern Europe in the 1520s and early 1530s, including the cities of Emden and likely Deventer, preaching a millenarian vision, baptizing adults and calling on true believers to separate themselves from the sins of the world and the flesh.[57] Stressing the centrality of Christ's incarnation, Hoffman argued that Christians could be reborn through voluntary believers' baptism and strive for moral perfection through good works and segregation from the fallen world. Sacraments, priests and the whole ecclesiastical apparatus in all its materiality hindered this process and were therefore to be rejected.[58] Settling in the imperial free city of Strasbourg, which was becoming home to a number of millenarians by 1530, he and other Anabaptists anticipated the imminent end of the world and the rise of the New Jerusalem, as predicted in the biblical book of Revelation.

Fancying himself a new Elijah, Hoffman directed apostles, who became known as Melchiorites, from the northwestern imperial town of Emden in 1530 westward into Groningen, Friesland and Holland, where his

---

[56] Williams, *The Radical Reformation*, pp. 212–286, 431–523. Recently historians of Anabaptism have questioned using the category "radical" to describe this particular stream of religious dissent; see Driedger, "Against the 'Radical Reformation.'"

[57] Zijlstra, *Om de ware gemeente en de oude gronden*, p. 95.

[58] Zijlstra, *Om de ware gemeente en de oude gronden*, pp. 88–94.

movement booked its biggest successes, gaining a following among the artisans and tradesmen of Amsterdam in particular.[59] These social groups especially had been badly affected by a general downturn in the Netherlandish economy in the 1520s and 1530s, and many of them turned to the eschatological promises of the Melchiorites "out of a profound sense of crisis."[60] Amsterdam was one of the few cities in the Low Countries enjoying economic growth in the period, and the political regime there was relatively forbearing in its treatment of suspected heretics, much to the annoyance of the provincial government. It was thus possible for Melchiorite disciples to preach and baptize inside that city with relative impunity.[61] At least some of those attracted to the new sects appear to have come out of evangelical and sacramentarian circles; they perhaps found sympathetic the uncompromising nonconformity and zealous spirituality of these new apostles.[62] Smaller Melchiorite conventicles were reported in other regions such as Zeeland, Brabant and Flanders, but the movement seems to have concentrated especially in the northern Netherlands, where the mechanisms of judicial persecution were more lax than in the south, though substantial Melchiorite communities could be found in Maastricht and Liège (a likely member of the latter group was Idelette de Bure, the future wife of John Calvin, who fled to Strasbourg in the 1530s with her first husband, Jean Stordeur, in order to escape persecution).[63] As the apostles' prophetic message spread among informal professional and familial networks, more and more enthusiasts came to Amsterdam in growing apocalyptic expectation. In late 1531, however, the provincial Court of Holland executed ten apostles for heresy, an act that shocked Hoffman into suspending baptisms for two years. Soon, however, a native prophet began to draw more attention: Jan Matthijsz (1500–1534), a baker from Haarlem, who on his own initiative resumed baptizing believers and sent out Melchiorite emissaries to spread the radical message to audiences across Holland, Friesland and Groningen. Far more so than earlier dissident groups, the Anabaptist movement derived great momentum from such charismatic figures. The number of people attracted to the radical message may have outstripped those drawn to milder evangelical or sacramentarian ideas of reform. The Anabaptists' passion and message of spiritual liberation appealed to a small but rapidly growing number of Netherlanders in the early 1530s.

---

[59] Deppermann, *Melchior Hoffman*, pp. 321–342.   [60] Waite, *David Joris*, p. 29.
[61] Mellink, *Amsterdam*, pp. 18–26.   [62] Mellink, *Amsterdam*, p. 21.
[63] Verheyden, *Anabaptism in Flanders*, pp. 15–18; Halkin, "Protestants des Pays-Bas et de la Principauté de Liège réfugiés à Strasbourg," p. 299.

That passion had dramatic consequences. Some of the Netherlandish Anabaptists made their way across the eastern border into the empire to the Westphalian city of Münster, where under the leadership of local reformers an evangelical coup was underway that had overthrown the ruling prince-bishop. In early 1534 Jan Matthijsz sent disciples there who preached and baptized and rapidly gained a following within the municipal population. He then came himself and proclaimed Münster to be the New Jerusalem once predicted by Melchior Hoffman (who had believed it would be Strasbourg), and his followers took over the city and tried to refashion it into an earthly paradise where private property, debts and money were abolished. Although Münster was a city in the Holy Roman Empire, it was Netherlandish Anabaptists who led the revolution in the city – first Jan Matthijsz himself and then after he was killed by besieging troops in April 1534, Jan Beukelsz van Leyden (1509–1536), a tailor and merchant from southern Holland.[64] Jan van Leyden styled himself king of the New Jerusalem, continued the practice of community of goods and, more notoriously, introduced polygamy into the city. Many Melchiorites were convinced that the New Jerusalem was merely the beginning of a worldwide transformation, the beginning of the end of days. This tumultuous experiment to create a theocracy along Old Testament lines sparked considerable alarm both outside and inside Münster. Eventually the city, bereft of food and rife with disorder, succumbed to combined Catholic and Lutheran besieging forces in the summer of 1535, and Jan van Leyden and his fellow leaders were tried and executed in 1536.[65] In both Catholic and Protestant legend "Münster" became a notorious byword for reformation run amok, with anarchy, bloodshed and destruction as the result. The Münster Anabaptists were denounced by all sides as dangerous heretics. Disciplinary authorities in churches both Catholic and Protestant took more care in future to control their flocks more carefully lest similar chaos ensue.

The fact that the Anabaptist kingdom of Münster's leadership was largely Dutch was perhaps less important than the effect the kingdom had on the Anabaptist movement inside the Netherlands during 1534–1535.[66] Among followers, that effect was electrifying. Conventicles popped up by the dozens in northern towns. Many of their members believed the end of the world might be at hand and sought to prepare themselves spiritually. These gatherings were led exclusively by laity, another difference with the evangelicals, who still tended to look to clergy

[64] Panhuysen, *De beloofde stad*, pp. 140–148.
[65] Zijlstra, *Om de ware gemeente en de oude gronden*, pp. 111–125.
[66] Mellink, *De wederdopers in de noordelijke Nederlanden*, pp. 20–101.

for leadership. This was a decidedly more revolutionary, sectarian and separatist dissent from the established church.[67] More so than earlier evangelicals, the Netherlandish Anabaptists felt the need for organization and community, often expressed in terms of a covenant.[68] Anabaptist congregations were led by lay elders and deacons, the latter of whom provided for less fortunate brethren. They demanded godly behavior from their members in anticipation of the Second Coming of Christ and his final judgment. While the New Jerusalem in Münster flourished thousands of Netherlandish Anabaptists, especially from Holland, tried to make their way there in anticipation of the end of days. Many of them failed, captured by authorities en route. The Anabaptist regime in Münster sent out emissaries as far away as Antwerp to ask for and collect munitions and provisions in order to hold out against the siege. Debates swirled within Anabaptist circles about whether taking up arms for the cause of the gospel was possible.

Many appear to have thought so, for many incidents of religious exaltation, some of them bizarre and even violent, erupted across the northern provinces during the years 1534 and 1535. In March 1534, for example, a group of Anabaptists ran through the center of Amsterdam waving unsheathed swords and calling on the godless to repent. Almost a year later in the same city a conventicle of a dozen or so Anabaptists, female and male, denounced material goods, stripped and threw their clothes in a fire and then ran naked in the streets in a fit of desperate religious ecstasy, much to the befuddlement and alarm of the authorities and inhabitants alike.[69] In 1535 uprisings and rebellions by Anabaptist conventicles flared up in a number of places in the provinces of Groningen, Friesland and Holland, inspired by the takeover of Münster. Once again, the ever-restive dissenters of Amsterdam stirred up trouble, trying to stage a desperate coup: in May 1535 a group of forty armed Anabaptists tried and failed to take over the town hall, an assault that traumatized the burgomasters considerably. They immediately retaliated, with the coup plotters either killed in battle or later hanged.[70] When Münster fell in June 1535 the apocalyptic movement effectively collapsed and severe government repression set in. The Melchiorite strain of millenarian Anabaptism, which had captured the energy and imagination of many in the Netherlands for a few brief years, was in effect quashed, along with its dream of a New Jerusalem.

---

[67] Duke, "Moulded by Repression," p. 91.
[68] Augustijn, "Anabaptism in the Netherlands," p. 205.
[69] Mellink, *Amsterdam*, pp. 31–32, 46–48.
[70] Mellink, *Amsterdam*, pp. 53–75; Zijlstra, *Om de ware gemeente en de oude gronden*, pp. 141–144.

With the fall of the kingdom of Münster and subsequent repression, Netherlandish Anabaptism lapsed into, in the words of its most recent chronicler, an "identity crisis."[71] Militant apocalypticism had failed; what was left of the promise of spiritual and social reformation? In the face of harsh governmental reaction many followers of course recanted and returned to the established church. The small numbers who were left over splintered into a variety of factions and sects that disagreed with each other on a number of questions, such as the licitness of using armed force, but they all retained a certain measure of the spiritualist and separatist legacies of Hoffman. The Batenburgers, named for their leader Jan van Batenburg (1495–1538), scion of a bastard branch of a noble family from Overijssel, carried on the violent apocalypticism of the Münsterites most directly. Styled the new King David who would defeat the ungodly (i.e., the Catholic church), Jan van Batenburg led what amounted to gangs of bandits in the plundering of churches and monasteries in the northeastern Low Countries in the later 1530s. His followers called themselves the "children of Jacob" and believed they were God's chosen. The sect disappeared after Jan van Batenburg was executed by authorities in 1538. Meanwhile the more pacifist heirs of the Melchiorite tradition grouped themselves around the Frisian surgeon Obbe Philips (1500–1568), who had been baptized by Jan Matthijsz's emissaries in 1533, and were concentrated in Friesland and Groningen; they remained a small and marginalized group, especially when Philips recanted his Anabaptism in 1540.[72] They were particularly known for their high standards of piety and behavior and for their strict self-segregation from public life.[73]

The most significant Anabaptist leader to emerge in the immediate post-Münster era was the Delft glass painter David Joris (1501–1556). He started his reforming trajectory as a sacramentarian evangelical and by the early 1530s became a Melchiorite sympathizer. By 1534 Joris had been rebaptized, and Obbe Philips made him an elder in the movement. He stayed well away from the Münster debacle and by 1536 was convinced through visions that God was calling him to preach the true meaning of the gospel. Joris's stress was on the internalizing of faith, and thus he regarded questions of ecclesiology as of little importance. The kingdom of God was instead to be cultivated in the heart of the believer, who was free to conform to whatever outward church necessary to keep safe. Joris's intense spiritualism also had a strong messianic streak, and by the 1540s he had drifted into a mysticism well removed from his

[71] Zijlstra, *Om de ware gemeente en de oude gronden*, p. 147.
[72] Zijlstra, *Om de ware gemeente en de oude gronden*, pp. 151–157.
[73] Woltjer, *Friesland in Hervormingstijd*, pp. 87–88.

Anabaptist beginnings.[74] Until about 1540 he was the acknowledged leader of what was left of the Anabaptist movement in the Netherlands and northwestern Germany.[75] Joris had a particularly strong following in Holland, and his prominent role at various gatherings of Melchiorite leaders abroad (in Bocholt and Strasbourg) propelled him to the forefront of the spiritualist wing of Netherlandish Anabaptism. He claimed to receive divine visions and increasingly insisted that because of these revelations his role was one of prophet. Scripture, he argued, should be understood in the light of his visions, what he called the "living word."[76] Small Davidite communities were particularly concentrated in the cities of the provinces of Overijssel, Utrecht, Holland and Brabant, and they comprised members from the artisanal classes in particular. Joris and some of his disciples settled in Antwerp between 1539 and 1544, where he found patronage and protection among noble families. During his time in Antwerp his theology grew more mystical and more starkly emphasized the distinction between flesh and spirit. Styling himself a new king David, he claimed for himself a greater and more apocalyptic spiritual authority that alienated some Melchiorites. The threat of persecution prompted Joris to leave Antwerp and move to the Swiss city of Basel in 1544; by removing himself geographically from Netherlandish Anabaptism he came to enjoy less and less influence over the movement.[77] By the later 1540s the predominant figure within Netherlandish Anabaptism was the Frisian ex-priest Menno Simons (1496–1561), who would become the spiritual and doctrinal father of one of the most important and enduring strains of Anabaptism in the Low Countries, Mennonitism.

Reaction

One of the events that had impelled Simons to abandon his priestly vocation and join the Anabaptist reformation was the 1531 beheading for heresy of a tailor in Leeuwarden who had been rebaptized. The emergence of various Protestant heresies in the Netherlands provoked a strong and sustained political and juridical reaction by the Habsburg government.

Although the new ideas of religious reform circulating in the 1520s and 1530s attracted the allegiance of a relatively small number of Netherlanders, political and ecclesiastical authorities did not stand idle in the face of what they saw as extremely dangerous dissent that

[74] Waite, *David Joris*, pp. 113–138.
[75] Zijlstra, *Om de ware gemeente en de oude gronden*, p. 167.   [76] Waite, *David Joris*, p. 133.
[77] Waite, *David Joris*, p. 177.

threatened the very fabric of Christendom. In the Holy Roman Empire the imperial Diet of Worms of 1521 had declared Luther both a heretic and a rebel, and not long after this those who expressed interest in or approval of his ideas soon found themselves subjected to the selfsame suspicions. The earliest Netherlandish evangelicals may have thought themselves faithful Christians who remained within the body of Christ, but the leadership of the Catholic Church was having none of that. Nothing less than the salvation of souls was at stake. Outside the church, so ran centuries of tradition, there was no salvation. Heresy, according to medieval definitions, included both intellectual and contumacious elements: it both disagreed with church teaching and rejected church authority.[78] Canon law thus made heresy the religious counterpart to treason, regarding it as rebellion against God. As far as the church universal was concerned, these dissenters and nonconformists, however small their numbers, however innocent their intentions, were potential heretics who posed a direct threat to Christendom by questioning and in some cases denying the veracity of fundamental doctrine. The treasonous nature of their offenses made it easier for the law to deal with them harshly, including the use of torture. The dissenters seemed to come from all strata of society, from renegade priests to discontented intellectuals to restless common folk. The more they gathered in secret, the more evangelicals seemed to be, as Alastair Duke nicely described it, "drifting into a sort of unintentional separatism."[79] The further disorders wrought by the radical Anabaptists hardened the resolve of authorities to suppress any religious dissent or nonconformity. The heretics brought with them the prospect of schism in the body of Christ. And for most right-thinking people of the time, particularly those serving in governing bodies charged with maintaining public order, heresy was a grave danger to the social fabric and to traditional values. Uniformity of belief, so ran the conventional thinking of the time, was the surest means to ensure social and political harmony.

In the Netherlands the official reaction to heresy would be almost immediate and would come directly from the top. The child Charles of Ghent inherited the Netherlands in 1506, and in 1519 the teenager Charles V was elected de facto Holy Roman Emperor. The imperial constitution limited Charles's ability to combat heresy in the German territories, but in his patrimonial lands in the Low Countries he had a much freer legal and political hand to deal with dissent than in the Empire proper. As a loyal Catholic and sworn protector of the church, he

---

[78] Goosens, *Les Inquisitions modernes*, vol. 1, p. 29.
[79] Duke, "Moulded by Repression," p. 87.

strongly believed he had a duty to suppress heresy in his native lands.[80] Furthermore, Charles's policy, like that of his predecessors, was to con- solidate his dynasty's authority over the Low Countries; a campaign against heresy, marshaling judicial power over recalcitrant subjects, fit in nicely with this goal.[81] The prosecution of heretics therefore became an instrument of Habsburg state-building in the Netherlands.[82] As a consequence, the judicial machinery to extirpate heresy would be more elaborately orchestrated in the Netherlands than anywhere else in Europe north of the Alps, though it was nowhere nearly as well organized or effective as the Mediterranean inquisitions.[83] Consequently, one of the defining characteristics of the Netherlandish Reformation was the severe and sustained persecution that Protestant sects of varying stripes endured there during the course of the sixteenth century. The first Protestant heretics in the Low Countries, as we have seen, were executed in 1523, and the last one would be executed in 1597. To a degree not seen in other regions of Europe, the Reformation in Netherlands would be, in the apt phrasing of Duke, "molded by repression."

The Netherlandish church's and government's offensive against heresy therefore began almost immediately; already in 1519 the theological faculty of the university of Leuven formally condemned Luther's doctrine of justification by faith.[84] In October 1520 the prince-bishop of Liège, a firm Habsburg ally, promulgated an edict condemning what the church began calling "Lutheran" ideas.[85] That same month the Leuven theolo- gians orchestrated a public burning of heretical books, including Luther's; similar bonfires were soon lit in other cities such as Ghent, Antwerp, Courtrai, Amsterdam and Utrecht.[86] Such displays were intended to send a vivid warning to those who might dabble with heresy. Charles V promulgated the 1521 imperial Edict of Worms, which con- demned Luther as a rebel and heretic, separately in the Netherlands, in order to underscore the greater direct authority he wielded in this partic- ular part of his dominions.[87] As the denunciations of evangelical ideas increased and spread, Netherlandish enthusiasts of the new ideas grew increasingly nervous. It became riskier to hold or even sympathize with heterodox ideas, even if one thought of oneself as a loyal Christian. The

[80] Blockmans, *Emperor Charles V*, p. 80.
[81] Fühner, *Die Kirchen- und antireformatorische Religionspolitiek*, pp. 89–166.
[82] Monter, "Heresy Executions in Reformation Europe," pp. 49–50.
[83] Gielis and Soen, "The Inquisitorial Office in the Sixteenth-Century Habsburg Netherlands," p. 65.
[84] Gielis, "'Post exactam et diligentiam examinationem.'"
[85] Halkin, *La Réforme en Belgique sous Charles-Quint*, p. 33.
[86] Visser, *Luther's Geschriften in de Nederlanden tot 1546*, pp. 13–15.
[87] Fühner, *Die Kirchen- und antireformatorische Religionspolitiek*, pp. 185–198.

Christian humanist Cornelius Grapheus, the town secretary of Antwerp, once so optimistic about the prospect of reform in Christendom through the revival of good letters, was made to recant his evangelical beliefs in 1522 and was subsequently dismissed from office and jailed.[88] It was clear that the central government in Brussels was in no mood to brook dissent, let alone heresy.

The first line of defense against heresy and its dangers was of course the regular legal system. Civic and provincial courts across the Netherlands had the task of prosecuting heresy because it was a threat to the civil and ecclesiastical order, and it was the secular arm of justice that carried out the punishments mandated by canon law. There had been an inquisition in the Low Countries, as there was in the rest of Latin Christendom since the Middle Ages, but it was of at best uneven effectiveness against these new, more aggressive brands of sixteenth-century heresy.[89] Additionally, inquisitors were obliged to try to save souls and allow suspects the chance to recant their errors; from their point of view a reconciled sinner was the preferred goal to a punished traitor. Local secular courts therefore carried the lion's share of the burden of enforcing religious uniformity. This responsibility included implementing the growing number edicts and placards against evangelical ideas issued by the Brussels government in the 1520s and 1530s.[90] The most important of these placards was Charles V's edict of October 1529, which reaffirmed and expanded the proscriptions against heresy: it remained a capital crime and the property of heretics was to be confiscated by the state. The placard further forbade the printing or possession of heretical books, attending secret conventicles, offering hospitality to a heretic in one's domicile, or discussing the Bible unless one was a theologian.[91] This Caroline legislation did not attack heresy per se, but instead was a measure directed against the spread of heretical ideas among the population. Habsburg policy insisted that judicial rigor in enforcing placards such as these was the only sure way to suppress disorder and to save souls.

As the evangelical movement swelled in the 1520s, and then as strains of it took a more militant turn in the 1530s, it became clear to the central government in Brussels that more urgent, concerted and concentrated judicial measures against religious malcontents were needed. The various provinces did not automatically register the placards officially, and so they

---

[88] Duke, "Moulded by Repression," p. 79.
[89] Goosens, *Les Inquisitions modernes*, vol. 1, pp. 38–40.
[90] Duke, "The 'Inquisition' and the Repression of Religious Dissent in the Habsburg Netherlands 1521–1566," in *Dissident Identities*, pp. 107–108.
[91] Halkin, *La Réforme en Belgique sous Charles-Quint*, pp. 48–49.

were not in force uniformly across the whole Netherlands.[92] Local courts
were enforcing the placards unevenly at best. In cities such as Antwerp
and Amsterdam, for example, magistrates often turned a blind eye to
dissenting groups within their populations. The confederate nature of
sixteenth-century Netherlandish local sovereignties meant that setting up
a more coherent and comprehensive judicial apparatus to suppress heresy
would be as challenging as any other political innovation there, though
since the fifteenth century the Burgundian–Habsburg regime had made
some headway in the centralization of princely justice.[93] There was little
also love lost between the Habsburg government and the Netherlandish
episcopacy, which mistrusted the Brussels court's centralizing ambitions.
Charles V had set up regents to govern the Netherlands in his absence; his
aunt Margaret of Austria (r. 1519–1530) and sister Mary of Hungary
(r. 1531–1555) tangled frequently with local bishops, provincial
estates and town governments in an ongoing contest over the question
of centralized powers. It was clear that ineffective traditional ecclesiastical courts and recalcitrant provincial courts were not going to make it
easy for the Brussels government to combat what was increasingly, and
indiscriminately, being called "luthery" (lutherij).[94]

At first in 1522 Charles V tried to set up a national agency for all his
Netherlandish possessions with a general commissioner given inquisitorial powers, the Brabant jurist Frans van der Hulst, put in charge, but Van
der Hulst managed to blunder across local privileges and sensibilities so
much that protests from provincial estates prompted Margaret of Austria
to dismiss him in a little over a year. Instead the regent lobbied for and got
from the papacy a separate inquisitorial office under Habsburg control
headed by a native churchman assisted by advisers from provincial courts.
In 1525 this hybrid imperial-papal inquisition was given jurisdiction by
the pope over all the Netherlands in the question of heresy, a provision
intended to circumvent the objections of the local courts. Additional
inquisitors and provincial delegates were added later to give the organization still more coherence and reach. The inquisitors-general had the
power to visit all provinces and to interrogate anyone in matters of heresy,
and they were to supervise all clergy, teachers and printers. In effect the
Netherlandish inquisition functioned as an office rather than a tribunal.[95]
The inquisitors were investigators rather than prosecutors who lent their

---

[92] Gielis and Soen, "The Inquisitorial Office in the Sixteenth-Century Habsburg
Netherlands," p. 53.
[93] De Schepper, "The Burgundian–Habsburg Netherlands," pp. 509–511.
[94] Tracy, "Heresy Law and Centralization under Mary of Hungary," pp. 284–285.
[95] Gielis and Soen, "The Inquisitorial Office in the Sixteenth-Century Habsburg
Netherlands," pp. 52–58.

expertise to civil courts in the campaign against heresy. In all their actions they were expected to cooperate with secular provincial judicial bodies.[96] In practice the imperial-papal inquisition worked alongside secular courts, both provincial and civic, to enforce canon law against heresy and to prosecute those who violated the Caroline religious placards.

It is in fact something of a misnomer to give the Habsburgs' anti-heretical policy the blanket label of "inquisition," with all the sinister connotations later Protestant propaganda would try to attach to that word; it was more a collection of evolving and multilayered political, ecclesiastical and legal measures the central government instituted, not always consistently or effectively, to prosecute the sin and crime of heresy. In some respects it operated as haphazardly as all the other central mechanisms the Habsburg government implemented in the Netherlands during the sixteenth century. For all its theoretical fearsomeness, the imperial-papal inquisition's reach was not uniform everywhere; it still had to reckon with the sensibilities of tetchy local authorities. It remained very much captive to the Netherlands' diffused political culture.[97] Overlapping jurisdictions sometimes hampered the effective exercise of inquisitorial authority. The execution of justice was one of the privileges that provincial and civic officials believed were part of their own bailiwick. Many local governing authorities found the severity of the anti-heresy legislation troubling, and more than one local magistracy, particularly that of cosmopolitan Antwerp, was accused of being soft on heresy.[98] Local political circumstances made the implementation of the new inquisitorial apparatus uneven; it did not pertain in Groningen (only recently annexed to the Habsburg Netherlands) and Luxemburg, and it barely touched the county of Namur and the duchy of Brabant, the latter of which contained the important cities of Antwerp and Brussels.[99] Indeed the Brabantine provincial estates successfully asserted their rights to fight the establishment of any permanent inquisitorial offices in their duchy.[100] And where the inquisitors did visit and investigate their successes were decidedly mixed. The inquisitors who came to Friesland in the 1550s, for example, to deal with Mennonite Anabaptists by offering them pardon if they reconciled, found that many suspects had either already broken with the movement or had found safety in exile. Meanwhile the provincial Court of Friesland refused

[96] Duke, "'Inquisition,'" pp. 103–105; Goosens, *Les Inquisitions modernes*, vol. 1, pp.137–145.
[97] Gielis and Soen, "The Inquisitorial Office in the Sixteenth-Century Habsburg Netherlands," p. 57.
[98] Duke, "Salvation by Coercion: The Controversy Surrounding the 'Inquisition' in the Low Countries on the Eve of the Revolt," in *Reformation and Revolt*, pp. 153–154.
[99] Duke, "'Inquisition,'" pp. 105–106.
[100] Goosens, *Les Inquisitions modernes*, vol. 2, p. 79.

to allow the inquisitors to take stricter measures. At best the inquisitors came up with dozens of recantations or punishments rather than the hundreds they had expected.[101] Likewise a sub-inquisitor visiting Zeeland in the 1550s and 1560s found himself frequently hindered by various checks that anxious city governments there put on his investigations, including requiring civic officials to accompany him at his interrogations.[102] The States of Holland successfully appealed to the Brussels government in the 1520s that all those Hollanders accused of heresy had to be tried in their home province.[103] The decentralized nature of the Netherlandish polity limited the central government's effectiveness in imposing a general anti-heretical legal regime on all of its subjects. Most of the actual prosecution of heresy cases was in local hands and was thus uneven at best. Perhaps the only exception to this rule was in the county of Flanders, where the inquisitor Pieter Titelmans zealously pursued heresy with relative success between 1545 and 1572, for a total of roughly fifteen hundred cases, far more than any other inquisitorial region in the Low Countries. This was in part because he was able for a time to keep the interference of local judicial authorities in the Flemish cities to a minimum.[104] Flanders proved exceptional, and even there the inquisition failed in its mission to eradicate heresy.

The impact and effectiveness of the Netherlandish inquisitorial mechanism were therefore not as great as has sometimes been suggested or that later Protestant legend made it out to be. Charles V in fact enacted an extensive reorganization of the anti-heretical apparatus in the Netherlands during the 1540s in order to render it more effective. And his successor, Philip II, would likewise be frustrated by what he saw as the policy's uneven results.[105] Nevertheless the Habsburg regime was responsible for the executions for heresy of some thirteen hundred people from the 1520s to the 1560s, out of a total of roughly three thousand heresy executions for Europe as a whole in that same period.[106] Despite its mixed success, therefore, the prosecution of heresy was still more severe in the Netherlands than everywhere else in northern Europe at that time, a state of affairs that affected the course of the region's politics as the sixteenth century wore on. In the long term the state's reaction to

---

[101] Woltjer, *Friesland in Hervormingstijd*, pp. 111–115.

[102] Rooze-Stouthamer, *Hervorming in Zeeland*, pp. 174–177.

[103] Duke, "Salvation by Coercion," p. 165.

[104] Van der Wiele, "De inquisitierechtbank van Pieter Titelmans."

[105] Gielis and Soen, "The Inquisitorial Office in the Sixteenth-Century Habsburg Netherlands," pp. 58–61.

[106] Duke, "'Inquisition,'" pp. 100–101.

heresy would prove to be at least as damaging to the Netherlandish political fabric as the heresy itself.

For those subject to its exactions, of course, the government's policy to eradicate heresy seemed effective enough. Even if, in the long run, the anti-heresy measures proved unsuccessful in eliminating the heretical threat, they inflicted a large amount of suffering and damage on a considerable number of people in the interim. At least twenty and perhaps as many as thirty individuals were executed for heresy in the 1520s alone.[107] Though the executions of the two Augustinian monks in Brussels in 1523 were (intentionally) spectacular and extreme, the early evangelicals who came before the law paid in other painful ways. Janne Pier Kerstiaansdr of Middelburg, for example, was banned from the city in 1527 for two years, but only after part of her tongue was cut out because of blasphemies she spoke against God and the Virgin Mary.[108] Priests who had embraced Lutheran opinions, such as Henry of Westphalia in Tournai in 1528, were publicly degraded and stripped of the trappings of clerical office before being consigned to the flames.[109] Franchois de Jonghe, a painter in Ypres, was found in 1538 to possess copies of forbidden songs and books. He was publicly flogged and his books were burned in front of him. After two years' imprisonment he was decapitated by sword and his corpse put on display.[110] Lives could be severely disrupted; some of those convicted or even merely accused fled to friendlier jurisdictions. Johan Pael of the Overijssel town of Kampen, for example, was accused of possessing heretical materials by that city's magistracy in 1529. He asked for time to consider the charges against him and then promptly fled the city to safety in Emden in the northwest Empire. The magistracy convicted and condemned him in absentia; two years later he appealed for mercy and recanted his opinions, whereupon the aldermen allowed him to return and made him pay a substantial fine instead.[111] There were many more such abjurations and recantations; not all accused of heresy would remain steadfast in their convictions and it was possible to escape the worst penalties if one showed enough contrition. The severity of the government's response to heresy early on clearly terrorized many in the evangelical movement, enough to make some of them return to the traditional church.

For those who embraced the more radical turn of religious dissent in the 1530s, the persecution grew worse still. The violent disruptions of the

---

[107] Duke, "Face of Popular Religious Dissent," pp. 57–58.
[108] Rooze-Stouthamer, *Hervorming in Zeeland*, p. 53.
[109] Moreau, *Histoire du Protestantisme*, pp. 65–67.
[110] Decavele, *De dageraad van de Reformatie in Vlaanderen*, p. 222.
[111] Pol, *De reformatie te Kampen in de zestiende eeuw*, p. 97.

apocalyptic Anabaptists in the northern Netherlands and the attendant debacle in Münster provoked a severe judicial repression from authorities panicked by social rebellion. An intense period of persecution followed in the mid-to-late 1530s.[112] Local law officers and tribunals had fewer qualms about directly quashing perceived revolutionaries than they did about cooperating with a national inquisition. In the province of Holland, one of the epicenters of the Anabaptist movement, about two hundred Anabaptists were executed for heresy in the years 1534–1536; during the same period in Friesland, another epicenter, the number was about fifty.[113] Even the Amsterdam magistracy, which had been relatively forbearing of dissenters in the city, reacted harshly and gruesomely when Anabaptists tried to take over the city in May 1535; one of the Anabaptist leaders, Jacob van Campen, had his tongue and right hand publicly cut off before he was beheaded in front of the city hall.[114] Anabaptists who had taken part in uprisings in Friesland in 1535 were swiftly executed by the provincial court there; some young girls who had also been involved but recanted were spared death, but they had to wear a special sign on their clothing for a year.[115] A number of northerners who tried to escape the persecution by fleeing south to Flanders found themselves instead in the clutches of the inquisitors there in 1538.[116] The Anabaptist reformation in the Netherlands was nearly decimated by the repression of the later 1530s and seemed, at least for the time being, to have been effectively suppressed (Illustration 2.1). The deterrent effect of harsh prosecution seemed to be working, at least in the short term. Those who remained faithful to Anabaptism only survived in part by going underground, in part by fleeing to safe havens abroad, and in part by retreating into an interior, self-segregating type of religious piety such as that espoused by Menno Simons. By abandoning chiliasm and revolution, the Anabaptists made themselves less obnoxious to authorities, at least until a new round of persecution erupted in the later part of the century.

The early reformation in the Netherlands, initially inspired by both Christian humanism and the German reformers, was small in numbers but large in impact. What had begun as an interest in spiritual improvement, scriptural study and church reform among literate urban classes in the early 1500s was transformed within a couple of decades into

---

[112] This persecution, though harsh, was not nearly as severe as later Mennonite martyrologies would make it out to be; Zijlstra, *Om de ware gemeente en de oude gronden*, p. 110. For a fine-grained analysis, see Geraerts, "The Prosecution of Anabaptists in Holland, 1530–1566."

[113] Zijlstra, *Om de ware gemeente en de oude gronden*, p. 239.

[114] Krahn, *Dutch Anabaptism*, p. 154.   [115] Woltjer, *Friesland in Hervormingstijd*, p. 85.

[116] Decavele, *De dageraad van de Reformatie in Vlaanderen*, pp. 303–314.

Illustration 2.1 (Copy of?) Barend Dircksz, *Execution of two Anabaptists (Terechtstelling van twee wederdopers)*, 1525–1545. The judicial backlash against the Anabaptist movement was particularly harsh after the upheavals of the 1530s. Courtesy Amsterdam Museum

a multitude of like-minded groups calling for profound spiritual and ecclesiastical change. Some of them, inspired by a new understanding of scripture, went further still and called for social revolution as well as religious reformation. This early reformation was eclectic, drawing inspiration from a wide variety of sources and influences, and initially it lacked any theological or organizational cohesion. Until charismatic prophets appeared in the early 1530s, it had no authoritative figures such as Luther or Zwingli to guide it. Instead it was very much part of the *Wildwuchs* of religious protest that proliferated in northern Europe during these decades. At this early stage dissenters created no actual church per se; outside of a small, informal Lutheran congregation in Antwerp consisting mostly of German merchants, no distinctively Lutheran congregation developed in the Low Countries. Luther insisted that no church reform could take place in defiance of earthly powers, and the Habsburg rulers of the Netherlands, as one of those earthly powers, were determined to prevent the spread of heresy in their hereditary lands. Protestant movements that would ultimately succeed in the sixteenth-century Low Countries would be those that either learned to lived quietly alongside the civil order, like the Mennonites, or those that would find strong political allies against the Habsburgs, like the Reformed. For the vast majority of Netherlanders who remained loyal to the Catholic Church, religious dissidents were, at least initially, a curiosity, and then, with the radicalization of the 1530s, a danger to good order. That Charles V would erect a juridical apparatus to combat this danger was in itself not surprising; a Christian prince was after all supposed to defend the Christian church and protect the welfare of his subjects against their enemies. This judicial regime, for all its improvised character and the stumbling blocks it encountered, seemed to be working; by the 1540s the worst of the heretical threat, the Melchiorite militants, had been neutralized. The Reformation in the Netherlands might have vanished, or at least remained negligibly small, but for political factors that fostered growing discontent with the Habsburg regime, as well as a confessional shift that sharpened religious identity and opposition in the middle of the century.

3   The Confessional Turn

In the middle decades of the sixteenth century, between roughly 1540 and 1570, the Reformation in the Low Countries underwent a shift. If the 1520s and 1530s can be characterized as a confused initial period of questioning and disorder, then the subsequent era might be seen as a quest for more order and coherence among different groupings of Netherlandish Christians committed to religious reform. Like many others across Europe at this time they were searching for a more fixed religious identity, for what it was they believed. The question of *reformatio*, of reform both individual and institutional, took on greater urgency and more defined guises. That is to say, what had begun as a congeries of interrogations, dissatisfactions, yearnings for reform, gatherings, agendas, preaching, books, pamphlets, dissents, occasional violent acts and outright rebellions was evolving by mid-century into a variety of efforts to fashion more solidified, programmatic and theologically coherent movements, confessing to particular doctrines and calling for serious and systematic religious change. These efforts took place within the Catholic Church as well as outside it.

This broad trend toward consolidation of belief and formation of identity, which happened not merely in the Netherlands but all over Europe and could be applied to all religious groups, was first described as "confession building" (*Konfessionsbildung*) by the German historian Ernst Walter Zeeden.[1] The Reformation ushered in the era of confessional Europe, when an identifiable range of Christianities emerged as successors to the once unified Latin Christendom of the Middle Ages. These new Christianities rooted their identities in confessions – that is, authoritative statements of belief to which all church members promised to adhere. This internal confessionalization led to the slow and fitful emergence of distinctive types of Christian churches – Catholic, Lutheran, Mennonite, Reformed and Anglican – centered around

---

[1] Zeeden, "Grundlage und Wege der Konfessionsbildung im Zeitalter der Glaubenskämpfe."

developing and negotiating core expressions of belief and praxis, often in conscious contrast to other Christian groups. One of the concept's later theorists, Heinz Schilling, argued that this "confessionalization" later became tied to state-building. With the notable exception of the Mennonites, these confessions, at least in some places, would over the longer term, certainly by the seventeenth century, enter into alliances with early modern governments in order to manage religious life more effectively. This included disciplining popular behavior, though the results usually fell short of what church authorities may have wished. The various religious authorities' intention of achieving a clear confessional identity and spiritual uniformity was more aspirational than actual and often met with indifference or even resistance among individual believers.[2] The mid-sixteenth-century confessional turn in the Low Countries, however, concerned the formation of internal confessional identity rather than state-building.

The Reformation in the Low Countries, much like in the rest of Europe, started to see this confessional turn as the sixteenth century approached its midpoint. The inchoate, protean and sometimes anarchic evangelical and Anabaptist dissent that had characterized the period before 1540 elided, over the next three decades, into an array of three broadly organized religious streams – Mennonite, Reformed and Catholic – dedicated in various ways and by various means to the reform of the Christian church. How exactly the church was to be reformed these streams now tried to express in clearer, more crystallized fashion according to an increasingly concrete set of theological and ecclesiological ideas, sometimes expressed in comprehensive confessions of faith. These statements of faith – such as the Mennonites' *Foundation of Christian Doctrine*, the Reformed Belgic Confession and the canons of the Council of Trent of the Catholic Church – were held as normative by their authors, standards by which the reform of Christian beliefs and lives was to be measured, according to each stream. There was a growing attempt among many to create boundaries between acceptable and unacceptable doctrine, between true and false religion.[3] As a consequence of drawing such theological lines, for some reform-minded Christians positions became more hardened, differences grew clearer, conflicts became sharper.[4] These three currents were by no means absolutely monolithic or internally uniform, and we should not overstate their coherence; they are to

---

[2] Schilling, "Confessional Europe"; Lotz-Heumann, "Confessionalization"; Grochowina, "Confessional Indifference in East Frisia."

[3] On the notion of early modern religious boundary-making, see Luria, *Sacred Boundaries*, pp. xxvi–xxxii.

[4] Woltjer, *Op weg naar tachtig jaar oorlog*, pp. 263–293.

a certain extent constructed categories born of hindsight. Many Netherlandish Christians were dedicated to the idea of reform but refused to align wholly with any of these currents; not all were interested in conforming to boundaries. Nevertheless these three broad confessional categories, and those who tried to navigate them, would dominate the story of the Reformation in the Low Countries during the second half of the sixteenth century. Internal confessionalization, haphazard and halting, would come to predominate within these streams.

Accompanying this developing confessional polarization at mid-century was an increasing political polarization. The discomfort between princely and regional power only grew. Local officials continued to chafe at the Habsburg government's efforts to increase its authority at their expense, especially when the regime began imposing new taxes to finance its renewed wars with Valois France in the later 1550s. Over the course of the 1550s, the Brussels government and the provincial-local authorities grew ever more sharply at odds over questions of sovereignty and privilege, especially after Philip II succeeded his father, Charles V, as the Netherlandish sovereign in 1555. Philip, raised in Spain, was far less familiar with the region than his father, and this lack of intimacy complicated his relationships with local grandees.

One of the major points of contention would be religious policy, specifically how the central government handled the matter of heresy. The Brussels court had yoked heresy with treason and so believed it had greater power to override civic and provincial legal custom in dealing with such a grave offense. Magistrates were distinctly lukewarm to the idea of subjecting their citizens to the rigors of inquisitorial justice, and there was some uncertainty about which opinions and notions exactly constituted outright heresy as opposed to an innocent interest in the Bible or mere curiosity about new ideas.[5] Thus local cooperation in the war against heresy remained uneven at best. Also, in 1559 Philip initiated an extensive reform of the organization of the Catholic Church in the Netherlands, and this sparked further opposition among local ecclesiastical and political elites. So, even as religious identities and therefore polarizations began to harden, political discontent was growing. The search for identity and boundaries among some Netherlandish Christians coincided with the first signals that the Habsburg composite state in the Low Countries was being seriously challenged by its aggrieved subjects.

These polarizations also coincided with a detectable drop in traditional religious activity by layfolk. In Ghent, for example, there was a marked

---

[5] Spaans, "Reform in the Low Countries," pp. 121–122.

decline in interest and participation in confraternities by mid-century.[6] The shrine of Our Lady of the Seven Sorrows in Delft stopped reporting miracles after the 1520s.[7] Monastic vocations, the sale of indulgences and the founding of chantries all declined precipitously. The rise of dissident voices had perhaps caused many to reconsider what religious devotion should actually entail.[8] Traditional religion, in short, seemed to be losing its attractions for many Netherlandish Christians. For some, the dissenting streams that had begun to form distinct religious identities by the 1550s would offer an attractive alternative to age-old Catholic piety.

From the point of view of the Brussels government, the hard judicial response to heresy seemed to be working; in the 1540s evangelical dissent was in flux and had either scattered or retreated into quietism.[9] The crackdowns on dissidents after Münster had tempered nonconformist activity considerably. Many Anabaptists opted for pacifism and withdrawal after the tumultuous 1530s, or even reconciliation with the Catholic Church. Heresy, it appeared, had been subdued. It had not disappeared of course; evangelical sentiments could still be heard here and there, in the plays staged by chambers of rhetoric, for example. Reformist books still sometimes circulated (even though dissident presses in Antwerp had been effectively shut down), and heresy prosecutions continued. Pockets and cells of religious nonconformity among ordinary people were still being uncovered by authorities. Still, religious dissent was far from organized and seemed to be, after the alarming eruptions of the 1530s, on the retreat.

From Anabaptist to Mennonite

Within Anabaptist circles, there was considerable disarray in the years after the fall of the "new Jerusalem" of Münster. The apocalyptic Münsterites had dispersed; the roving bands of Batenburgers were largely vanquished. A movement that had accustomed itself to charismatic leadership seemed at a loss for luminaries. Obbe Philips, who had emerged as the leader of what was left of Melchiorite Anabaptism, abruptly recanted his beliefs in 1540 and left for northern Germany to resume his career as a barber-surgeon. Meanwhile the Melchiorite prophet David Joris's departure from Antwerp for Basel in 1544 and his increasing mysticism effectively removed him, geographically and theologically, as a leader of Netherlandish Anabaptists.

---

[6] Trio, *Volksreligie als spiegel van een stedelijke samenleving*, p. 191.
[7] Verhoeven, *Devotie en negotie*, pp. 180–184.
[8] Pollmann, *Catholic Identity and the Revolt of the Netherlands*, pp. 40–41.
[9] Augustijn, "Niederlande," p. 478.

What remained of the post-Münster spiritualist movements began to pay greater heed to the teachings of the Frieslander Menno Simons (1496–1561), who had been a Catholic priest in Leeuwarden before his conversion. In 1539 he published his major work, *The Foundation of Christian Doctrine* (*Dat Fundament des Christlycken Leers*). After the fall of the Münster kingdom he spent most of the 1540s and 1550s in safer imperial havens in east Friesland and the Rhineland, where he continued to write and publish his interpretations of scripture. During this period he also appointed elders who provided the leadership and pastoral care for Anabaptist congregations in the Netherlands, particularly in the northern provinces but also as far south as Tournai.[10] Menno's pastoral and theological labors in these decades paid off as his following grew. He never styled himself as a prophet and deliberately eschewed the Old Testament metaphors so beloved of the Melchiorites; he presented himself only as a preacher and teacher of the Bible.[11] So closely was he identified with the Anabaptist movement in this period that "Mennonites" became a common epithet used to describe his coreligionists, though they were also known more broadly as *Doopsgezinden* ("Baptists" or "Baptism-minded").

Menno Simons proved to be the sixteenth-century Low Countries' most influential native theologian. In his *Foundation* he provided Netherlandish Anabaptism with its first thorough and enduring exposition of doctrine. He emphasized the importance of penance and regeneration, the contrast between flesh and spirit, the centrality of scripture and the kingdom of God. The spiritually regenerate person strove to do good works, as instructed by Christ's words in the Bible: "such is the penitence which we teach, to die unto sin, and all ungodly works, and to live no longer according to the lusts of the flesh."[12] The believer's baptism was the outward sign of this regeneration. In this work of regeneration, the believer was aided and encouraged by the community, which as the body of Christ had to be "without spot or wrinkle." Church discipline, including a ban for unregenerate sinners, was exercised by elders to preserve this purity within congregations. The faithful had to distinguish themselves in behavior and belief from the sinful, fleshly world. This included sober clothing and demeanor ("never show off in gold, pearls, or costly apparel") and refusing to take up the sword or to hold any public office.[13] The godly community was to be insulated from the sinfulness of a fallen, carnal world by segregating itself from it as much as possible.

---

[10] Zijlstra, *Om de ware gemeente en de oude gronden*, pp. 178–181.
[11] Visser, "Mennonites and Doopsgezinden in the Netherlands," p. 304.
[12] Simons, "Foundation of Christian Doctrine," in *The Complete Writings*, p. 111.
[13] Simons, "Foundation of Christian Doctrine," p. 183.

Instead the Christian must patiently wait for the coming of God's kingdom and certainly not use force to bring it about, as had been tried so
disastrously in Münster.[14] In practice, with these basic tenets, the
Mennonites would try to tread a middle path between the extreme
worldly engagement of the Melchiorites and the extreme spiritualist
detachment of David Joris.

The Mennonites were among the most active Protestant movements in
the Netherlands in the 1540s and 1550s.[15] By the early 1540s
a Mennonite congregation was already established in Amsterdam,
which met secretly in a private home for preaching and Bible study.[16]
Within the decade similar congregations emerged in the towns of
Flanders and in the late 1540s in Antwerp. Itinerant elders from
Holland and Zeeland, operating clandestinely, guided these young congregations initially until a local leadership was trained and took over by
the 1550s.[17] These communities were small but grew relatively widespread. Antwerp, by virtue of its size and cosmopolitanism, functioned
very much as the center of the network of Mennonite congregations
across the southern provinces (especially Flanders).[18] Mennonite communities, however, were much more heavily concentrated in the Dutch-
speaking lands of the Netherlands than in the French-speaking areas,
especially in northern regions such as Friesland, Holland and
Groningen. The majority of devotees came from middling ranks of artisans and skilled labor; more than 75 percent of the Anabaptists prosecuted in Antwerp between 1550 and 1566, for example, belonged to this
economic group.[19] Nevertheless, the Mennonites found followers from
a broad spectrum of society, especially as the century progressed, and by
the 1560s they were the most predominant variant of Anabaptism within
the Netherlands.

These Mennonite congregations were likely not very large, but since
they had to operate clandestinely smaller numbers provided greater security against detection. They were served by mostly itinerant pastors and
elders, who often met with congregations under cover of the evening
hours; their principal tasks were baptizing and preaching God's Word.
The singing of hymns was also an important liturgical activity.[20] And of
course congregants gathered to aid each other in the process of

---

[14] Zijlstra, *Om de ware gemeente en de oude gronden*, pp. 187–196.
[15] Augustijn, "Anabaptism in the Netherlands," p. 205.
[16] Duke, "Moulded by Repression," in *Dissident Identities*, p. 95.
[17] Verheyden, *Anabaptism in Flanders*, pp. 25–27.
[18] Marnef, *Antwerp in the Age of Reformation*, p. 75; Decavele, *De dageraad van de Reformatie in Vlaanderen*, p. 515.
[19] Marnef, *Antwerp in the Age of Reformation*, p. 77.
[20] Zijlstra, *Om de ware gemeente en de oude gronden*, pp. 260–261.

regeneration by exercising moral discipline among their members, including imposing the ban on particularly stubborn sinners. Discipline also included, aside from the monitoring of the normal run of human error, a careful effort to make sure that the community remained segregated from the fallen, sinful world that belonged to the realm of Satan. Thus Mennonites were above all to avoid attending the Catholic Church. Similarly they could not swear oaths, hold public office or serve in militias. All these behaviors could of course draw the suspicion of local authorities, and so to commit to Mennonitism in this era of placards and inquisition was to live a life of considerable risk.[21] Congregations protected themselves by being tightly knit and carefully disciplined. Indeed, the moral seriousness and self-containment of Mennonite communities drew the grudging admiration of other reformist groups, Catholic and Reformed alike. Some of the Netherlandish Reformed in particular would come to see the Mennonites as potentially serious competitors for those souls inclined to more sober and more literal biblicist piety.

Thus, by the middle of the sixteenth century, with their focused doctrine and their rigorous church discipline, the followers of Menno Simons flourished as the principal heirs to the Anabaptist movement that had broken out in the Netherlands twenty years earlier. That very same stress on discipline, however, would eventually splinter the Mennonite congregations into different factions in the 1550s and 1560s, as well as later in the century, so they never were a monolithic bloc of believers.[22] The question of how the godly were to relate to the world vexed Mennonite elders in these decades, a debate that may have in part been a result of the Mennonites' success in establishing stable and enduring congregations. The practical considerations of how to exercise church discipline and the ban and how much involvement in the outside world was desirable were especially fraught questions. Serious disagreements about these issues led to splits within congregations and there was no recognized, overarching authority among them to adjudicate such disputes. This congregationalist preference led to a great deal of unraveling. By 1567 four major Mennonite or *Doopsgezind* factions (from most open to most strict: Waterlanders, High Germans, Frisians and Flemish) had emerged, whose definitions and enforcement of church discipline and interaction with outsiders ranged from broad to narrow. Still more schisms within these four streams would occur again in the 1580s, 1590s and 1610s. Yet despite their fierce arguments and divisions among themselves the

---

[21] Zijlstra, *Om de ware gemeente en de oude gronden*, pp. 262–265.
[22] Zijlstra, *Om de ware gemeente en de oude gronden*, pp. 270–298; Visser, "Mennonites and Doopsgezinden in the Netherlands," pp. 309–314.

Netherlandish Mennonites retained a basic common confessional identity of followers of the basic Anabaptist teachings of biblicism, believer's
baptism, penitence and self-segregation. Theologically they differed from
each other little, and their disputes were largely about church authority,
organization and order. Like other Netherlandish Christians in this
period, the Mennonites continued to sort out questions of identity and
boundaries.

To a far lesser degree, the spiritualist strain of early Netherlandish
religious Anabaptism would still manifest itself in the second half of the
sixteenth century, often dismissed as "libertine" by its detractors. The
works of David Joris remained popular in some small, scattered circles.
Another small spiritualist sect, the Family of Love, founded about 1540
by the Amsterdam merchant Hendrik Niclaes, retained in the second half
of the century a scattered following among a handful of intellectuals and
wealthy merchants who were attracted to its nondogmatic teachings and
its irenic rejection of sectarian boundaries. The renowned Antwerp
printer Christopher Plantin published Niclaes's books anonymously. By
century's end, however, the Familists, never very numerous, largely disappeared as a movement.[23]

Their deep sense of commitment, their dedication to a church "without
spot or wrinkle," helped the Netherlandish Mennonite communities
weather some of the harshest persecution the Habsburg judicial regime
meted out for the crime of heresy. The placards in particular forbade
rebaptism, absence from regular Catholic worship and lending aid to
Anabaptists. A particularly sharp "blood placard" issued in 1550 by
Charles V raised the punishments against heresy even more drastically
and reinforced inquisitors' right to detain and investigate anyone suspected of heresy. Some Mennonites fled to comparative safety in England
or Germany. In the county of Holland prosecution of dissenters was
especially harsh in the wake of Münster, where heresy and Anabaptism
were considered virtually synonymous in the 1540s.[24] In the county of
Flanders, the imperial-papal inquisitor successfully eradicated most of
the Anabaptist congregations during his tenure between 1545 and
1566.[25] Of the roughly thirteen hundred individuals executed for heresy
in the Netherlands between 1523 and 1566, a disproportionate number
of them were Anabaptists.

Reconciliation with the church remained an option for repentant heretics, of course, and several hundred former dissenters took that route, but

[23] Hamilton, *The Family of Love*; Mout, "The Family of Love."
[24] Duke, "Building Heaven in Hell's Despite: The Early History of the Reformation in the
Towns of the Low Countries," in *Reformation and Revolt*, p. 89.
[25] Duke, "The 'Inquisition,'" in *Dissident Identities*, p. 107.

many also simply refused to recant their beliefs.[26] The heavy persecution the Anabaptists endured helped fuel a martyrological tradition in Netherlandish Mennonitism, which served to strengthen its sense of confessional identity. The medium of print allowed Mennonites to circulate stories of heroic martyrs widely among their congregations. In 1562, in the Frisian town of Franeker, appeared in print a small octavo book called *The Sacrifice to the Lord* (*Het Offer des Heeren*), which was a collection of contemporary documents about Mennonite believers who had lost their lives for the faith.[27] These documents, largely unedited and offered with little commentary, included letters, testimonies, professions of faith and songs by and about the faithful who fell victim to Habsburg religious prosecution. *The Sacrifice to the Lord* proved exceedingly popular in Mennonite circles and went through many printings and editions to the end of the sixteenth century. Its stories (which begin with the account of Stephen the proto-martyr from the biblical book of Acts) may not have been completely accurate, but the martyrology's purpose was both hortatory and didactic: it provided congregations with encouraging stories of steadfastness and also prepared them for what they might face if captured by the authorities, a prospect that was all too likely in the 1550s and 1560s.[28] The rhyming songs included in the collection both enriched Mennonite culture and also allowed for illiterate believers to learn and communicate the stories even more widely.[29] The documents repeated traditional Mennonite themes of holiness, the rejection of worldliness and the judgment of God. In his testimony the condemned glazier Adriaen Cornelisz, imprisoned in Leiden in 1551, exhorted his friends. "Do not grieve because you have suffered for so long and must flee from one city to another, but realize instead that this is all to your salvation."[30] Mayken Boosers, condemned in Tournai in 1562, implored her children to "follow the Lord's will" and, like their mother, to seek not the honor of this world but instead find it in suffering on behalf of the Lord.[31] Such heartfelt, moving accounts were intended to reinforce a sense of Mennonite identity and common commitment, of solidarity in the face of persecution and trust in the righteousness of God. They were deliberately designed to instill a kind of emotional fellowship among believers. With such stories the Mennonites were reminded of their distinctiveness from other religious groups – through the construction of such boundaries came a sharper sense of identity.

---

[26] Soen, "De reconciliatie van 'ketters' in de zestiende-eeuws Nederlanden."
[27] "Het Offer des Heeren," *BRN*, vol. 2, pp. 1–486.
[28] Zijlstra, *Om de ware gemeente en de oude gronden*, pp. 248–249.
[29] Gregory, *Salvation at Stake*, p. 227.   [30] "Het Offer des Heeren," p. 197.
[31] "Het Offer des Heeren," p. 416.

Mennonite confessional identity was further honed and polished by the publication of a Dutch translation of the Bible for use in worship. The strong biblicism of the Mennonites demanded an accessible version of scripture for congregations to study, and in 1560 appeared the first edition of what became known as the Biestkens Bible, named for its Mennonite printer. This was a translation, by multiple Mennonite authors, of Luther's German Bible. Mennonite and *Doopsgezind* communities used this edition of scripture widely in the sixteenth and seventeenth centuries, favoring it over what they saw as the inferior translations of other confessions (Illustration 3.1).[32] Thus literature, in the various forms of theological books, martyrology and translated scripture, also helped further the Mennonites' sense of confessional distinctiveness. As a result, the various Mennonite/*Doopsgezind* groupings emerged by the later sixteenth century as one of the major streams of Netherlandish Christianity.

Reformed Protestantism

While in exile in East Friesland, Menno Simons had the opportunity in 1544 to meet with Polish nobleman Johannes a Lasco (1499–1560), the superintendent of the evangelical church in the city of Emden. The peripatetic Lasco had studied in Basel, where he had come to admire both Erasmian humanism and the burgeoning reform movement coming out of the Swiss and German cities. Under the patronage of Countess Anna of Oldenburg, regent of East Friesland, Lasco was attempting to establish a broader, more expansive alternative to both Catholicism and Lutheranism in the church of Emden. To that end he met and disputed with a number of religious dissenters, including Anabaptists such as Menno. After their meeting the two of them could only agree on a couple of points of doctrine – original sin and sanctification – and they later engaged in a brief polemic with each other in print.[33]

It was testimony to the growing influence of the Mennonite stream within sixteenth-century Netherlandish Christianity that a figure as important as Lasco felt the need to enter into discussion with Menno. At the same time, it was also indicative of the rise of yet another distinctive stream among Europe's growing number of evangelical dissenters, which historians have come to call Reformed Protestantism. Reformed Protestantism, a blanket label that comprised a wide array of doctrines and manifestations, had its origins in the Swiss lands, beginning with

---

[32] De Bruin and Broeyer, *De Statenbijbel en zijn voorgangers*, pp. 152–161; François, "De doopsgezinde Biestkensbijbel," pp. 318–322.

[33] Krahn, *Dutch Anabaptism*, pp. 179–180; Zijlstra, *Om de ware gemeente en de oude gronden*, pp. 219–220; Jürgens, *Johannes a Lasco in Ostfriesland*, pp. 254–271.

Illustration 3.1 Title page of Biestkens Bible, 1560. Vernacular Bible translation was an important part of the confessional formation of the Mennonite movement in the mid-sixteenth century. Courtesy University Library, Free University of Amsterdam

Huldrych Zwingli's reformation in the city-state of Zurich in the early 1520s. This Swiss evangelical proposed a more thoroughgoing transformation of the church than his contemporary Martin Luther, including a more rigorous adherence to the doctrine of *sola scriptura*. In practice that meant Zwingli was more readily prepared to do away with nearly every ecclesiastical practice or tradition that he could not justify by scripture, such as the use of images inside churches. Though his biblicism was not as radical as that of the Anabaptists, Zwingli reformed his church at a faster pace than Luther, with whom he also disagreed fundamentally on the question of the real presence in the Eucharist. This Zwinglian model of reformation made its way to other Swiss cities such as Bern and Basel and also found a prominent sympathizer and advocate in the person of Martin Bucer (1491–1551), the influential preacher and reformer in Strasbourg, one of the major free cities of the Empire. Reformed Protestantism's second generation would be most famously personified by the exiled French preacher in Geneva, John Calvin (1509–1564). Calvin was especially interested in the ecclesiological implications of reform and created in Geneva a basic model of Reformed church governance, structure and function that proved to be highly exportable and adaptable. Elders and preachers presided over congregations in a consistory, whose primary tasks were to preach the Word of God and to discipline congregants into leading godly lives, while a diaconate was charged with caring for the poor. Yet, unlike the Anabaptists, Reformed (or, as they were sometimes called, especially by their opponents, Calvinist) congregations were actively and deeply engaged in the world and had no interest in self-segregation.[34] In this regard Reformed Protestantism could posit itself as an evangelical "answer" to the perceived anarchies and disorders of Anabaptism. By the 1550s Reformed movements were in the forefront of European evangelical dissent, far surpassing Lutheranism in their reach, activities and influence across the continent. In contrast to the Lutherans, the Reformed offered a flexible, clear and highly adaptable blueprint of church organization – a true re-forming, as it were – while at the same time offering a more coherent, structured and dynamic vision of church life than the radicals. And its various church orders were designed to work alongside the civil order rather than be subjected to it, which later made it highly exportable to a variety of environments. Of all the sixteenth-century Protestant movements, the Reformed would prove the most successful in terms of both numbers and geographic spread.[35]

---

[34] Benedict, *Christ's Churches Purely Reformed*, pp. 9–109.
[35] MacCulloch, *The Reformation*, pp. 230–233.

Starting in the 1540s, some of those Netherlandish evangelicals who did not identify with either the militancy or the quietism of the Anabaptists and yet longed for church reform began to gravitate toward this growing and dynamic movement.[36] Representatives from evangelical groups in Tournai and Valenciennes traveled to Strasbourg, at that time the most important hub of European Protestantism, in the autumn of 1544, requesting leadership for their embattled communities. Reformed preaching thus made an initial foray into the Low Countries in the person of Pierre Brully (1518–1545), a former Dominican friar from Metz who had served as preacher to the French Reformed congregation in Strasbourg. After consultation with Bucer and Calvin, Brully agreed to travel northwestward to teach Reformed doctrine in those towns. For the next several weeks he preached, in private homes under cover of night, to evangelical conventicles in Tournai, Valenciennes, Douai, Arras and Lille. In Tournai he was arrested by local officials and then tried and executed for heresy in early 1545.[37] This initial foray of Reformed dissent into the Low Countries thus proved unsuccessful. As Brully's fate demonstrated, spreading Reformed ideas was a dangerous business in the Netherlands, and there was considerable discussion within evangelical circles about how open one could be about one's allegiances. John Calvin, always a great believer in orderly boundaries, insisted in a tract he had circulated among French and Netherlandish evangelicals in 1544 that "Nicodemism," adhering inwardly to Reformed beliefs while outwardly conforming to the Catholic Church, was unacceptable.[38] Simulation was playing at faith, and it earned Calvin's strongest rebuke; the only acceptable choices for Reformed Christians in Catholic lands, he sternly insisted, were either suffering for their faith or moving to a place where they could worship freely.[39] To be sure, this opinion was controversial, and not every Netherlandish evangelical, subject to one of the harshest anti-heretical regimes in Europe, was willing to make that choice. Still, between 1540 and 1570 a growing number of Netherlandish Christians chose to risk the exactions of Habsburg religious policy in order to worship God in a manner that they broadly identified as Reformed.

They were aided in this resolve by an increasingly sophisticated international Reformed movement, which by the 1550s comprised a constellation of churches in Switzerland, the Empire, France,

---

[36] Van Veen, *Een nieuwe tijd, een nieuwe kerk*, pp. 65–66.

[37] Moreau, *Histoire du Protestantisme*, pp. 91–110.

[38] Augustijn, "De opmars van de calvinistische beweging in de Nederlanden," pp. 427–429; Eire, *War against the Idols*, pp. 240–250.

[39] Augustijn, "De opmars van de calvinistische beweging in de Nederlanden," p. 428.

Scotland and England. This constellation provided a variety of ideas and models about how the church should be re-formed. Once again, the geographic and economic openness of the Low Countries facilitated the circulation of new ideas. Reformed literature, principally books and pamphlets written by such Reformed luminaries as Bucer and Heinrich Bullinger of Zurich, managed to find its way into the region via established trading routes. Evangelical conventicles in southern French-speaking towns such as Tournai and Valenciennes benefited early on from the northward spread of Huguenot missionaries active in the kingdom of France.

The evangelical community in Emden, superintended by Johannes a Lasco in the 1540s, readily received Netherlandish religious refugees and also provided an early and very proximate model of a Reformed church order, including a church council comprising preachers and elders to govern and discipline the congregation.[40] Following the execution of Pierre Brully, some of Tournai's evangelicals fled the city and found a home in Rhenish Wesel, whose city fathers, intent on welcoming economic talent and capital, allowed the establishment of a French-speaking Reformed church.[41] More and more, contact, exchange and migration among Netherlandish evangelicals of all stripes and their counterparts abroad became frequent and widespread.

The Tournai refugees in Wesel were among the earliest of many Netherlandish evangelicals in this period who, perhaps mindful of Calvin's condemnation of Nicodemism, chose to live and worship in safety abroad rather than suffer the further persecutory exactions of the placards. Habsburg religious policy remained resolutely anti-heretical well into the 1540s and 1550s, and more and more Netherlandish evangelicals opted to migrate to relatively safe havens in nearby regions where greater freedom to worship was available. This diaspora of tens of thousands of religious refugees abroad would prove a watershed moment in the development of mid-century Netherlandish Protestantism, especially its Reformed variants. Some Netherlanders who fled saw themselves as living in exile and eventually returned to the Low Countries, but many left home for good; they were migrants rather than exiles. For many of them, their time abroad proved to be one of education, as they tried in new environments to fashion new congregations or join existing ones, under the watchful eyes of their new host governments, that reflected their adherence to what they understood as biblical Christianity.[42] In exile some of the most committed among the

---

[40] Pettegree, *Emden and the Dutch Revolt*, pp. 32–34; Jürgens, *Johannes a Lasco in Ostfriesland*, pp. 281–325.
[41] Schilling, *Niederländishe Exulanten im 16*, pp. 70–71; Spohnholz, *Tactics of Toleration*, p. 28.
[42] See, for example, Gorter, *Gereformeerde migranten*.

Reformed continued to discuss and negotiate and argue with each other vexing questions of ecclesiology and doctrine; the shared experience of flight did not necessarily produce a uniform set of beliefs. For many (though not all) of these Netherlandish evangelicals, the search for identity and boundaries continued and was even accelerated by the experience of exile. Their experiences far from home would vary from place to place, but this time spent abroad would prove formative for the evolution of many Netherlandish Reformed Protestants.[43]

The most important centers for Netherlandish religious dissidents migrating abroad were in the Holy Roman Empire and England, in such cities as Emden, Wesel, Aachen, Frankfurt, Strasbourg, London, Norwich and Sandwich. Of these, London and Emden would assume greatest significance for the Netherlandish Reformed movement, for it was in these places that Netherlandish evangelicals for the first time fashioned churches of their own in an environment that was tolerant rather than hostile. In 1550 Johannes a Lasco left Emden for London, where under the regime of the reform-minded king Edward VI he established and supervised two "stranger churches," one for Dutch speakers and the other for French speakers. Together with two Netherlandish exiles, the Ghent refugees Maarten Micron, a preacher, and Jan Utenhove, an elder, Lasco created a church with a governing consistory of elders, a diaconate to help with the relief of the poor, regular preaching, translated confessions and scripture into the relevant languages and worship designed according to Reformed prescriptions. This church order derived inspiration from a number of others, including those of Geneva, Strasbourg and Zurich. It set up regular mechanisms of church discipline and demanded a high order of participation from its membership, who were catechized carefully before being allowed to join.[44] By 1553 membership in the two churches numbered between three and four thousand, mostly from the artisanal and commercial strata of society.[45] Except for an interruption during the reign of the Catholic queen Mary in 1553–1558, the London churches would serve as an important refuge and resource for Netherlandish coreligionists back home.

Like London the Emden congregation in the northwestern Empire would serve as a "mother church" to the growing evangelical population in the Low Countries during the mid-sixteenth century. Refugees found a spiritual home there, and aspiring preachers could receive training and logistical support. Equally important, Reformed literature and Bible

[43] Pollmann, "The Low Countries," p. 85; Spohnholz and Van Veen, "The Disputed Origins of Dutch Calvinism."
[44] Pettegree, *Foreign Protestant Communities*, pp. 46–76.
[45] Pettegree, *Foreign Protestant Communities*, p. 78.

translations in Dutch and French streamed from Emden's presses and made their way to Antwerp via well-established trade routes to Antwerp; half of Dutch vernacular evangelical literature printed between the mid-1550s and the mid-1560s came from Emden.[46] And, starting in the 1560s, Emden's church fathers found themselves aiding the small but growing number of Reformed communities inside the Low Countries, principally in the southern provinces, who risked judicial prosecution to establish their own secret local congregations.[47]

The growth of Netherlandish Reformed communities abroad was soon accompanied by growth at home. The expansion of Reformed Protestantism within the Low Countries in the 1560s was spurred in part by two political events: the succession of Elizabeth I to the English throne in 1558 and the signing in 1559 of the Treaty of Cateau-Cambrésis that ended the war between Spain and France. Elizabeth's more sympathetic regime allowed the Dutch and French stranger churches to reopen in England after the Marian hiatus, and they in turn would provide invaluable moral and logistical support to their harassed coreligionists in the Netherlands. Cateau-Cambrésis opened up the southern border with France, thereby allowing a much easier traffic between Huguenot preachers and missionaries and their coreligionists in the Francophone Netherlands. Taking advantage of these political circumstances, the international Reformed network reasserted itself with vigor and enthusiasm to missionizing in the Low Countries.

The Reformed congregations formed in the Netherlands starting around 1560 could be found from the French border northward to Brabant and Zeeland, in the provinces with the greatest wealth and highest density of population. No organized congregation appeared further north before 1566, possibly because of the already long-established Anabaptist presence there.[48] The teeming commercial behemoth of Antwerp naturally took the lead. From some time in the early 1550s there are traces of an organized, if underground Reformed congregation in that metropolis. By 1555 the Mechelen preacher Gaspar van der Heyden (1530–1586) had created a structured congregation in Antwerp that was in regular contact with coreligionists in Emden.

The congregants met in small groups for prayers, Bible lecture, psalm-singing and preaching. The congregation fashioned a church order modeled on exile communities. Within a few years the demand for evangelical worship was great enough to require a second preacher, Adriaan van

---

[46] Pettegree, *Emden and the Dutch Revolt*, p. 104.
[47] Pettegree, *Emden and the Dutch Revolt*, pp. 57–86.
[48] Woltjer, *Op weg naar tachtig jaar oorlog*, p. 288.

Haemstede (1525–1562), though he and Van der Heyden sometimes disagreed about how strict the congregation should be about allowing sympathizers, as opposed to those who had made a full confession of faith, to attend meetings. Van der Heyden, one of those reformers who was increasingly inclined to draw boundaries, insisted that members abandon their Catholic ties completely, while Van Haemstede preferred a less exclusivist approach. By the late 1550s a French-speaking Reformed church was established in Antwerp as well. This congregation had close contacts with the French exile church in Wesel, and both communities worked closely with the London stranger churches that were restored in 1559 after the accession of Elizabeth I.[49] Antwerp's churches "under the cross," as they were called, took on a leading role in the establishment of other underground Reformed congregations across Brabant and Flanders. The Antwerp churches also served as refugee congregations for those evangelicals fleeing persecution in other parts of Flanders and Wallonia.

By 1560 Reformed congregations were also established in the major cities of the county of Flanders – Ghent and Bruges – as well as the manufacturing towns of the Westkwartier in the far southwestern part of the province, despite the severe prosecutions the inquisition enacted there. Native evangelicals from this province who had fled to Emden and London carefully returned home, usually via Antwerp, to help form secret Reformed congregations. In the towns and villages of the Westkwartier, in particular, Reformed dissidents were very active setting up conventicles; thanks to its proximity to England, west Flanders saw exiles from the stranger churches in London and especially Sandwich slip into its towns to help with the building of congregations there. These congregations would later be among the most brazen and aggressive in defying the strictures of the Habsburg regime.[50]

In the French-speaking south, the towns of Tournai, Valenciennes and Lille formed the core of Reformed activity. Tournai in particular took on a leading role, especially its energetic and formidable preacher from Hainaut, Guy de Bray (1522–1567), who had sojourned in London, attended Johannes a Lasco's church there and later studied in Geneva. De Bray served the Tournai church from 1559 to 1561 and thereafter functioned as an itinerant preacher in the surrounding region. Following Lasco's models he and his pastoral colleagues set up a functional Reformed consistory and diaconate in Tournai and soon gathered a large number of followers, mostly from the middling ranks of society,

---

[49] Marnef, *Antwerp in the Age of Reformation*, pp. 61–64.
[50] Decavele, *De dageraad van de Reformatie in Vlaanderen*, pp. 322–434.

such as artisans, lawyers and merchants, as well as several members of the grander families of the city. The church met initially entirely in secret, usually in small gatherings in private homes under cover of night. These meetings usually consisted of prayers, psalm-singing and Bible lecture; the sacraments of baptism and communion were administered on occasion.[51] Such small, simple gatherings were deliberately designed to echo the experiences of the early, apostolic church and recreate its spirituality.[52]

De Bray is also traditionally associated with one of the earliest programmatic statements of Netherlandish Reformed Protestantism, the *Confession de foy* of 1561, known later as the Belgic Confession. Evidence suggests De Bray compiled it in collaboration with his coreligionists in Antwerp. It borrowed heavily from the French Huguenot confession of faith published not long before.[53] Among those Reformed seeking sharper boundaries between themselves and other religious groups, especially the Anabaptists, this was a welcome document. Within a few years of its composition a secret synod of Netherlandish Reformed churches meeting in Antwerp obligated all members to subscribe to its tenets.[54] In a preface addressed to King Philip II, the Confession insisted its followers were loyal subjects who wished only to "live in purity of conscience, serve God, and reform ourselves according to his divine Word and holy Commandments" – that is, they were both obedient and orthodox.[55] The Belgic Confession itself reiterated in thirty-seven articles particular points of Reformed doctrine: the sovereignty of God, the sole authority of Scripture, the salvific nature of Christ, election and reprobation, justification by faith, a disciplining conciliar church order and the sacraments of baptism and communion.[56] Here, on paper, written in straightforward, declarative language, was an early attempt to establish Netherlandish Reformed identity. As a creedal statement the Belgic Confession, proclaiming the beliefs of the "true" church, allowed its subscribers to distinguish themselves from both the Catholic Church and their Mennonite rivals.

Reformed church expansion took on a more rapid pace as the 1560s wore on. Congregations grew substantially larger, though no firm numbers exist in the historical record. The town of Mons in Hainaut may have

---

[51] Moreau, *Histoire du Protestantisme*, pp. 144–152; Braekman, *Guy de Brès*, pp. 75–85.
[52] Crew, *Calvinist Preaching and Iconoclasm in the Netherlands*, pp. 61–62.
[53] Moreau, *Histoire du Protestantisme*, p. 156; Braekman, *Guy de Brès*, pp. 193–204; Bakhuizen van den Brink, *De nederlandse belijdenisgescrhiften*, pp. 8–10; Gootjes, *The Belgic Confession*, pp. 13–58.
[54] Marnef, *Antwerp in the Age of Reformation*, p. 71.
[55] Bakhuizen van den Brink, *De nederlandse belijdenisgescrhiften*, p. 63.
[56] Bakhuizen van den Brink, *De nederlandse belijdenisgescrhiften*, pp. 60–146.

had about two thousand Reformed adherents in 1566.[57] Tournai's congregation was (over)estimated by one contemporary at about twelve
thousand five hundred in a city of twenty-five thousand, though this
figure probably included sympathizers and the curious as well as full
church members.[58] Antwerp's congregation likely numbered in the hundreds, but the city's place as the Netherlands' leading metropolis meant
that its influence, especially among coreligionists in surrounding Brabant
and Flanders, was substantial.[59] Several underground meetings of
Reformed leaders, called synods, took place in Antwerp to formulate
common statements of faith and ecclesiology. The synods borrowed
substantially from French Huguenot blueprints of church organization
and discipline, but stressed more heavily the centrality of the local congregation and took on a sharper anti-Anabaptist tone, fearing perhaps the
competition from the latter's reputation for strict moral discipline.[60] By
the early 1560s the key centers of Reformed Protestant activity could be
found in Tournai, Antwerp and the Westkwartier of Flanders, which was
heavily supported by the migrant congregations in East Anglia.[61] From
these core regions the movement spread through Hainaut, Brabant,
Flanders, Artois and Zeeland.

Not only were the Reformed Protestants growing in numbers, they
were also growing bolder in action. In the early 1560s some of them
started to stage open manifestations of their convictions. Participants in
these actions may have been encouraged by events in France, where the
Huguenots were going more and more public with their faith and where in
January 1562 they won a limited legal toleration from the Valois monarchy. Some of their Netherlandish coreligionists likewise took steps to
demonstrate their faith openly. In the fall of 1561 several hundred
Reformed Protestants in Valenciennes and Tournai began to stroll the
streets of their cities in the evening while singing French translations of
the Psalms. Song was a popular and powerful medium of expression for
religion dissenters in the sixteenth century; as noted earlier, Martin
Luther's earliest hymn had been inspired by the Brussels martyrs of
1523. By mid-century the Reformed in particular had embraced psalm-
singing as an effective and easy means to spread their message.[62] The
leaders of these *chanteries* were hot-headed young deacons impatient with
having to worship in secret. These aggressive acts deeply disturbed the

---

[57] Crew, *Calvinist Preaching and Iconoclasm in the Netherlands*, p. 80, n. 114.
[58] Moreau, *Histoire du Protestantisme*, p. 151.
[59] Marnef, *Antwerp in the Age of Reformation*, p. 67.
[60] Knetsch, "Church Ordinances and Regulations of the Dutch Synods."
[61] Esser, *Niederländische Exulanten in England*, pp. 238–243.
[62] Pollmann, "'Hey ho, let the cup go round!'"

preacher De Bray, whose recently composed *Confession de foi* had stressed what good burghers the Reformed were, and he disavowed them. Perhaps inevitably, a government crackdown ensued and the Tournai Reformed were driven underground while De Bray was forced to flee to safety in France.[63] The Reformed in nearby Valenciennes grew still bolder; in 1562 they staged a spectacular rescue of two of their condemned fellow believers from the stake at the very last minute.[64] In the spring of 1563 they consciously cultivated the following they had accrued from the *chanteries* by staging several open-air *grands prêches* in the countryside around the city; according to reports as many as six thousand people may have attended.[65]

In the Westkwartier of Flanders in the early 1560s the local Reformed believers, led by returning exiles from the English stranger church in Sandwich, were likewise growing restless.[66] Turmoil accompanied executions for heresy in the region and local authorities took to having armed guards present on these occasions.[67] In the spring of 1561, a group of Reformed men broke into the prison of Mesen south of Ypres and freed one of their coreligionists arrested for heresy. At least half a dozen more prison breaks took place in the Westkwartier over the following year; such guerilla tactics alarmed authorities considerably.[68] During the summer of 1562 in the village of Boeschepe a lay preacher publicly led worship for two hours, under armed escort, in the local cemetery while the mass was celebrated inside the church nearby. He too had eventually to flee abroad to escape harsh reaction.[69]

The brazenness of these actions took local authorities off guard and they feared a more widespread heretical rebellion. Repression ensued, especially in Flanders, where inquisitors scoured the countryside for heretics. Some congregations went underground while many of their preachers fled abroad. After 1563 there were few public manifestations by the Reformed until the outbreak of iconoclastic riots across the Netherlands in 1566. Within Reformed circles, especially in the churches abroad, there was some debate about whether violent acts on behalf of the true faith, such as storming prisons or executions, were permissible; should force be used to make Netherlandish authorities legally recognize the Reformed religion? Militants within the stranger church in Sandwich

[63] Moreau, *Histoire du Protestantisme*, pp. 168–191.
[64] Clark, "An Urban Study during the Revolt of the Netherlands," pp. 274–288.
[65] Clark, "An Urban Study during the Revolt of the Netherlands," pp. 179–181.
[66] Backhouse, *Flemish and Walloon Congregations at Sandwich*, pp. 137–147.
[67] Decavele, *De dageraad van de Reformatie in Vlaanderen*, pp. 414–415.
[68] Decavele, *De dageraad van de Reformatie in Vlaanderen*, pp. 418–419, 425.
[69] Decavele, *De dageraad van de Reformatie in Vlaanderen*, pp. 428–429.

insisted that resistance to religious tyranny was licit, while a more pacifist camp within the London congregation argued that rebellion was detrimental to the cause of true religion.[70] Calvin's admonitions against timid Nicodemites still rang in the ears of some, while others insisted that lawful government, whatever its religious policies, had to be obeyed. Not until a much more polarized set of political circumstances obtained in the late 1560s would Netherlandish Reformed Protestants unite around the idea of armed resistance to the central government.

During this period of growing religious agitation in the 1550s and 1560s, the Reformed search for identity and boundaries, like that of the Mennonites, was encouraged by the publication of martyrologies. In 1554 the Arras lawyer Jean Crespin (1520–1572), who had many ties to the Netherlandish Reformed, published the first edition of his *Histoire des Martyrs*, and five years later the industrious Antwerp preacher Adriaan van Haemstede wrote *De geschiedenis en de dood der vrome martelaren* (*The History and Death of the Pious Martyrs*).[71] These two books became enormously popular in Reformed circles and went through many printings in the sixteenth century long after their respective authors' deaths. Crespin recounted stories of both French and Netherlandish Reformed Protestants who had lost their lives for their faith, while Van Haemstede more ambitiously placed the Netherlandish martyrs within the longer history of Christian martyrdom, starting with Jesus Christ himself.[72] Crespin was supplied with information about Netherlandish martyrs by such preachers as De Bray, while Van Haemstede in some cases described the executions of his own friends and acquaintances.[73] The latter wrote his work while serving the church under the cross in Antwerp, and the perils attending such a precarious position lent vividness to his prose.[74] One of victims he may have known personally was Cornelis Halewijn, who was imprisoned for his beliefs in Antwerp in 1559 and who, under interrogation, insisted like a good Protestant that he would only accept charges of error against him if they could be proven through scripture. His executioners told him that if he held a wooden cross in his hands he would receive a more merciful death by sword rather than fire, but he cast the "idolatrous" cross aside and declared that he would die in witness to the truth of God.[75] Many more such stories filled these collections, and they

---

[70] Backhouse, *Flemish and Walloon Congregations at Sandwich*, pp. 138–140; Muylaert, *Shaping the Stranger Churches*, pp. 105–114.

[71] Crespin, *Histoire des martyrs*; Van Haemstede, *Geschiedenis der martelaren*.

[72] Jelsma, *Adriaan van Haemstede*, pp. 234–236.

[73] Jelsma, *Adriaan van Haemstede*, p. 259.

[74] Pettegree, "Adriaan van Haemstede," p. 60.

[75] Van Haemstede, *Geschiedenis der martelaren*, pp. 683–685.

emphasized both the steadfastness of the martyrs and the rightness of their cause. Designed to stir an emotional response in their readers, these tales tried to reinforce the fellowship of feeling among beleaguered Reformed Netherlanders. The martyrs believed they were dying for true religion and therefore formed a legitimate continuation of the long history of Christian heroism throughout the ages. The martyrologies of Crespin and Van Haemstede reassured their Reformed readers that they were indeed the true heirs of the early church, rather than the Catholics. Their martyred coreligionists had not died for error, these books declared, but for truth. As was the case with the Mennonites, martyrologies sought to sharpen confessional identity by allowing the Reformed to differentiate themselves from their religious antagonists and rivals.

Like the Mennonites, the Reformed also produced a distinctive vernacular version of the Bible for use by their communities. Eschewing the Catholic Vulgate, Reformed versions of scripture turned instead to Martin Luther's German Bible and the Genevan Bible for inspiration. Ultimately the various translations and revisions by Reformed divines were put together in the early 1560s into an edition known as the Deux-Aes Bible, which Reformed communities and congregations in the Netherlands used well into the mid-seventeenth century. By arming themselves with such literary tools – confession, martyrology, Bible – the Reformed sought, like their Mennonite competitors, to fashion for themselves a distinctive confessional identity.[76] A variety of opinions and approaches remained among them, particularly on how churches should be organized and how the authorities should be dealt with, but it was clear that by the 1560s there was a stream of Christianity within the Low Countries that could be increasingly recognized as Reformed.

Catholic Reform

The search for identity was not confined to the dissenters alone. The Catholic Church, the church of the vast majority of Netherlanders, would also try to draw sharper boundaries and adopt clearer statements of belief as it sought both to reform itself and defeat heresy during the course of the century. The question of *reformatio* had preoccupied the church seriously long before the outbreak of the various Protestant heresies; from numerous quarters both inside and out, from the religious orders to princes to the humanists, came the call for renovation of church practice and

---

[76] De Bruin and Broeyer, *De Statenbijbel en zijn voorgangers*, pp. 180–191; Den Hollander, "Edition History of the Deux Aes Bible," pp. 41–72; François, "De doopsgezinde Biestkensbijbel," pp. 335–340.

organization.[77] The widespread lay desire for greater participation in religious life had also fueled the growing demand for religious reform. When the Protestant rebellion broke out in the sixteenth century, the issue of church reform took on much greater urgency and relevance. The Catholic Church thus also embarked on a search for identity and boundaries at mid-century as it sought to distinguish itself more vigorously from the manifold heresies of the Protestants. In the Netherlands this effort to establish clearer boundaries was to a large part driven by the Habsburg government, especially the new sovereign Philip II of Spain, which very much saw itself as the defender of true religion. Arguably, it was the state almost as much as the church itself that drove Catholicism's mid-century reformation in the Low Countries.

To be sure, Catholic ecclesiastical authorities had not been idle as heresy spread in the region; the prince-bishop of Liège, for example, had condemned Luther's books and ordered them burned already in the fall of 1520.[78] Ruard Tapper, a leading theologian at the University of Leuven, added to the chorus by arguing that a reformed and disciplined clergy would do much to halt the spread of the heretical contagion.[79] Not all bishops remained impassive; the aristocratic bishop of Cambrai, Robert de Croÿ, made sincere efforts to introduce reform measures in his diocese, as did his successor, Maximilien de Berghes.[80] The most aggressive measures against religious rebellion, however, came primarily from governmental rather than ecclesiastical quarters.[81] The diffused episcopate of the Netherlands prevented any centralized campaign against heresy by the bishops; only the state would have the resources to mount a coordinated and sustained offensive against dissenters, and even that had proven only partially successful. Emperor Charles V, as sovereign in the Low Countries, assumed the lead in combating the heretical threat in his patrimonial lands. Starting in the 1520s, as we have seen, a barrage of anti-heretical edicts, placards and legislation issued from the Brussels court; inquisitorial judicial mechanisms were set up across many provinces. While clerics certainly worked within this legal apparatus, the Netherlandish anti-heretical effort was principally a state-driven affair. Charles's legislation equated heresy with divine lese-majesty, which meant that heresy, in addition to being a sin, became a crime against the state.[82] That in turn meant

[77] Rummel, "Voices of Reform from Hus to Erasmus."
[78] Verheyden, *Le Martyrologe Protestant*, p. 18.
[79] Gielis, "Een pleidooi voor klerikale herbronning."
[80] Van de Meulebroucke, Soen and François, "Robrecht van Croÿ"; Soen and Hollevoet, "Le 'Borromée' des anciens Pays-bas?"
[81] Pollmann, *Catholic Identity and the Revolt of the Netherlands*, p. 45.
[82] Duke, "Salvation by Coercion: The Controversy Surrounding the 'Inquisition' in the Low Countries on the Eve of the Revolt," in *Reformation and Revolt*, pp. 161–162; Goosens, *Les Inquisitions modernes aux*, vol. 1, pp. 47–68.

that the central authorities had far greater legal latitude to override local laws and privileges when prosecuting heretics, including trying them outside their home jurisdictions and confiscating their property. This brusque nullification of local privileges would become a sticking point with the growing political discontent with the Habsburg government.[83] A large portion of the Netherlandish political establishment simply failed to support the work of the inquisitors, and Habsburg anti-heresy policy never gained much sympathy from the general population.[84]

The parish clergy in the Netherlands, who were at the front lines in this struggle with heresy, initially remained oddly quiescent, appearing reluctant to stir up their parishioners too much against the threat. In contrast to France, where priests passionately denounced Huguenot doctrine in the pulpit and in print to the Catholic faithful early on, Netherlandish priests took a much more passive stance. While Protestant polemical literature flooded the book and pamphlet market, Catholic imprints before 1566 were almost entirely devotional rather than apologetic in nature. There seems to have been a consensus among priests that discussing heresy with the laity would only encourage the spread of heterodox notions; it was better to exhort parishioners to be good Catholics, to repent and to leave the fight against heresy to church professionals. Layfolk should focus on personal, moral reform; it was safer to ignore heretics, priests told their parishioners, than to answer them. This may have seemed like a prudent strategy at the time, but the failure of the clergy to garner more popular support, to create a more sectarian Catholic party among the laity as it were, would backfire when religious violence broke out in 1566.[85]

Yet even if Netherlandish priests and prelates seemed reluctant to mobilize lay support in the effort to burnish a more distinctive Catholic identity, the wider spread of Protestant heresy, especially its Reformed variant, across Europe forced the Catholic church to confessionalize more generally in order to counter it. In this sense Catholic reform formed part of the larger effort to establish identity and boundaries among Christian groups that was now preoccupying the reformation in the Low Countries. The ecumenical Council of Trent, which met in the course of three gatherings at mid-century (1545–1547, 1551–1552, 1562–1563), reaffirmed traditional church doctrine and thereby delineated more sharply and more insistently the boundaries between Catholic and Protestant belief. That heresy could spread so rapidly and gain such a substantial following suggested to many reform-minded Catholics that the church

[83] Pollmann, *Catholic Identity and the Revolt of the Netherlands*, pp. 45–46.

[84] Duke, "The 'Inquisition' and the Repression of Religious Dissent in the Habsburg Netherlands 1521–1566," in *Dissident Identities*, p. 116.

[85] Pollmann, *Catholic Identity and the Revolt of the Netherlands*, pp. 44–67.

was failing in its pastoral tasks; the most trenchant critics of priestly abuse and neglect often came from inside the first estate itself. Indeed, much of the work of the Council of Trent concentrated on the reformation of clergy, making the bishop and the priest central to the rejuvenation of the church and the struggle against heresy.[86] The Trent decrees or canons were first printed with royal imprimatur in the Netherlands in 1564, though it would take the work of years to implement them to any effective degree. The Trent canons required, for example, regular visitations of parishes by the bishops; the first such event did not take place in the Low Countries until 1570, when the bishop of Utrecht visited the parishes of the town of Culemborg (and only after he was pressured by the Habsburg government to do so). Seminaries for the proper education of priests were also mandated by the canons; the first one in the Low Countries was established by the bishop of Ypres in 1565.[87]

Other measures of Catholic reform came to the Low Countries in mid-century as well, many of them sponsored by the Habsburg government. In 1562, for example, the Netherlands' second university was set up at Douai in the southern province of Artois to serve the Francophone provinces. The location was a deliberate choice, for the surrounding regions (which included the cities of Tournai and Ypres) were hotbeds of evangelical activity, and the Habsburg government hoped the new university would counterbalance native heretics as well as Huguenot influences streaming in over the nearby French border. A number of the new institution's staff were Catholic exiles from England who had fled the Protestant regime of Elizabeth I. For many decades following the university of Douai flourished as a bulwark of Catholic scholarship and printing.[88]

The demand for *reformatio* also encouraged the creation of new religious orders. The order most closely associated with Catholic reform, the Society of Jesus, soon came to the Netherlands as well. The first Jesuits arrived in the Low Countries in 1542 at the University of Leuven, encouraged by its energetic vice-chancellor, Ruard Tapper, a mere two years after their order was officially approved by the pope. Within a few years they had recruited several new members into the order from Leuven students and clergy. Tapper persuaded Philip II to recognize the order formally in the Low Countries in 1556, and by 1565 the Society of Jesus had its own college in Leuven, which coexisted uneasily with the university's theology faculty until the order's suppression in the eighteenth

---

[86] Bireley, *Refashioning of Catholicism*, p. 57.
[87] Spiertz, "Succes en falen van de katholieke reformatie."
[88] Löwe, "Richard Smyth and the Founding of the University of Douai"; Soetaert, *De katholieke drukpers in de kerkprovincie Cambrai*, pp. 39–63.

century.[89] A specific Jesuit province for the Netherlands, called *Germania Inferior*, was set up in 1564, though the subsequent troubles of the next two decades retarded its progress. Prevented from moving further north by the wars, at the sixteenth century's close the Society was a presence in nearly every major town in the southern Netherlands, with established colleges for boys and sodalities dedicated to the Virgin Mary for all types of social groups, including students and unmarried women.[90] The Jesuits soon became important motors of Catholic education in the southern Netherlands and the vanguard in the movement for moral and spiritual reformation among Catholics.

The most significant and most controversial contribution of the Habsburg government to Catholic reform in the Netherlands was its reorganization of the region's episcopal infrastructure.[91] It had long been a goal of the Habsburgs, as part of their larger project of consolidating power over the region, to reorganize and rationalize the Netherlands' sprawling and distended bishoprics, whose boundaries still followed diffused medieval lines that in no way matched the composite state Charles V had successfully achieved by the 1540s.[92] Introducing new bishoprics thus nicely dovetailed their twin aims of reforming the church and extending their power. Negotiations between Philip II's counselor, the Brabantine theologian and inquisitor Franciscus Sonnius (1506–1576), and Rome began in the 1550s to replace the Netherlands' eight traditional dioceses with a more tightly arranged system. The current diocesan boundaries, everyone agreed, had led to ineffective local pastoral situations. Valenciennes, for example, sat squarely on the jurisdictional line between the bishops of Arras and Cambrai, and neither one ever gained the upper hand of authority over the city's parishes. Instead these were largely controlled by powerful local abbeys.[93] Creating smaller bishoprics, Sonnius argued, would make them more manageable and encourage bishops to become more accountable for the parishes they superintended. Bishops, according to Tridentine prescriptions, were to make visits to parishes, ensure that their priests were better schooled and prepared, and act as more effective shepherds for their flocks overall. Such a thoroughgoing reform of the Netherlandish church's organization could also only help in the ongoing war against heresy, or so Philip II hoped.

What Sonnius's negotiations in Rome finally produced in 1559 was a bull from Pope Paul IV, *Super universas*, which created an entirely new

[89] Roegiers, "Awkward Neighbours," pp. 155–157.
[90] Spiertz, "Succes en falen van de katholieke reformatie," p. 70.
[91] Postma, "Nieuw licht op een oude zaak," pp. 11–12.
[92] Dierickx, *De oprichting der nieuwe bisdommen in de Nederlanden*, pp. 32–48.
[93] Clark, "An Urban Study during the Revolt of the Netherlands," pp. 141–142.

diocesan structure for the Habsburg Netherlands.[94] It approved the scrapping of the old system and the creation of fifteen new bishoprics for the Low Countries: Groningen, Deventer, Leeuwarden, Haarlem,

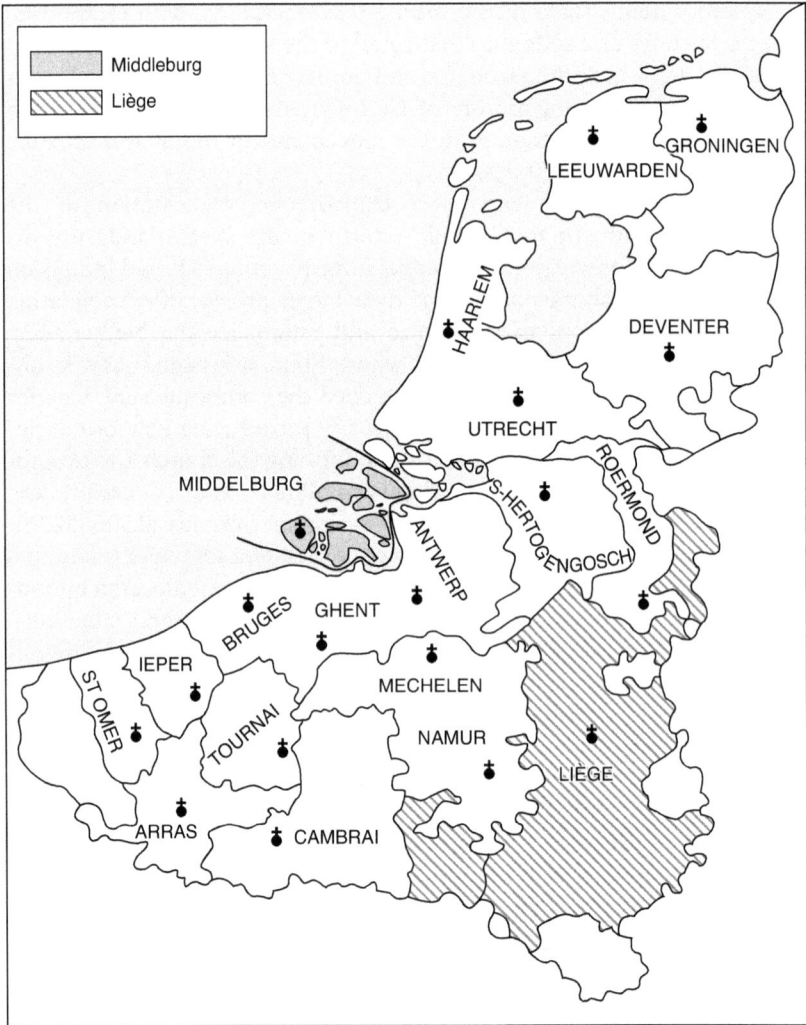

Map 3.1 Diocesan boundaries in the Low Countries after 1559

[94] Dierickx, *De oprichting der nieuwe bisdommen in de Nederlanden*, pp. 62–69.

Middelburg, Antwerp, Bruges, Ghent, 's-Hertogenbosch, Ypres, Roermond, Arras, Tournai, St. Omer and Namur. These in turn incorporated into three new archbishoprics: Utrecht, Mechelen and Cambrai. Philip II was granted the power to name all these bishops except Cambrai, which the papacy reserved for itself; aside from this proviso, foreign prelates outside of Habsburg control would no longer have any jurisdiction within the Netherlands, as the boundaries of the new bishoprics would now fall within those of the Habsburg Low Countries.

The actual implementation of this scheme proved to be an extremely fraught process; there were a number of entrenched political and ecclesiastical interests whom such changes would put at a severe disadvantage.[95] The archbishops of Cologne and Reims, who stood to lose their influence in the region, naturally fought it tooth and nail, though to little avail. The Netherlandish high nobility also voiced strong objections: the spirit behind the reorganization insisted that the prospective candidates for bishops, as well as their cathedral canons, be better credentialed and seriously reform minded, a requirement that disqualified some younger aristocratic sons who normally were automatically favored for these kinds of high ecclesiastical appointment. The already restive grandees believed that the crown was using the excuse of church reform to yet again chip away at their natural privileges of leadership, and they resented that they had been excluded from negotiations with Rome.[96] And indeed Philip II named to the new episcopal seats mostly non-noble men who were both irreproachable and loyal to the Habsburg regime (Sonnius, for example, was rewarded with the miter of 's-Hertogenbosch).

The additional stipulation that each new diocese was to appoint its own inquisitors further disturbed both nobles and magistrates, among whom rumors flew that the reorganization might introduce a more effective and more severe inquisition against heresy, perhaps based on the infamous Spanish model. The inquisition-averse magistracy of Antwerp went so far as to protest in 1562 to the regent Margaret of Parma that their city, the largest in the Netherlands, did not really need its own bishop.[97] The Netherlandish monastic establishment was also unhappy with the reorganization, which called for the incomes from rich abbeys to fund the new bishoprics; in effect each new bishop would become abbot of at least one of the great abbeys in his diocese. The wealthy and powerful abbeys of the duchy of Brabant in particular, which would bankroll the primate-archbishop of Mechelen, resisted this arrangement strenuously. Making

---

[95] Postma, *Viglius van Aytta*, pp. 227–242.
[96] Soen, "Between Dissent and Peacemaking," p. 741.
[97] Dierickx, *De oprichting der nieuwe bisdommen in de Nederlanden*, pp. 168–169.

the bishops abbots effectively imposed secular priests as leaders of monasteries, something to which the religious orders strongly objected.
Brabant's nobles joined them in their protest, for the assumed abbacies
would make the archbishops disproportionately powerful members of the
clerical chamber in the provincial estates. The prickly estates of the
northeastern provinces, Friesland, Groningen, Guelders and Overijssel,
who twenty years after the fact still referred to their annexation by the
Habsburgs as "the recent conquest," resisted the installation of the new
bishoprics entirely, as they regarded it as an incursion of princely power
into local affairs.[98] Because of these various entrenched parties of resistance, the last of the new bishops was not installed until 1570, and by then
the Netherlands was engulfed by war. The reform of the bishoprics, the
centerpiece of the Habsburg push to confessionalize the Catholic Church
in order to strengthen it against heresy, proved at best a mixed success.

   These kinds of measures of reform, theological, institutional and pastoral, sought to strengthen the Catholic Church, to shore it up against its
growing number of heretical enemies and to reaffirm its authority. The
Trent canons, the new religious orders, educational initiatives and infra-
structural change were all designed to make clear distinctions between the
true, traditional church and its heretical opponents. In this way Catholic
reform can also be seen as a type of confessional turn, an awakened
concern with identity and boundaries. By the 1560s the disparate streams
of Christianity in the Netherlands had distinguished themselves quite
clearly from each other. More and more the tendency among many
Netherlanders who took their religion seriously (be they Catholic or
Protestant) was to draw sharper and sharper lines between what they
saw as true and false religion.

   Mennonite, Reformed, Catholic – these are, to be sure, broad and
imprecise umbrella categories; within each remained considerable varie-
gation and even disagreement. The Mennonites splintered into various
groups already in the 1560s, the Reformed movement was not uniform in
its agreement on all points of doctrine or ecclesiology, and among
Catholics there was still a range of opinions about the need for and
direction of reform. Nor were all Netherlanders inclined to lend their
enthusiasm to a more sharply polarized religious landscape. The eminent
historian Juliaan Woltjer posited that a religious center of sorts did exist,
"middle groups" of people who wanted neither Protestant nor Catholic
sectarianism and who did not identify themselves completely with any of
the three slowly emerging confessions.[99] The moderates were not a party

[98] Dierickx, *De oprichting der nieuwe bisdommen in de Nederlanden*, p. 188.
[99] Woltjer, *Friesland in Hervormingstijd*, pp. 90–101; Woltjer, "Het beeld vergruisd?"

in and of themselves and were certainly not monolithic in their religious opinions or beliefs, which could run from late medieval ideas of
reformatio through humanism to spiritualism.[100] Some of them were
protestantizing Catholics, often priests who remained loyal to the
church but eschewed selected doctrines such as purgatory or prayers
for the dead. A pastor named Steven Silvius working in Friesland in
the 1550s, for example, instructed his parishioners to attend the sermons to hear God's word but not to go to mass, since he was not
certain that the actual body of Christ was present there.[101] Despite the
confessional turn, it was still possible for some to float between religious convictions, to sympathize with the desire for reform without
giving up ecclesiastical allegiance. The eclectic Reformation of the first
part of the sixteenth century, which picked and chose particular religious ideas it found congenial, lived on in these groups. At most what
these moderates shared was an affinity of sentiment; they wanted to
avoid "the choice between Trent and Geneva."[102] They felt at home
neither in hidebound, entrenched Catholicism, nor in sectarian,
aggressive Reformed Protestantism, nor in quietist, self-segregating
Mennonitism. They seem instead to have sought a less doctrinaire
form of Christianity, one that perhaps sought to marry the enveloping
universality of the church of Rome with the serious piety of the
Mennonites and the Reformed. They were mirrored by an equally
amorphous group of political moderates, men in authority such as
the Netherlands' principal grandee William of Orange, who rejected
heresy but deplored the heavy-handedness of Habsburg policy and
hoped to negotiate some sort of change to it. And in his case there
were already indications by the 1560s that, though he had not openly
broken with the Catholic Church, his theological sympathies were
leaning back to the Lutheranism of his early German upbringing.[103]
These vague middle groups, defined mostly by what they were not –
confessional Catholics or Protestants – would find themselves eclipsed
once armed rebellion broke in the Low Countries in the late 1560s.[104] As
political and religious circumstances became more polarized and more
violent in the 1570s, the middle groups' hopes for religious reconciliation
and political compromise would be dashed. Confessionalism, with all its

---

[100] Woltjer, "Political Moderates and Religious Moderates in the Revolt of the
Netherlands," in *Reformation, Revolt and Civil War in France and the Netherlands*, p. 195.
[101] Woltjer, *Friesland in Hervormingstijd*, pp. 91–92.
[102] Woltjer, "Het beeld vergruisd?" p. 137.
[103] Klink, *Opstand, politiek en religie bij Willem van Oranje*, pp. 147–150.
[104] Smit, "The Present Position of Studies Regarding the Revolt of the Netherlands," p. 51.

attendant boundaries and political consequences, would win out. The inchoate Reformation of the earlier part of the century was disappearing as different religious movements each sharpened their sense of identity. With polarization inevitably came conflict. What ultimately brought the most dramatic religious change to the Low Countries was war.

4   War

In the later 1560s, religious dissent and political discontent in the Low Countries coalesced into a general rebellion against the Habsburg government. Reformed Protestants, who by then formed the most conspicuous group of religious dissenters, ultimately threw in their lot with the growing political opposition that had emerged to the policies of the Brussels court. For the next generation reformation in the Low Countries would be attended by armed conflict.

This conflict, usually called the Revolt of the Netherlands or Dutch Revolt, was by turns (and often at the same time) a rebellion, a civil war, a religious war and a great-power struggle. This period, from the late 1560s through the early 1590s, saw the first eruption of sustained confessional violence in the region and also the first establishment of protected Protestant churches on Netherlandish soil.

The Revolt *in* the Netherlands, as Anton van der Lem has more judiciously termed it, arose out of a political crisis, the contest between the Habsburgs and regional leaders, and it would be exacerbated by religion. The centralizing policies of Charles V had been unpopular among the Netherlands' aristocratic and civic elites, and under his son and successor, Philip II, the discontent and resentment deepened and sharpened. Philip had brought an end to the long-running French wars in 1559, but debts from military expenditure had accrued significantly and the central government was effectively bankrupt. The States-General balked at the amount of taxation the king demanded to address the financial crisis and insisted on greater oversight in fiscal affairs, something Philip refused. Every measure Philip took to try to ease his fiscal burdens and garner more revenue was met with resistance and protest by provincial elites. After the peace negotiations with France ended, he left the Netherlands to attend to Spanish and Mediterranean affairs; he named his half-sister Margaret of Parma (1522–1586) as regent but really trusted only the confidants and jurists he had installed at the Brussels court to run Netherlandish affairs properly. He made his Burgundian loyalist Antoine Perrenot de Granvelle (later rewarded with the newly created archiepiscopal see of Mechelen) her chief councilor to ensure the enforcement of royal policy; this job made him so unpopular among the nobility that the ever-prudent Philip was obliged to remove him from office in 1564. The *grands seigneurs* of the Netherlands, who believed that governing the country was in fact their natural due, found themselves shut out of the high councils of leadership. The high nobility, led by its ranking member William, prince of Orange (1533–1584), repeatedly and unsuccessfully petitioned the king in the early 1560s for a greater role in governing their lands. They were stymied by Philip's resistance and their resentment grew accordingly.[1]

The religious issue made things worse. The Reformed Protestant movement was growing bigger and more organized during the early 1560s, although its adherents remained a small minority of the popula-tion. Despite the spread of Reformed conventicles and clandestine churches, Habsburg anti-heresy policy grew more unpopular among the general population. The governments of cities and even entire provinces, such as Friesland and Groningen, citing age-old traditions of local privi-lege, refused to execute convicted heretics or even to promulgate the anti-heresy placards. The severity of the religious legislation, which equated heresy with treason and thus allowed for harsher punishments (including confiscation of property and trial outside of one's own hometown) that rode roughshod over local justice, deeply vexed local nobles, magistrates and jurists, and led many of them to engage in passive resistance. Local rights and jurisdictions, so jealously guarded, hampered the efficient prosecution of heresy. Inquisitors complained of local municipal autho-rities' lack of cooperation, and indeed many town governments appear to have unofficially relaxed their application of the placards. The loyalty of local leaders to the sovereign was severely tested by the harshness of the anti-heretical campaign.[2]

From the standpoint of Philip II, all this recalcitrance was deeply troubling. An unwavering Catholic, he saw his inheritance in the Netherlands surrounded by heresy: Lutherans were tolerated to the east in the Holy Roman Empire, England to the west was now ruled by a heretical queen, and, perhaps most alarming, savage religious war had broken out just to the south in France. The heretics who escaped his placards could easily find refuge in these lands and his French-speaking southern provinces now lay exposed to the baleful influences of the Huguenots. Reformed Protestantism was gaining ground throughout

[1] Van der Lem, *Revolt in the Netherlands*, pp. 35–57.
[2] Duke, "Salvation by Coercion," in *Reformation and Revolt*.

northern Europe in the 1550s and 1560s. To stem this tide Philip strongly advocated reform within the Catholic Church; enforcing the renewing initiatives of Tridentine Catholicism in his lands was another way to counter heresy, so he avidly pushed, for example, the reorganization of the bishoprics. On a more geopolitical level, the Ottoman Turkish empire was becoming a serious strategic threat to his Mediterranean interests. Philip could not lose religious and political control of his patrimonial Low Countries, the source of so much wealth, while having to fight a war for dominance of the Mediterranean Sea. There were all sorts of solid religious and political reasons to keep a firm line against heresy, so he remained resistant to repeated appeals from the Netherlandish grandees to relax the placards.[3] "Considering the condition of religious affairs in the Netherlands as I understand it," he wrote Margaret of Parma in a widely publicized letter in the fall of 1565, "this is no time to make any alteration."[4]

Philip's stern line on religious policy made governing the Netherlands that much more difficult for his half-sister and the Brussels court, given the unpopularity of the placards. Though nearly all of them were Catholic and had little sympathy with Protestant ideas (a few had wives who were Lutherans, however), the grand nobles were deeply troubled by the crown's uncompromising policy against heresy and the social and legal disruptions it was causing in their lands. For them religion was a political issue, and as local authorities they were in part responsible for carrying out royal anti-heresy policy. As vassals to the king they believed that it was their obligation to mitigate what they saw as increasingly harmful royal actions in the localities they were responsible for governing.[5] They feared that these actions might in turn provoke violence and even rebellion; the common welfare of the land was under threat. Their already long-simmering political unhappiness with Philip was compounded by widespread popular discontent with the placards; some of them even proposed an arrangement of religious coexistence or toleration to safeguard public order, as was currently being attempted in France.[6] Royal authority was eroding; by the close of 1565 a general sense of political crisis was brewing among Netherlandish elites.

---

[3] Parker, *Grand Strategy of Philip II*, pp. 115–121.
[4] "Petition of 5 April 1566," in Kossmann and Mellink, *Texts concerning the Revolt of the Netherlands*, p. 55.
[5] Van Nierop, "The Nobility and the Revolt of the Netherlands: Between Church and King, and Protestantism and Privileges," in Benedict et al., *Reformation, Revolt and Civil War in France and the Netherlands*, p. 87.
[6] Soen, "Between Dissent and Peacemaking," pp. 735–758.

It was, however, the lesser nobility, the *gentilshommes*, rather than the grandees, who made the first overt, collective demonstration of protest to Philip's religious policies in this pivotal decade. The lesser nobility had less direct access to court and did not sit in the States-General, but they often served as sheriffs, bailiffs and judges in the countryside, which put them in the front lines of the application of anti-heresy law. By the 1560s a number of gentry were openly sympathetic to the Reformed cause, and a handful of them went so far as to convert to the Reformed faith. These in turn hosted Reformed preaching on their manors, protected nascent congregations in their jurisdictions and supported ministers and consistories. By December 1565, when it became clear how adamant the king was about upholding the anti-heresy laws, a series of meetings among these gentlemen, under the leadership of the Reformed nobles Hendrik van Brederode, lord of Vianen (1531–1568), Jan van Marnix (1537–1567), lord of Toulouse, and Louis of Nassau (1538–1574), the younger brother of William of Orange, led to the creation of a "Compromise" of the nobility, a coalition of lesser nobles that formally protested the government's religious policies. Specifically, the petition of the Compromise warned against the strengthening of what it called the "inquisition" by the crown, including the unfounded rumor that Philip intended to introduce the Spanish Inquisition into the Netherlands: "Not only is this inquisition iniquitous and against all divine and human laws surpassing the worst barbarism ever practiced by tyrants, it will also most certainly lead to the dishonoring of God's name and to the utter ruin and desolation of these Netherlands."[7] The letter warned that "open revolt and a universal rebellion" were imminent because of the unhappiness of the people with the placards. The Compromise carefully avoided all mention of heresy or Protestantism and instead couched its concerns in terms of the general welfare of realm and church. The text was circulated among noble family and clientage networks, and altogether about four hundred signatories, Catholic and Protestant alike, pledged their allegiance and assistance to each other in this cause. Then, in April 1566, in a carefully staged event redolent of the pageantry of the Habsburg court, two hundred of the noble signers solemnly entered Margaret of Parma's palace in Brussels and presented her with the petition document, pressing her to persuade her half-brother to suspend the placards and the inquisition lest widespread disorder break out in the Netherlands (Illustration 4.1).[8] Although one of Margaret's courtiers dismissed the petitioners as mere "beggars" (*gueux* or *geuzen*), she countered with a proposal to moderate the government's religious policy, ultimately allowing for a temporary

---

[7] "Petition," *Texts*, p. 60.   [8] Arnade, *Beggars, Iconoclasts, and Civic Patriots*, p. 77.

Illustration 4.1 Frans Hogenberg, *Presentation of the Petition by the Compromise of the Nobility*, 1566–1570. Hogenberg produced a number of images depicting the Netherlandish wars in his Cologne workshop in the 1570s. Courtesy Rijksmuseum Amsterdam

suspension of the placards. In their triumph the Compromise nobles eventually took up, in a neat bit of social and cultural inversion, the sobriquet "Beggars" as a badge of honor; a few of the more theatrical among them even walked around in long gray cloaks and carried beggars' bowls.[9] Those who opposed the king and eventually organized an armed rebellion against him were known as the "Beggars" for the rest of the Netherlandish wars.

It was the issue of religion, therefore, that sparked the crisis that led to revolt against the Habsburg regime; the Compromise was first of all a denunciation of Philip's anti-heresy policies.[10] At the same time, as we have seen, Reformed Protestant groups in the Netherlands had not been idle in this decade. During the 1560s their spread and organization grew more marked and they rapidly became the most numerous

[9] Van Nierop, "Beggars' Banquet."
[10] Secretan, *Les privileges, berceau de la liberté*, p. 21.

and well-organized of all the dissenting evangelical groups in the Low Countries. They started to set up their own local structures of church government – that is, consistories made up of elders and deacons. Despite their small numbers they were an increasingly loud and public minority. Their growing success at attracting adherents in virtually every province, especially in the core western regions, was one of the reasons that prompted the lesser nobility to organize the Compromise. With Guy de Bray's Belgic Confession the Reformed movement had a clear, normative statement of belief, and its adherents grew more and more vocal and brazen in their public expressions of faith, flouting the placards in many instances. In the city of Ghent, for example, where a certain degree of unofficial magisterial tolerance reigned, the local Reformed congregation in the spring of 1565 even dared to ask the city fathers for permission to secure their own church building.[11] Reformed Protestantism appeared to be making rapid progress everywhere, and the religious question was now the driving force in Netherlandish political life.

The Wonderyear

As word of Margaret of Parma's moderating of the placards spread during the spring of 1566, Protestant activity became even more visible. Across the land it became clear that though public meetings of evangelicals remained officially prohibited, there would no longer be any prosecution of heretical beliefs.[12] The informal gathering of Antwerp Lutherans, most of them German merchants, immediately constituted itself into an official congregation, for example.[13] Emboldened Reformed preachers streamed back into the country from their exile in England and the Holy Roman Empire. Proselytizing proceeded apace, and not just by mouth: one of the notable developments of this year was a flurry of pamphlets, prints, broadsides and propaganda supporting religious dissent, denouncing royal policy and satirizing the Catholic Church, which issued forth from presses both within and outside the Netherlands. Indeed, according to Alastair Duke, more titles issued from Netherlandish presses in 1566 than in any other single year in the sixteenth century. By the summer of 1566 such material, which once would have been confiscated as heretical or seditious, was openly peddled on the streets and markets of most major towns.[14] For a few shillings ordinary folk could buy pamphlets and prints

[11] Decavele, *De dageraad van de Reformatie in Vlaanderen*, pp. 334–335.
[12] Parker, *Dutch Revolt*, pp. 70–71.
[13] Van Manen, *Lutheranen in de Lage Landen*, pp. 70–77; Brall, *Konfessionelle Theologie und Migration*, pp. 61–85.
[14] Duke, "Posters, Pamphlets and Prints," in *Dissident Identities*, pp. 157–177.

criticizing or satirizing both state and church. From the pen of a Brabantine evangelical schoolmaster named Petrus Bloccius, for example, came a trenchant pamphlet, whose title, "More Than Two Hundred Heresies, Blasphemies and New Dogmas That Have Come from the Mass," effectively conveyed the sentiment of its contents.[15] One widely noticed sacramentarian print, entitled "The Burial of the Mass," depicted the mass carried in a coffin by two Beggars to a gravesite, followed by a cortege of grieving priests and nuns (Illustration 4.2).[16] More decorously, the Antwerp Reformed preacher Franciscus Junius published a solemn tract addressed to Philip II defending the sincerity of Reformed believers and urging him not to oppress consciences.[17] Likeminded texts and images abounded in the bookstalls of urban markets across the Low Countries, and they circulated widely.

Illustration 4.2 Anonymous, *The Burial of the Mass (De begrafenis van de mis)*, 1567. This polemic print depicts two Beggar rebels carrying a coffin with the accoutrements of the Catholic mass (or "the pope's invention," as the caption beneath them has it) to an awaiting grave, trailed by weeping monks and nuns. Courtesy Royal Library, Brussels

[15] Van Gelderen, *The Political Thought of the Dutch Revolt*, p. 83.
[16] Horst, *De Opstand in zwart-wit*, pp. 45–47.
[17] "A Brief Discourse Sent to King Philip," *Texts*, pp. 56–59.

As the spring and summer of 1566 wore on, Reformed Protestants grew still bolder in their public actions. Episodes of *chanteries* or psalm-singing were reported in a number of public civic spaces. Many Reformed organized open-air sermons held safely outside city walls – "hedge-preaching" – that sometimes attracted large crowds. Already in May open-air preaching took place outside Ypres in western Flanders, attracting as many as a thousand listeners.[18] In the Reformed hotbeds of the French-speaking south, Tournai and Valenciennes, such *prêches* likewise brought in hundreds of onlookers at a time. The message of these sermons was defiant; a preacher outside Tournai told his listeners: "we pray to God that that He may grant the destruction of this papist idolatry; be of good heart for we are strong ... and we pray God the He may keep the people ... in their convictions."[19] In late July the Reformed of Tournai made a conspicuous public display of their power: several hundred of them entered the market square in orderly formation, demanding from the magistracy permission to build themselves a church (*temple*) just outside the city walls where they could worship during the cold winter months.[20] By mid-summer public preaching was taking place as far north as Amsterdam, Haarlem and Hoorn in the county of Holland.[21] In June nearly five thousand people gathered to hear sermons preached just outside the city walls of Antwerp; by July that number reached a spectacular twenty-five thousand.[22] It was not clear to what extent these crowds included both the committed and the merely curious, but the Reformed were well on their way to becoming a mass movement. Local authorities did little to stop these activities and the government in Brussels grew increasingly nervous. The fiery rhetoric preached at these gatherings to sometimes thousands of people suggested that dissent and defiance were finding resonance. Worse still, in the minds of authorities, with that defiance might come disorder.

When violence did break out, it was not in one of the great cities but in the remote, rural Westkwartier in the far southwest corner of Flanders, which had been a hotbed of Reformed activity since the early 1560s and whose Reformed Protestants had close ties to the English exile churches in Sandwich and Norwich just across the water. Economic conditions had gotten increasingly worse there as trade wars with England shut off precious wool supplies that were the lifeblood of local small-scale textile manufacture. Wars in the Baltic Sea region also cut off grain supplies to

---

[18] Crew, *Calvinist Preaching and Iconoclasm in the Netherlands*, p. 7.
[19] Duke, Lewis and Pettegree, *Calvinism in Europe*, p. 144.
[20] Woltjer, *Op weg naar tachtig jaar oorlog*, p. 379.
[21] Duke and Kolff, "The Time of Troubles in the County of Holland, 1566–67," in *Reformation and Revolt*, p. 129.
[22] Marnef, *Antwerp in the Age of Reformation*, p. 88.

the Netherlands, and the result was that across the countryside grain was both scarce and expensive. Such economic straits may have made local artisans and craftsmen more receptive to the radical and fiery sermons of the Reformed preachers who flooded the area in the spring and summer of 1566 and capitalized on the general discontent. As economic, political and religious tensions grew over the course of the summer, it was clear to contemporary observers and authorities that trouble was brewing.[23]

The dam finally burst on August 10, 1566, the feast day of Saint Laurence. From the village of Steenvoorde in the Westkwartier two Reformed preachers led a group of armed followers into the Saint Laurence chapel just outside the town, where they proceeded to destroy all the paintings and statues inside, decrying them as idols.[24] Three days later a similar act of violence took place in the nearby village of Bailleul, and within ten days roving bands of iconoclasts attacked churches, religious houses and images throughout western Flanders, reaching eastward to Tournai and Valenciennes by August 23–25.[25] By late September dozens of iconoclastic attacks erupted across the length and breadth of the Low Countries, from Ypres to Amsterdam and Groningen to Maastricht. As had happened elsewhere in Europe where religious dissenters gained a following, the violence was directed at sacred spaces and objects.[26] The attacks and destruction seemed to follow no particular pattern and varied from place to place. In some cases they were carried out by highly disciplined bands of iconoclasts paid by the Reformed consistory of Antwerp; other incidents were the work of angry and often drunken mobs perhaps fueled in part by economic distress. Sometimes a Reformed preacher's impassioned sermon denouncing idolatry was the spark; sometimes the attack was carefully plotted out in advance. In 's-Hertogenbosch in north Brabant the iconoclasts set to their destructive work while singing psalms in Dutch.[27] Some attacks were committed brazenly and in public; others happened under cover of night. In some instances magistrates got word about what was going to happen and managed to remove the most precious pieces of art from their churches before the attacks began; in other cases civic militias, whose members could include sympathetic citizen-soldiers, refused to stop the iconoclasts. This "iconoclastic fury" (*beeldenstorm*) struck most of the major towns of the Netherlands, with a few notable exceptions such as the cities of Brussels, Lille, Leuven and Bruges, where Catholic resistance was

[23] Parker, *Dutch Revolt*, pp. 73–74.
[24] Backhouse, *Beeldenstorm en bosgeuzen in het Westkwartier*, p. 54.
[25] Deyon and Lottin, *Les "Casseurs" de l'Été 1566*, pp. 44–53.
[26] Cools, "De Beeldenstorm," pp. 160–162.
[27] Van Gurp, *Reformatie in Brabant*, p. 80.

stauncher. Yet on the whole there was astonishingly little resistance to the attacks; in some towns civic militias, within whose ranks sympathizers could be found, turned a blind eye while iconoclasts did their work. There seems to have been a general collapse of local authority in the face of this wave of violence, which was mostly directed against objects rather than persons (Illustration 4.3).[28]

The *beeldenstorm* appeared to have, as Peter Arnade has put it, its own "repertoire of violence," with various carnivalesque combinations of destruction, desecration, mockery and pillage.[29] Iconoclasts attacked principally religious materials, not just paintings and statuary of Mary and the saints but also stained-glass windows, candelabras, crucifixes, altars and priestly vestments. Communion wafers were trampled underfoot and eucharistic wine gleefully quaffed. Church property and treasure were plundered. Sacred objects were mocked; urinating into a eucharistic

Illustration 4.3 Frans Hogenberg, *Iconoclastic Fury in Antwerp*, 1566–1570. Courtesy Rijksmuseum Amsterdam

[28] Parker, *Dutch Revolt*, pp. 75–81; Van der Lem, *Revolt in the Netherlands*, pp. 61–63; Crew, *Calvinist Preaching and Iconoclasm in the Netherlands*, pp. 10–12.
[29] Arnade, *Beggars, Iconoclasts, and Civic Patriots*, p. 125.

chalice was reported more than once. One Amsterdam iconoclast hurled her slippers at an image of the Virgin Mary.[30] The iconoclasts shared the widespread belief that such objects possessed spiritual power and therefore attacked them for what they saw as their demonic and idolatrous potency. Statues of saints had their heads cut off and eyes gouged out as if that destroyed their power. The iconoclasts justified their violence as an attack on idolatry. "What little gods these people have!" exclaimed one attacker while crushing consecrated hosts underfoot. "If he were God he would bite my toes."[31] The rioters mocked the authority of the church and oftentimes shouted "Vivent les Gueux!" during their ransacking, thereby yoking their violence not only to the Reformed attack on Catholicism but also to the aristocratic opposition to Philip II.[32]

The violence, speed and range of the iconoclastic fury, as well as the local authorities' uneven response to it, shocked contemporaries, especially Margaret of Parma. On August 23, under pressure from the grandees, who insisted that the crisis required a change in religious policy, she reluctantly signed an "Accord" allowing Reformed preaching to continue freely where it was already taking place.[33] The Reformed communities took this to mean full freedom of worship, and they pressed their local authorities for worship spaces and official recognition. The question of just how much toleration was granted to the Reformed was a crucial one; Margaret expected them to confine themselves to private preaching and not to disturb Catholic worship, while the Reformed clearly expected to be able to worship with the full administration of the sacraments and to establish orderly church polities, as their coreligionists in Reformed lands had done. In some cities local grandees brokered a religious peace (*religievrede*) among the confessions; William of Orange, for example, arranged for the freedom of worship for Reformed and Lutheran Christians within the city of Antwerp, of which he was viscount. It became increasingly apparent, however, that the Reformed would not be content with any limited toleration; the most radical among them expected eventually to supplant the Catholic Church and not just simply coexist with it, much to the displeasure of Margaret of Parma.[34]

To dismayed Catholic authorities, 1566 indeed seemed a year of terrible wonders, the dangerous consequence of tolerating heresy. Reformed communities in the Netherlands came to see it as miraculous as well, but

[30] Kaptein, *De beeldenstorm*, p. 7.
[31] Quoted in Duke, "Calvinists and 'Papist Idolatry': The Mentality of the Image-Breakers in 1566," in *Dissident Identities*, p. 188.
[32] Arnade, *Beggars, Iconoclasts, and Civic Patriots*, pp. 90–124.
[33] Parker, *Dutch Revolt*, p. 81.
[34] Crew, *Calvinist Preaching and Iconoclasm in the Netherlands*, pp. 13–16.

for very different reasons. Although the iconoclastic violence was the work of a radical minority among them, all congregations immediately exploited the possibility of greater freedom to worship. In the late summer and fall of 1566 Reformed congregations across the Netherlands arose in more organized form, appointing elders, securing buildings for preaching and sacraments, creating diaconates to help with the relief of the poor, but also arming themselves for protection. Rumors circulated that some congregations were even planning to take over local municipal offices.[35] It proved to be a brief season of liberty, however, as it became clear by the fall that the Habsburg government, after an initial period of shock and disarray, was determined to respond to what it characterized as disorder and rebellion, and most of the great nobles supported this response.[36] To pacify the region Philip II dispatched an army headed by Fernando Álvarez de Toledo (1507–1582), the duke of Alba, a councilor who had argued that the king needed to take direct action to stop what was rapidly turning into a widespread rebellion against his authority.[37] After four months' march up the "Spanish Road" from Italy to the Netherlands, Alba entered Brussels at the head of the ten-thousand-man army of Flanders in August 1567.

The Revolt in the Netherlands thus ignited over the question of religion and its first skirmishes were fought by religious rebels. It was Reformed congregations and their allies among the Compromise nobility who, anticipating the coming backlash, led the first attempt at armed rebellion against the central regime. Reformed nobles such as Louis of Nassau, younger brother of Orange, solicited help in the form of troops and arms from sympathetic Lutheran princes in the Holy Roman Empire. Reformed groups in Tournai and Valenciennes as well as in the Westkwartier of Flanders organized for battle as the winter of 1566–1567 approached. In December 1566 the Reformed synod of Antwerp resolved that armed rebellion was now justified, and it set about raising money for the coming fight.[38] From his base in Amsterdam the nobleman Hendrik of Brederode raised a Reformed army and became the new protector of the movement. Reformed consistories in the west and south frantically raised cash to pay for troops. These rebel armies proved ineffective, however. Margaret of Parma's troops decisively quashed the rebels in western Flanders and then laid siege to Valenciennes, which finally surrendered to royal control in March 1567. That same month Brederode's Reformed army was defeated at the strategic village of

[35] Crew, *Calvinist Preaching and Iconoclasm in the Netherlands*, pp. 15–16.
[36] Soen, "The *Beeldenstorm* and the Spanish Habsburg Response."
[37] Parker, *Dutch Revolt*, pp. 87–89.
[38] Van Roosbroeck, *Het Wonderjaar te Antwerpen*, pp. 212–220.

Oosterweel outside of Antwerp; William of Orange, seeing their cause as hopeless, prevented Antwerp's Reformed from leaving the city to aid their coreligionists, an action that would cause much Reformed wariness toward him in coming years.[39] By late spring the armed rebellion, such as it was, was largely put down and royal authority reestablished in towns where the Reformed had been briefly dominant. Reformed Protestants reconverted, Reformed churches were destroyed, and consistories were disbanded. Many rebels, both political and religious, fled into the safety of exile in England and Germany. By the time of Alba's arrival in Brussels the brief initial phase of the armed rebellion had ended with a decisive royal victory.[40]

Repression and Exile

Philip II had given the duke of Alba a free hand to take all necessary steps to end the troubles in the Netherlands. In protest Margaret of Parma quickly tendered her resignation to Philip, and Alba became the new governor of the Netherlands. He set up the Council of Troubles, a central court that overrode all local jurisdictions and was authorized to deal with cases of rebellion. Functioning in effect as a political tribunal, the Council's commissioners proceeded against every troublemaker they could find, great or small, and paid little concern to the customs or niceties of local justice. It sparked considerable fear among the population, who referred to it as the "Council of Blood."[41] Most notoriously it arrested two of the region's greatest magnates, the counts of Egmont and Hornes, tried them for treason and then executed them publicly in Brussels in 1568. A substantial portion of those convicted by the Council were inhabitants of the large cities of the south where Reformed activity had been most marked: Tournai, Antwerp, Valenciennes and Ypres. Many noble signers of the Compromise were also condemned, often in absentia. The aristocratic opposition to Philip was also sentenced, including William of Orange, who had prudently retreated to his ancestral estates in Germany and by 1568 was acknowledged as the leader of the political opposition, building up an army of Beggars to pursue rebellion against Philip II. Civic patricians who had joined the opposition were likewise condemned and many of them fled into exile in Germany or England as well. In total the Council tried more than twelve thousand people for their role in the events of 1566–1567;

---

[39] Parker, *Dutch Revolt*, pp. 93–98.
[40] Van der Lem, *Revolt in the Netherlands*, pp. 65–67.
[41] Verheyden, *Le Conseil des Troubles*, pp. 14–39; Maltby, *Alba*, pp. 138–158; Kamen, *Duke of Alba*, pp. 75–105.

nine thousand were condemned to confiscation of their goods, mostly in absentia, and more than a thousand were executed.[42] Although Alba carefully insisted that he sought to punish rebellion rather than heresy, a plurality of those whom the Council condemned or banned were Reformed Protestants, nearly 50 percent.[43] Both Philip and Alba were convinced that this stern justice was necessary to save the region; piloting the ship of church and state through the dangerous waters of heresy and sedition was their preeminent goal (Illustration 4.4).

In addition to these judicial measures, Alba did what he could to further Philip's goal of church reform in the Netherlands; in this regard he was very much an instrument for Catholic reformation in the region. The reorganization of the Netherlands' bishops, first announced in 1559, had still not been completed, in part due to foot-dragging by provincial estates. By the time of Alba's arrival in 1567 only eight of the new bishops had been installed wholly or in part. Alba forced through the appointment of the remaining six, and by 1570 all fourteen new dioceses in the Netherlands had new bishops fully appointed and installed. The duke himself had a hand in deciding on the kind of men elevated to bishop; he appreciated that responsible pastoral men were needed if the reform of the church was ever to move forward.[44] To that end some of the new bishops pressed Alba to issue a general pardon for the whole Netherlands, which he issued in 1570. But it contained so many exceptions (no pardon for iconoclasts, elders and deacons of consistories, exiles) that its effect on popular opinion fell far short of expectations. Nevertheless, the bishops claimed that thousands of former heretics in their dioceses were reconciled to the church.[45]

Many opponents, however, were not interested in reconciliation and sought refuge abroad. An estimated thirty thousand to sixty thousand individuals, comprising both political and religious rebels, fled the Netherlands and found safety in exile havens in England, East Friesland, the Palatinate and the Rhineland.[46] In these places religious dissidents, Reformed, Mennonite and *Doopsgezind*, found congregations of like-minded Protestant compatriots. For the Reformed Protestant movement in particular the post-1566 period of exile would prove a pivotal moment in its development. It was while in exile that some of the Reformed, especially those militants who hoped someday to return to their homeland, first imagined a broadly national, reformed church for

---

[42] Parker, *Dutch Revolt*, p. 108.   [43] Verheyden, *Le Conseil des Troubles*, p. 116.

[44] Parker, *Dutch Revolt*, p. 113; Dierickx, *De oprichting der nieuwe bisdommen in de Nederlanden onder Filips II*, pp. 253–291.

[45] Soen, "Reconciliatie," pp. 350–352.

[46] Pettegree, *Emden and the Dutch Revolt*, p. 148.

Illustration 4.4 Anonymous, *Allegory of the Ship of State*, late sixteenth century. An allegorical painting about the Netherlandish revolt. The ship, representing the Habsburg state and the Catholic Church, navigates through a treacherous archipelago full of dangers. The figures standing in the ship's center may represent the Netherlands' ecclesiastical and political leadership, including the duke of Alba and king Philip II. Courtesy Royal Museums Greenwich

the whole of the Low Countries, and they drew up blueprints accordingly. Exile, despite its constraints and depredations, provided a period of "recovery and reorganization" for many in the Reformed cause.[47] One

---

[47] Pettegree, *Emden and the Dutch Revolt*, p. 147.

of the leading historians of Netherlandish Reformed exiles argues that this period brought new vigor and commitment to the movement, sharpened its ecclesiology, clarified its doctrine and therefore further confessionalized what was gradually turning into the Reformed church.[48] There is evidence, though, that exile did not radicalize every refugee. The Haarlem humanist and freethinker Dirck Volckertz Coornhert, for example, who fled to Cologne because of his opposition to the Habsburgs, remained as moderate as ever in his religious opinions and rejected the extremism of those he derisively called Calvinists.[49] And of course some Reformed refugees fled abroad with no interest in ever returning back home. More recent scholarship has questioned the long-standing narrative of the "reformation of the refugees" and argued that it was largely a construction of nineteenth-century neo-Calvinist historians engaged about contemporary debates on religious liberty.[50] Still, there was a fair degree of discussing, meeting and planning about the future among some Netherlandish religious exiles in the years immediately following 1566. It might be more accurate to suggest that those evangelicals who were already firmly committed to their cause found in this exilic period an opportunity to consolidate their organization – that is, to transform themselves from a movement to a church. For some Reformed, being dispersed from their homeland made the search for confessional identity all that more urgent.

The brief season of liberty Netherlandish congregations had enjoyed following the iconoclastic fury of 1566 revealed a variety of practices and approaches to church building as well as to some differences over points of doctrine. Many Reformed leaders in exile, most of whom had been pastors in major southern cities such as Antwerp and Ghent, made efforts to sort out differences and establish more explicitly normative doctrine and organization. The energetic preacher Petrus Dathenus (1531–1588), for example, who had translated the Psalms and the Heidelberg Catechism into Dutch, had traveled widely across Reformed Europe, and had actively aided underground churches in the Netherlands until forced to flee to Germany in 1567, likely composed a draft set of articles for a possible church order that circulated widely in Reformed exile circles in already in 1568.[51] Reformed ministers also sought out and received the support of William of Orange, who, despite his own lukewarm religious convictions, was coming to realize how vital the support of the religious refugees was to his cause.[52] The most militant Reformed leadership in

[48] Pettegree, *Emden and the Dutch Revolt*, pp. 243–244.
[49] Van Veen, "Dirck Volckertz Coornhert."
[50] Spohnholz and Van Veen, "The Disputed Origins of Dutch Calvinism."
[51] Spohnholz, *Convent of Wesel*, pp. 40–65.   [52] Spohnholz, *Convent of Wesel*, pp. 28–29.

turn saw Orange and his insurgents, despite doubts about the depth of their religious commitment, as their best means for returning home. It was while in exile that the alliance between evangelical and political opponents to the Habsburg regime was truly sealed.

For the Reformed movement perhaps the most important event to occur during this period was the Synod of Emden, held in October 1571. To achieve greater consensus on doctrinal issues exiled leaders from southern Netherlandish congregations in particular pushed for a meeting. The initiative was especially spearheaded by Antwerp preachers such as Gaspar van der Heyden, currently residing in the Palatinate, and it won the endorsement of William of Orange, who wanted to see as much unity as possible among his sometimes fractious Reformed allies. Thirty delegates, most of them exiled preachers and elders from Holland, Flanders, Brabant, Tournai and Hainaut, met in Emden in early October and eventually negotiated agreement on key questions. They formally subscribed to both the French Confession of Faith and the Belgic Confession and recommended the Genevan and Heidelberg Catechisms as sources for sound doctrine; in doing so the Synod placed itself very much in the mainstream of what was becoming an increasingly international Reformed Protestantism.[53] The Synod further outlined a common ecclesiology, with consistories governed by elders and poor relief directed by deacons and prescriptions for the orderly training and appointment of preachers. This ecclesiology was effectively based on what was already common practice in some of the diaspora churches.

Finally, the Synod imagined a blueprint for a future Netherlandish church complete with provincial synods and regional classes, in effect a copy of the structure of the Huguenot churches already in place in France. In its effort to provide a doctrinal foundation and an ecclesiological model, the Synod of Emden proved to be of enduring influence on what eventually would become the Dutch Reformed church. It also represented a considerable organizational success for the communities of Netherlandish Reformed in Germany, who were by no means completely unified on all ecclesiastical questions or practices. That the consensus was achieved in Emden without major disagreement or dissent was testimony to the commitment of the delegates who deliberated the thorny questions there.[54] What remained uncertain as the Synod closed was whether the church they imagined there would ever be realized in their homeland.

---

[53] Prestwich, "The Changing Face of Calvinism," in Prestwich, *International Calvinism 1541–1715*, pp. 1–14.

[54] Pettegree, *Emden and the Dutch Revolt*, pp. 182–186.

Revolutionary Reformation

As it turned out, the opportunity to test out their Emden blueprint came to the Reformed exiles far more quickly than anyone expected, about half a year after the Synod's close. On the first day of April 1572 the Sea Beggars, the naval privateering arm of the Orange's ragtag land forces, took over the coastal town of Brielle in South-Holland on the mouth of the Meuse after having been kicked out of their English havens by Elizabeth I.[55] From this accidental, unplanned success in Brielle the privateers quickly moved inland. Within months most of the major towns of South-Holland and Zeeland surrendered to the Beggar soldiers' control and the Beggars declared them to be under the lordship of the prince of Orange. Unexpectedly the Revolt now had a foothold on Netherlandish soil; for the first time in a century large parts of Zeeland and Holland were independent of Habsburg overlordship. For the next decade, during years of bitter and destructive war, the armed rebellion against Philip enjoyed considerable military success, winning territory from Flanders to Groningen.

These changes in the fortunes of the war had in turn a direct effect on the fortunes of the evangelical opponents to the Habsburgs, for with revolt came reformation. The year 1572 offered them the opportunity to transform themselves from a rebellion to a church.[56] Reformed exiles quickly followed Beggar armies back into these conquered territories and declared them for "true" religion. From 1572, when Holland and Zeeland first came under rebel control, until 1585, when royalist forces retook Antwerp and most of the south, the Reformed movement in the Netherlands engaged in a period of what has been aptly called "revolutionary reformation."[57] In core western regions of the Netherlands where the rebel forces gained control during this period – Holland, Zeeland, Flanders, Brabant, Utrecht – returning Reformed leaders established congregations, set up church polities and disrupted Catholic worship. It seemed as though a radical new ecclesiastical regime was succeeding, on the heels of warfare, in bringing to the Netherlands a reformation of church and society long hoped for by many fervent evangelicals and long feared by many more faithful Catholics. Yet the revolutionary nature of this religious shift proved to be the very undoing of the political rebellion it had supported. The radical wing within the Reformed movement in the period 1572–1585 would ultimately undermine the uneasy, still mostly Catholic rebel coalition against the Habsburgs and turn the

---

[55] Doedens and Houter, *De Watergeuzen*, pp. 151–153.
[56] Van Veen, *Een nieuwe tijd, een nieuwe kerk*, p. 84.
[57] Enno Van Gelder, *Revolutionnaire Reformatie*.

Netherlandish revolt into a civil war and, in some respects, a religious war as well.

Almost immediately in the spring and summer of 1572 political and religious exiles returned to Holland and Zeeland on the heels of the Beggar takeover of major towns. Magistrates, mayors and town councilors who had fled the Netherlands for opposing royal policy now returned to reassert their authority in the cities, while those loyalist political elites who had supported the crown were forced in turn to flee to Catholic territories into an exile of their own. The political disarray and military chaos caused by Beggar armies prompted a meeting in Dordrecht in July 1572 of the States of Holland. The urban patricians gathered there formally (and illegally, since there was a Stadholder already in place) recognized William of Orange as Stadholder, governor-general of the province, since he was the only figure with enough prestige to restore law and order.[58] The States also decreed that henceforth within the province Catholic and Reformed Christians would both enjoy full freedom to worship. This was in keeping with the policy of Orange, who brought a *politique* sensibility to questions of religion and who was determined to introduce a general religious peace in the regions his forces controlled. He had promised Catholics, still very much the majority of the population in Holland and Zeeland, that their faith would be protected. At the same time he had agreed to his Reformed allies' demand for religious liberty in the independent provinces. His preference was to allow Catholics and Protestants both complete freedom of worship; he was keenly aware that he needed the support of as much of the population as possible to prop up what was still a very precarious insurgency.[59]

Orange's hoped-for religious peace, however, virtually died on the vine. The pent-up sectarianism fostered by years of oppression and exile came into destructive and murderous flower. Beggar troops plundered Catholic churches and monasteries and confiscated their goods, including valuable ornaments taken for the war effort. Despite Orange's orders, his commanders in the field allowed Beggar troops to harass and even murder priests, to say nothing of plundering and damaging churches and cloisters. Catholic clergy and religious in lands controlled by the Beggars found themselves subject to a reign of terror throughout 1572 and 1573.[60] Beguines from the northern town of Hoorn, for example, were assaulted and raped by Beggar soldiers.[61] The Augustinian friar Wouter Jacobsz, who had fled Gouda for Amsterdam, which was still under

---

[58] Swart, *William of Orange and the Revolt of the Netherlands*, p. 45.
[59] Swart, *William of Orange and the Revolt of the Netherlands*, pp. 34–36.
[60] Van Nierop, *Treason in the Northern Quarter*, pp. 140–143.
[61] Van Nierop, *Treason in the Northern Quarter*, p. 177.

loyalist control, dolefully recorded the attack on Catholic worship in Holland: "God's temples were destroyed, the holy images were broken, God's servants, priests, religious and honest Catholics despised, hunted, despoiled and horribly murdered and finally also the worship of God and the holy sacraments obstructed, slandered and scandalously abused."[62] Monasteries and convents were invaded and ransacked, and religious women and men had to escape to safety in Catholic regions; the Poor Clares of Alkmaar, for example, fled their convent in the dead of night, carrying with them the eucharistic host safely ensconced in a cypress box.[63] The most notorious atrocity Beggar soldiers committed in this period was the summary arrest and hanging in Brielle of nineteen priests and friars from the Holland town of Gorinchem in July 1572. To Catholic minds this heinous crime created martyrs out of its victims, and it only increased their panic and despair. The prolonged terror across city and countryside in the early 1570s profoundly demoralized Holland's Catholics as priests fled to safer havens and churches were closed and confiscated by civic authorities.[64]

It was not only soldiers who engaged in this anti-Catholic assault. Close on the heels of political exiles returning to Holland and Zeeland came the religious refugees, most of them zealous Reformed Protestants. They had allied with Orange's political opposition in return for the promise of religious liberty, and very soon prominent Reformed ministers and layfolk began appearing in the towns in the rebel-held provinces agitating for accommodation and space.

Already in May 1572 in Zeeland's towns Reformed preachers reappeared on the streets after years spent abroad in congregations in East Anglia.[65] Within a month of the city of Leiden's cooption into the insurgency the first public Reformed preaching was held in one of the city's three parish churches.[66] Iconoclastic riots, which included both soldiers and Reformed sympathizers, often accompanied the takeover of ecclesiastical space. Rumors of Catholic plots abounded. In Delft, where William of Orange had set up his headquarters, mobs attacked churches twice in spring 1573, partly out of frustration with his attempts to guarantee local Catholic rights of worship.[67] Magistrates in some cities, such as Gouda and Leiden, closed down ecclesiastical buildings entirely in order to restore some civic order. Such scenes were repeated all over Holland and Zeeland. By late 1572 open Catholic worship had virtually

[62] Van Eeghen, *Dagboek van Broeder Wouter Jacobsz*, vol. 1, p. 3.
[63] Fagel and Spaans, *Nonnen verdreven door Geuzen*, pp. 26–27.
[64] Kooi, *Calvinists and Catholics during Holland's Golden Age*, pp. 25–27.
[65] Rooze-Stouthamer, *De opmaat tot de Opstand*, pp. 226–227.
[66] Kooi, *Liberty and Religion*, p. 32.   [67] Abels, *Nieuw en ongezien*, p. 128.

disappeared in all the areas under rebel control as Catholic clergy fled and churches were appropriated. Despite the best intentions of William of Orange, his radical Reformed allies had succeeded in virtually shutting down the Catholic Church in the insurgent provinces. This triumph would be sealed and legalized in February 1573, when the States of Holland outlawed the celebration of any Catholic sacrament throughout the entire province and granted only the Reformed Church the right to worship God publicly.[68] Those Catholic priests and religious who had not fled were forcibly retired and given modest pensions. William of Orange's dream of a religious peace among Hollanders and Zeelanders of all confessional stripes crumbled before the anti-Catholicism of his most militant Reformed partners.

Instead revolutionary reformation prevailed. Orange's most zealous evangelical allies were determined to create a new ecclesiastical order in the provinces they saw as freed from popery. Returning Reformed Protestants wasted little time in setting up their own church polities as war raged in Holland; they were still very much in the minority, and their precarious position spurred them to set up solid ecclesiastical organizations along the model of the Synod of Emden's church order as soon as feasible. Within a year of the Beggar takeover of Holland and Zeeland, Reformed congregations in most towns not only had a least one Reformed preacher installed in the pulpit but also established consistories of elders and in some cases diaconates. The church in turn set up classes, which were meetings of regional church leaders charged with examining and disciplining clergy, though at the first Reformed provincial synod held at Dordrecht in June 1574 military exigency prevented many of the classes from sending delegates. Consistories, under the Emden model, were charged with governing the church and disciplining the congregation, while diaconates cared for and supported less fortunate church members. In these early years the congregations over which they presided were very small; communicant rolls, even in larger towns, ran at most into the low to mid-hundreds.[69] The new political regime did not force anyone to join the new church, and Reformed consistories insisted that any adult who wished to join had to profess publicly his or her faith and also submit to ecclesiastical discipline. And many were uninterested in such a submission, like the Delft printer whose wife told the consistory there that "he wanted to be free to print and to sell whatever books he pleased."[70] These factors may have kept the number of members small,

---

[68] Koopmans, *De Staten van Holland en de Opstand*, p. 160.

[69] Duke and Jones, "Towards a Reformed Polity in Holland, 1572–78," in *Reformation and Revolt*, p. 211.

[70] Quoted in Duke and Jones, "Towards a Reformed Polity in Holland, 1572–78," p. 214.

but there is evidence that far more people attended services than just those who had formally joined the church. These *liefhebbers* (sympathizers) filled the churches on Sundays but could not take communion, which required full membership. The small sizes of congregations did not seem to bother the church leadership, which never equated success with numbers. But it did lead to the anomalous situation of the Reformed Church, which became in 1573 the privileged church of Holland, attracting only a small minority of the population. Aside from the *liefhebbers*, the rest of the population was Catholic, Mennonite, Lutheran or unchurched entirely.

The men in authority in insurgent Holland, the civic magistrates and town councilors, also had to adjust to how the province's new religious settlement was working itself out. The States of Holland, which these patricians dominated, assumed control of formerly Catholic ecclesiastical property, out of which they paid for the salaries of ministers, and granted the Reformed church use of most ecclesiastical buildings.[71] Many of the urban regents had hoped for an inclusive, open church that embraced all inhabitants along the model of the Church of England, but instead they got a Reformed Church order that guarded its boundaries very jealously, especially when it came to questions of how the church was to be governed. Evidence suggests that many of the patricians who ruled Holland's cities were at best lukewarm in their commitment to the new church, and some did not attend it at all. They also expected, as city fathers, to exercise some supervisory authority over the public church, including the power to appoint ministers or even elders. Meanwhile Reformed consistories, perhaps remembering the years of persecution, expected independence from political control. The town council of Gouda, for example, was reluctant to completely suppress Catholic worship within city walls, despite the belligerence of the Reformed. It also tried very hard to control the appointments of ministers to the city's Reformed pulpits, to make sure that only congenial personalities with sympathetic opinions served in the public church.[72] Church leaders chafed at what they saw as political meddling and only grudgingly acquiesced to the idea of a national, civil church that offered baptism and marriage to anyone who asked.[73]

Puzzling out the relationship between church and magistracy in towns across the insurgent provinces proved to be one of the thornier problems of what was slowly evolving into a new ecclesiastical settlement in the 1570s. Two parties who had once been allies during rebellion and exile,

---

[71] Koopmans, *De Staten van Holland en de Opstand*, pp. 160–161.
[72] Hibben, *Gouda in Revolt*, pp. 89–93, 111–120.
[73] Pettegree, "Confessionalization in North Western Europe," p. 113.

the political opponents to Habsburg overreach and the evangelical dissenters from the Catholic Church, now found themselves in uncomfortable negotiation with each other in the wake of their success. The political leaders of the revolt believed they had fought for liberty or "*libertatis ergo*," as their propaganda put it; the religious opponents believed they had fought for religion or "*religionis ergo*." Now, in the regions wrested from Habsburg control, those two goals seemed sometimes to conflict. What did reformation now mean in these altered circumstances? Political authorities wanted a church they could superintend while church leaders wanted as much autonomy as possible. The result of the complicated negotiation between these two parties in Holland and Zeeland in the 1570s was that the Reformed Church became the public church, which was the only one allowed to worship openly, but which coexisted with an array of private congregations, Lutheran, Mennonite and Catholic. A similar ecclesiastical settlement would eventually pertain in the other provinces that came under permanent rebel control by the end of the century. The independent provinces would have a public church but not a universal one.

Habsburg forces struggled, with little success, to retake the insurgent regions, and by the mid-1570s Philip's financial ability to continue waging war in the Netherlands was proving increasingly parlous. The fighting between royal and rebel forces was causing greater and greater civilian destruction and death. Most notoriously in November 1576 mutinying soldiers plundered Antwerp in a "Spanish fury" and put at least hundreds if not thousands of its inhabitants to death.[74] These murderous and destructive rampages had shocked many loyalist provincial elites into protesting that royal policy was ruining the Netherlands. Anti-Habsburg feeling grew, even among those loyal to the traditional church. There was a growing middle-group party of moderates, the vast majority of them Catholic, among the provincial elites, led by the States of Brabant, who wanted some sort of peace settlement with the rebels that would end the mutinies, withdraw the Army of Flanders and restore the governance of the Netherlands to provincial authority. Representatives of the States-General, who had assembled on their own initiative to protest royal policy, and of William of Orange met in Ghent in November 1576, not long after the "Spanish Fury" in Antwerp, to sign an agreement. This Pacification of Ghent was in effect a peace treaty between insurgent Holland and Zeeland and the rest of the Netherlands, with the shared goal of ridding the land of Spanish troops. Once the country was pacified and freed from Spanish armies the thorny issue of religion could then be settled.[75] Nearly all of the

---

[74] Fagel, "Origins of the Spanish Fury at Antwerp."
[75] Groenveld, "Mislukte matiging, 1575–1581," pp. 103–106.

seventeen provinces were now, however briefly, united against crown policy (Luxemburg, Limburg and Namur did not sign the agreement). The States-General, styling itself "patriots," made common cause with the rebels against the Habsburg regime in order to end what had become a very destructive and disruptive war.[76] For the first time in a century of state-building, the Habsburgs got what they wanted, a united Netherlands; unfortunately, it was a Netherlands united against *them*.

The Pacification of Ghent stipulated that outside of the provinces of Holland and Zeeland the Catholic status quo would be maintained, but it also effectively suspended the anti-heresy placards throughout the Low Countries. Freedom of conscience therefore by default became the law of the land.[77] Emboldened, the more zealous Reformed in the rebellion saw this moment as an opportunity to evangelize further; the freedom of conscience clause in the Pacification, from their perspective, allowed for the further spread of revolutionary reformation. Missionaries proselytized their message in Flanders and Brabant, the old heartlands of evangelical agitation before the 1566 Wonderyear. Reformed Protestants still remained a demographic minority in the Netherlands, but thanks to their alliance with the new regime they secured a privileged position. As the decade drew to a close it was clear that the Reformed Church had successfully established itself as the dominant confession of the new revolutionary order. This dominance would be the undoing of the shaky alliance of the Pacification.

When the preachers and elders of Reformed congregations in the insurgent Netherlands met at their first national synod in the South-Holland town of Dordrecht in June 1578, they were likely heartened by how much progress their church had made in the Low Countries in the past six years. After many years of persecution and exile, it was perhaps dizzying to them how far their revolutionary reformation had come – to the north and east in Utrecht, Overijssel, Guelders, Groningen and Friesland and to the south in Flanders and Brabant. The western core lands of the Netherlands, plus a few regions on the northeastern periphery, were now in rebel hands and reformation was proceeding there apace. The delegates at Dordrecht faced a twofold task: to consolidate the gains already booked in the northern provinces over the past six years, and to strengthen the newer congregations in the southern cities. Two weeks of discussion produced a church order that the members of the synod believed would meet those two challenges – it would help achieve unity in doctrine and conformity in practice. Building from

[76] Van der Lem, *Revolt in the Netherlands*, pp. 110–115.
[77] Van der Lem, *Revolt in the Netherlands*, p. 111.

the Emden blueprint, the Dordrecht church order established a hierarchy of congregational consistories, regional classes and provincial synods to ensure universal norms of proper governance, ministerial training, ecclesiastical discipline and church doctrine. It also strongly affirmed the independence of the Reformed Church from any control by local or provincial government, yet at the same time clearly expected political authority to support the public church.[78]

With the 1578 church order the Reformed Church in the Netherlands created for itself its first normative and authoritative statement of ecclesiology. It represented a triumph for the most zealous faction within the church that wished to follow Genevan and French models of church polity as closely as possible, advocates sometimes disparagingly termed Calvinists by those who disagreed with them. Whether all leaders of the Reformed Church would conform to the synod's prescriptions was, however, another question. Not all preachers within the Reformed Church, especially in Holland, were necessarily in complete agreement about doctrine.[79] A minority of preachers, sometimes called Libertines by their opponents, questioned the majority consensus on doctrine, creedal documents, discipline and the proper relationship between church and state. For all the Dordrecht synod's apparent uniformity and consensus, building up a church proved an exceedingly fraught process, especially in towns and cities where ruling magistrates expected to have a hand in the overseeing the public church, especially with regard to the appointment of ministers since they administered the funds created from confiscated Catholic wealth from which ministers were paid.

A handful of cities in the north would in fact see serious controversies over ecclesiology and doctrine erupt between Calvinists and Libertines in the late 1570s and early 1580s within their Reformed congregations, most notably in Leiden, Gouda and Utrecht. In Leiden the dispute that pitted magistrates against Calvinist ministers in 1579 and 1580 was the question of consistorial autonomy – that is, whether the public church should be allowed to appoint its own leadership, specifically elders and deacons, without magisterial approval. The dispute proved so acrimonious that it split the congregation for over a year. One of the city's preachers, Caspar Coolhaes, supported the magisterial position, and in the ensuing decade he became the target of a prolonged Calvinist effort to have him stripped of his clerical privileges.[80] Likewise the magistrates of Gouda, no great sympathizers with the Calvinist faction of the church, steadfastly

---

[78] Nauta, "De Nationale Synode van Dordrecht."
[79] Nijenhuis, "Variants within Dutch Calvinism in the Sixteenth Century."
[80] Kooi, *Liberty and Religion*, pp. 55–101.

supported their own clerical supporter, Herman Herbertsz, throughout the 1580s despite serious synodal efforts to have him censured for doctrinal opinions the Calvinists deemed unorthodox.[81] In the city of Utrecht the magistrates there imposed the most extreme solution to intra-church discord by setting up two separate public churches, one Libertine and one Calvinist, in the period 1578–1586 as a means of supporting their preferred minister, a spiritualist named Hubert Duifhuis who allowed open communion.[82] In all these cases magistrates, accustomed to a long tradition of particularist privilege and supported by the Libertine ministerial faction, were insistent on their right to superintend city churches, while the most zealous Calvinists, with long memories of state persecution, were equally insistent on the independence of the true church. The States of Holland, in an effort to resolve these disputes, organized an extraordinary series of formal disputations between spokesmen from both sides in the late 1570s and early 1580s, but these accomplished little.[83] These conflicts beset only a minority of the new congregations in rebel-held lands, almost all in Holland and Utrecht; in most other regions churches and magistrates cooperated largely harmoniously in the work of church building.

Radicalization was not confined to Reformed congregations in the north, however. The 1578 national synod of Dordrecht also petitioned the States-General to allow the formation of a Reformed congregation anywhere in the Netherlands where at least one hundred families asked for it.[84] This was a direct response to what was happening in Flanders and Brabant, where the anti-heresy placards had been suspended with the Pacification of Ghent. Religious refugees flooded into these provinces from exile, and before long the partisans of revolt and reformation were taking over the major cities there. In the autumn of 1577 Reformed militants, led by the patricians Jan van Hembyze and François van Ryhove, overthrew the city government of Ghent with the tacit approval of William of Orange and immediately set about instituting a radical Reformed government, the first of the so-called Calvinist Republics. Their intent was to create a godly commonwealth "which aims to reform the church of God in our city so that she will be an example for the whole Netherlands," as the Ghent consistory exultantly put it.[85] The new regime proceeded, in violation of the Pacification, to suppress Catholic worship by plundering Catholic churches, arresting the bishop and executing monks on charges of sodomy.[86] Not only did the Reformed

[81] Hibben, *Gouda in Revolt*, pp. 120–129.
[82] Kaplan, *Calvinists and Libertines*, pp. 156–175.   [83] Roobol, *Disputation by Decree*.
[84] Bremmer, "De nationale betekenis van de Synode van Dordrecht," pp. 92–100.
[85] Marnef, "From Prosecuted Minority to Dominance," p. 227.
[86] Despretz, "De instauratie der Gentse Calvinistische Republiek."

control the city but from there they engineered coups in the two other major cities of Flanders, Bruges and Ypres. Before long the Ghent radicals fomented political agitation that spread to the neighboring duchy of Brabant, and by 1580 most of the major cities there, including Antwerp, Mechelen and Brussels, were in the grip of radical Reformed regimes.[87] These governments, relying mostly on support from guilds and civic militias, stripped Catholic churches of images, gave worship space to Reformed Protestants, plundered monasteries and expelled priests and religious orders.[88] As had happened with their coreligionists in Holland and Zeeland, Flemish and Brabantine Catholic burghers found themselves relegated to a distinct second-class status in their own hometowns.

Another consequence of the establishment of revolutionary reformation and Catholic disestablishment was that it became the turn of Catholic Netherlanders to flee their homes for safety in exile. Religious exile was not a purely Protestant phenomenon in the case of the Low Countries. Thousands of displaced Catholics fled oppression and harassment to find safety in the Catholic territories of the Holy Roman Empire or in northern France. In the Rhineland cities such as Cologne and Kalkar served as bases for émigré Catholics for many years. Some remained in their new homes; others returned to those southern Netherlandish regions that were later retaken by Habsburg armies. Those who did eventually return were often reinvigorated in their Catholic piety and contributed significantly to the work of re-catholicization.[89]

For William of Orange this turn toward revolutionary reformation endangered the fragile unity of his coalition against the Habsburgs. In the summer of 1578, supported by the national synod being held at Dordrecht, he proposed a religious peace to the States-General, which was supposed to protect freedom of conscience and which prescribed mutual accommodation and parity between Reformed and Catholic in the towns where the rebels gained control, but this stipulation had not been observed in Holland or Zeeland nor was it being respected by the Calvinist republics in Flanders and Brabant, most of which outlawed Catholic worship by 1581. The States-General declined to adopt the religious peace, leaving it instead to city governments to decide whether to implement such arrangements. Staunchly Catholic royalist cities in southern provinces such as Artois, Namur and Hainaut, where the rebellion had been soundly quashed already in the late 1560s, had little interest in reintroducing Reformed heresy inside their walls, while Reformed

[87] Marnef, "Brabants calvinisme in opmars."
[88] Marnef, "From Prosecuted Minority to Dominance," pp. 227–244.
[89] Janssen, *Dutch Revolt and Catholic Exile in Reformation Europe*.

strongholds further north, especially the Calvinist Republics in Flanders and Brabant, had no wish to see Catholic idolatry permitted once again within their communities.

Over the next few years about thirty towns across the Netherlands adopted some version of religious peace, but by the 1580s such arrangements were mostly abandoned. Religious peace, the policy of the moderate parties that had negotiated the Pacification of Ghent, was a dead letter.[90] Triumphant Calvinists were not interested in it and fearful Catholics were suspicious of it. The ultimately unsuccessful religious peace of 1578 was the last effort to legalize some sort of official confessional coexistence in the whole of the Netherlands in the early modern era; a variation of it would later live on in the Dutch Republic.

Catholic nobles within the States-General, who dominated the French-speaking rural Netherlandish provinces, had entered into the Pacification of Ghent in 1576 with the hopes of ending the mutinies in the Army of Flanders, ridding the land of foreign troops and allowing the aristocracy to resume its due place as the rulers of Netherlandish affairs; their interest in the alliance against crown policy was purely political.[91] They looked with growing dismay at the increasing militancy of the Reformed party, especially when it imposed radical regimes in the Flemish and Brabantine cities and attacked priests and sacked churches. These Catholic grandees had been fighting for liberty, not religion; heresy left them distinctly discomfited. The new governor-general, Alexander Farnese, prince of Parma (1545–1592), was authorized by Philip II to offer these discontented nobles what they wanted most, a restoration of their privileges and dignities. The result in early 1579 was the Union of Arras, in which the southern Catholic political elite, led by the counties of Artois and Hainaut, abandoned the rebel alliance and formally reconciled with Philip II.[92] This was explicitly a Catholic union; there was no discussion in the treaty of freedom of conscience or tolerating Protestantism by the signatories. Quite the contrary – it stipulated the "preservation of the Roman, Apostolic, and Catholic religion" as one of its principal goals.[93] The Pacification of Ghent, which had briefly united nearly the whole Netherlands against the king in a fragile and tetchy alliance under the auspices of the States-General, came to a quick end thanks to a combination of Reformed aggression and Catholic fear.

[90] Ubachs, "De Nederlandse religievrede van 1578."
[91] De Schepper, "De mentale rekonversie van de Zuidnederlandse hoge adel naar de Pacifikatie van Gent."
[92] Van der Lem, *Revolt in the Netherlands*, pp. 123–125; Parker, *Dutch Revolt*, pp. 190–193.
[93] "Articles de la Paix concluë entre les Députéz du Prince de Parme et les Provinces Valonnes," in Rowen, *The Low Countries in Early Modern Times*, p. 261.

That same year those regions that remained in rebellion to Philip negotiated a defensive alliance of their own, the Union of Utrecht. The Union eventually came to comprise Holland, Zeeland, Utrecht, Guelders, Friesland, Groningen, Overijssel and several of the major cities of Flanders and Brabant. When it came to the thorny issue of religion, the rebel leadership came down on the side of toleration: the Union stipulated that each region was to regulate its own religious affairs and that no one's conscience was to be violated.[94] For the first time anywhere in the Low Countries the principle of private religious freedom was officially endorsed, a reflection of William of Orange's desire for religious peace. The Reformed Church, as a critical ally to the political rebels, nevertheless insisted on its primacy. In practice this meant that in these independent northern provinces the Reformed Church, though still a demographic minority, came to dominate the north's religious affairs and that Catholic worship continued to be outlawed, hindered and suppressed (though the severity of this varied from region to region). By the early 1580s Reformed Protestantism enjoyed the exclusive right to worship publicly in the lands of the Union of Utrecht, even though its articles insisted that "no one [be] persecuted or questioned about his religion."[95] The principle of toleration may have been established, but its practice proved far more complicated. Religious peace of a sort would come to the insurgent provinces, but only under the condition that the Reformed Church enjoy privileged status. The Union became, in effect, a Reformed alliance, as well as the nucleus of what later became known as the United Provinces or Dutch Republic. By the late 1580s the insurgency in the north evolved into an occasionally uneasy confederacy of sovereign provinces, with the urban regents of Holland dominating it economically and politically.

The abandonment of the Pacification of Ghent and the concomitant creation of the Unions of Arras and Utrecht meant that the rebellion, stumbling on the question of religion, had metamorphosed into both a civil war and a religious war. The dream of opposing Habsburg authority while simultaneously preserving religious peace, so hoped for by Orange and the moderate middle groups, proved chimerical. Instead polarization prevailed, and religious questions once again influenced the course of the war. Catholic political elites in the south rejected the militancy of the radical Calvinists, and the latter in turn increasingly suspected that most Catholics wished to remain loyal to the crown. There was no room for accommodation or compromise from either side. Revolutionary

---

[94] Boogman, "Union of Utrecht."
[95] "Treaty of the Union," in Kossmann and Mellink, *Texts concerning the Revolt of the Netherlands*, p. 170.

reformation had provoked a backlash that sparked a new round of warfare, colored again by the passions of confessional antagonism.

Reconquest and Consolidation

The Reformed movement reached the height of its geographical success in the Low Countries from 1572 until 1585; the ensuing decades witnessed a period of reconquest, retrenchment and consolidation. Once again war determined the path of religious change in the region. In the 1580s Spanish forces, led by governor-general Alexander Farnese, the prince of Parma, successfully reconquered a substantial portion of Flanders and Brabant from rebel occupation. The Calvinist republics would all disappear as a triumphant Catholic Church returned to those cities in the wake of Parma's armies. The military rebellion retreated further north and confined itself largely to the independent provinces, with Holland dominating. There the Reformed Church continued its process of church building, negotiating with local powers about its still ambiguous place in polity and society as the public church.

Of all of Philip II's governors-general, the prince of Parma proved to be the most capable militarily. In the first half of the 1580s Parma won a series of victories in Flanders and Brabant that restored Habsburg governance to those cities that had been taken over by radical Calvinist regimes, culminating in the triumphant recapture of Antwerp after a long siege in the summer of 1585.[96] The Calvinist republican regimes came to an end, and Parma restored royal authority to the cities while promising to respect their privileges. The governor-general also handled the religious question with more delicacy than had been past Habsburg practice: the Catholic Church was of course returned to its full rights, but Parma modulated the placards against heresy. He offered to Protestants in these retaken cities amnesty for any acts of rebellion or violence and a grace period in which either to reconcile with the Catholic Church or sell their goods and emigrate. For committed Protestants, of course, this meant leaving their homes to settle elsewhere; in their eyes this may have hardly seemed gracious or generous, but they had little choice.[97]

Paired with this policy of clemency came a program of vigorous re-catholicization. Churches were cleansed of Reformed trappings, holy spaces were reconsecrated, heretics who had been buried inside churches were reinterred in unconsecrated ground.[98] Clerics and religious orders

---

[96] Parker, *Dutch Revolt*, pp. 209–216.
[97] Soen, "Reconciliatie," pp. 355–357.
[98] Spicer, "After Iconoclasm," p. 432.

returned to claim their property and houses, as did lay Catholics who had fled the Calvinist regimes into exile in such safe havens as Cologne. Parma oversaw the task of re-catholicizing the cities with care and attention, meeting with priests, monks and bishops about the proper ways to reconcile heretics as effectively as possible. The right of emigration of course emptied these cities of many of their Protestants, but the project of reconciliation to the old church proved relatively successful as well; the bishop of Antwerp reported that more than ten thousand former heretics eventually returned to the Catholic fold.[99]

The right to emigrate granted by Parma resulted in the eventual departure of well over one hundred thousand people, many of them Protestants, from reconquered Flanders and Brabant during the 1580s and 1590s, depriving the southern Netherlands of a large portion of its wealth and talent and contributing to dramatic, short-term economic stagnation there. Southern cities lost significant portions of their populations in the later 1580s: fifteen thousand left Ghent, ten thousand left Bruges, thirty-eight thousand left Antwerp and six thousand departed Tournai.[100] It was not just the Reformed who left; the Lutheran community of Antwerp, mostly German merchants, migrated principally to Amsterdam, and the city's Portuguese New Christians, many of them crypto-Jews, departed for safer havens as well. Tens of thousands of these émigrés went north to the independent provinces, where the Reformed Protestants among them were assured freedom of worship in the public church and the entrepreneurial among them might find work or fortune in the north's increasingly expanding economy. Northern cities, especially those in Holland, welcomed this influx of labor and capital, and the Reformed Church welcomed new members into its congregations.

The Reformed Church in the rebel provinces was experiencing its own growing pains in the 1580s, as political and ecclesiastical elites negotiated with each other over its political and social role as the public church, and a large inflow of new, staunchly Reformed southern refugees did not necessarily make things easier. The regents of Holland's cities in particular were wary of the militant Reformed demand for church autonomy. Thanks to Parma's military successes the rebellious north was very much on the defensive during the 1580s. The rebellion suffered from a lack of clear leadership: the States-General was riven by political faction, and then William of Orange was assassinated in 1584. Thereafter Queen Elizabeth's favorite, the Earl of Leicester, briefly served as governor-general for two years. His tenure proved disastrous, as he quarreled with the powerful

[99] Soen, "Reconquista and Reconciliation in the Dutch Revolt," pp. 14–18.
[100] Briels, *Zuid-Nederlanders in de Republiek 1572–1630*, pp. 28, 47, 80, 92.

Holland regents who dominated the north's politics. His failures on the battlefield did not help, nor did the fact that he took up the cause of the militant Reformed party and half-heartedly attempted a coup against Holland's cities that failed utterly. In 1587 he left the country in disgrace.[101]

In some northern cities and communities the work of reforming the church went relatively smoothly when Reformed and civic elites worked harmoniously with each other.[102] But in other places disagreements over church governance, discipline and doctrine made church building a fraught process in this decade. The Union of Utrecht, which was slowly becoming by default the foundational document of the insurgent provinces, had stipulated that the regulation of religious questions was to be left to local jurisdictions. The powerful civic magistrates of Holland, the most populous and richest of the northern provinces, took effective control of the political leadership of the independent provinces. These patricians, though they had been fervent political opponents of Philip II, were generally lukewarm toward the new ecclesiastical regime. They wanted as inclusive a public church as possible and expected to exercise some oversight over the public church, particularly the calling of ministers, and were dismayed when the most zealous leaders within the Reformed Church tried to thwart this goal. As noted earlier, in the cities of Gouda, Leiden and Utrecht serious controversies broke out over the precise relationship of the public church to civil authority. The Reformed Church in turn was disappointed that civil authorities did not provide more cooperation in the disciplining of society and only grudgingly conceded that as the public church it was required to offer the rites of baptism and marriage to anyone, whether or not they were church members.[103] The ambivalent status of the public church would get resolved locally and temporarily in various places, but no general settlement could quite get established. In 1591 a committee of political and ecclesiastical delegates tried to create a church order for the province of Holland, but several city governments rejected it because they thought it offered the public church too much autonomy.[104] The problem lay dormant but continued to simmer. A generation later the same unresolved, intractable issues were to be revived again during the far more divisive Arminian controversy of the 1610s.

Another challenge the young public church faced was the recruitment of a qualified corps of clergy. Through the 1610s the Reformed Church

---

[101] Groenveld, *Tachtigjarige Oorlog*, pp. 120–127; Dunthorne, *Britain and the Dutch Revolt*, pp. 82–83.

[102] In Haarlem, for example, relations between magistrates and ministers were relatively amicable in the late sixteenth century. Spaans, *Haarlem na de Reformatie*, pp. 82–89.

[103] Pettegree, "Confessionalization in North Western Europe," p. 113.

[104] Hooijer, *Oude kerkordeningen der Nederlandsche Hervormde Gemeente*, pp. 324–350.

battled with a chronic shortage of preachers to meet congregational demand, especially outside the large towns. The provincial synods and regional classes tried to oversee the recruitment and training of candidates to the ministry, but resources were often lacking. In the early decades ex-priests and religious who had converted formed a significant minority of local preachers. In the countryside these clergy were of sometimes uneven quality, especially those appointed in some of the seigneuries of local gentry.[105] This sometimes led to situations that church authorities found disturbingly heterodox. In 1604 the classis of Dordrecht, for example, learned to its consternation that an ex-priest named Goswinus Johannis was literally crossing the confessional divide along the military frontier south of the city: he celebrated mass for Catholics in Brabant in the mornings and then in the afternoons traveled north of the border into Holland to preach in the Reformed manner to village congregations.[106] Such unauthorized ministries were possible in less supervised rural areas. In addition, complaints from congregations about unlettered or untrained ministers reached classes across the country. Universities set up in Leiden (1575) and Franeker (1585) were designed to ameliorate the problem of unlettered clergy by providing more thorough theological schooling, but the building up of a professional clerical caste was a slow, generational process that extended well past the turn of the century.[107]

The Reformed Church held two more national synods in the 1580s, one in Middelburg in 1581 and another in The Hague in 1586. Both of them wrestled with the thorny questions of church polity and discipline, as well as with cases of preachers whom the clerical majority accused of being insufficiently orthodox. Some dissenting voices within the church were stilled: the Leiden preacher Caspar Coolhaes, who supported the Leiden magistracy's insistence on subordinating the public church to civil authority, was excommunicated by the Reformed Church in 1582.[108] The Utrecht minister Herbert Duifhuis, a favorite of the magistracy there, likewise endured tremendous pressure from his Calvinist opponents to amend his preaching, which they saw as dangerously spiritualist and libertine.[109] By 1590 the public church appeared to have settled its internal divisions, or at least quieted them.

---

[105] Duke, "The Reformation of the Backwoods: The Struggle for a Calvinist and Presbyterian Church Order in the Countryside of South Holland and Utrecht before 1620," in *Reformation and Revolt*, pp. 242–245.
[106] Kooi, *Calvinists and Catholics during Holland's Golden Age*, p. 44.
[107] Van Deursen, *Bavianen en slijkgeuzen*, pp. 34–42.
[108] Gottschalk, *Pleading for Diversity*, pp. 89–106.
[109] Kaplan, *Calvinists and Libertines*, p. 85.

Although the organization of the Reformed Church grew more consolidated and uniform, it still struggled with the vestiges of what it called popery. It was all very well for the church to set up a more streamlined polity and build a consensus on doctrine; the greater challenge was to win the hearts and minds of the population. Resistance or indifference to ecclesiastical discipline was widespread and old ways lingered. As had been the case since before the wars, the Reformed were in the minority. Consistories, classes and synods complained repeatedly the persistence of Catholic "idolatry" in communal life, be it the leftover customs of Saint Nicholas Day in December or actual clandestine worship by neighborhood Catholics in private homes and spaces.[110] To anxious Reformed leaders it seemed very much as though popery was everywhere, and they continually demanded that the government suppress it. The leadership also complained about the presence of Mennonite congregations in their communities, though with less ferocity. All non-Reformed worship was officially illegal, but as long as it occurred privately and municipal peace was not disturbed, local authorities were not much inclined to enforce the rules very stringently. Persecution of Catholics was sporadic, localized and inconsistent; nevertheless a halting, slow, but palpable de-catholicization of the public sphere was underway.[111]

Although the northern provinces, which were slowly evolving into the Dutch Republic, were now officially Reformed, the public church did not gain large numbers of committed adherents in the 1580s. We have no reliable sources for numbers, though politicians in the States of Holland claimed in 1587 that only one in ten Hollanders belonged to the public church.[112] In most localities the Reformed made up a minority of the population. This was due to a number of factors, both external and internal. The Reformed Church, intent on establishing as pure a household of God as possible, set strict standards for membership, requiring both a public profession of faith and submission to consistorial discipline. At the same time the governments of the rebel provinces, mindful of the Union of Utrecht's stipulation about freedom of conscience, required no one to join the public church. Consequently, few inhabitants in the north joined the church, though the evidence suggests that far more people, the *liefhebbers*, attended Sunday worship without committing to full membership. These sympathizers likely outnumbered

[110] Duke, "The Reformation of the Backwoods," pp. 227–230.
[111] Kooi, *Calvinists and Catholics during Holland's Golden Age*, pp. 99–108; Parker, *Faith on the Margins*, pp. 46–54.
[112] Duke, "The Ambivalent Face of Calvinism in the Netherlands, 1561–1618," in *Reformation and Revolt*, p. 269.

professed members considerably.[113] Many inhabitants of the Dutch Republic, for whatever reason, chose not to be a part of the public church, whether out of indifference or allegiance to another confession. The privileged, public church was a minority among minorities, a demographic fact that would persist until the later seventeenth century.[114]

The most far-reaching consequence of the war for reformation in the Low Countries was that, starting in 1572, it enabled Protestant churches to establish a permanent, secure home in the region. A second consequence of the wars was that Netherlandish Reformed Protestantism reached, for a brief dozen or so years, its greatest geographic extent in the Low Countries, from Artois to Groningen, from Holland to Limburg. A third consequence was that the vicissitudes of the wars, starting in the 1580s, shifted the center of Reformed Protestantism from its original nucleus in the south – Brabant, Flanders, Hainaut – to the north. Whereas once Antwerp, Tournai and Ghent were the incubators of native evangelical movements in the period up through the 1566 Wonderyear, in the last quarter of the sixteenth century Reformed Protestantism in the Netherlands found a permanent home instead in such northern cities as Amsterdam, Leiden, Kampen, Groningen and Utrecht, where it had little been in evidence before 1566. What had once been a broad, Netherlandish Reformed movement was after 1585, thanks to exigencies of war and migration, more narrowly concentrated in the lands of an independent northern republic.

Not only did the wars affect reformation, reformation in turn affected the course of the wars. The wars convulsed the Habsburg Low Countries and ultimately bifurcated them. They were destructive and bloody, involving massacres of noncombatants and the terrorizing of whole communities. Countless numbers of buildings, religious and secular, were laid waste. Much of this turmoil was tinged by religious passion (of all kinds) that made the fighting all the more desperate and extreme. Zealotry led to violence. Contemporaries understood just how much religious passion fueled the bloodiness of the conflict; the provincial Council of Hainaut, in a report to the Brussels government in 1587, summed up the situation concisely: "The present wars are not common and ordinary wars in which princes are fighting each other. They rather are wars searching to impose God's glory."[115] Religious questions, specifically the Habsburg government's policies toward heresy, sparked the first open opposition. Religious militancy sustained the coalition against the Habsburgs in

---

[113] Van Deursen, *Bavianen en slijkgeuzen*, pp. 128–131.
[114] Bergsma, *Tussen Gideonsbende en publieke kerk*, pp. 415–421.
[115] Quoted in Simon, "Council of Trent," p. 206.

exile when the energetic and organized Reformed movement threw in its lot with the rebel Beggars, but once the rebellion moved on to Netherlandish soil, the coalition rapidly broke down over that selfsame Reformed militancy. Reformation, as it turned out, was an uncertain and fickle political ally. War to impose God's glory made sustained Protestant reformation possible in some parts of the Low Countries, while in other parts it quickened the ongoing process of Catholic reformation.

5   Schism

By the beginning of the seventeenth century war had split the old Burgundian–Habsburg Netherlands into two states, one Catholic and the other Protestant. The military front divided the region, including the vital western core provinces, in two, and some one hundred thousand people emigrated from north to south.[1] Not only was this a political separation, it was also in effect a schism.

Three decades of war had destroyed the religious and political unity of the Low Countries. Although militant parties on both sides of the border dreamed one day of reuniting the whole of the Netherlands politically and religiously, this separation of identities, as Jonathan Israel calls it, first tacitly acknowledged by the Twelve Years Truce reached by the two sides in 1609, would prove permanent.[2] During the Truce (1609–1621) the religious divide would be further reinforced by the consolidation of the Reformed Church in the north and the revitalization of the Catholic Church in the south. Although the Truce had little to say on the subject of religion, the temporary cessation of hostilities brought with it the time and space for sharpening separate confessional identities. The bifurcated Low Countries grew apart from each other into two discrete political-religious entities.[3]

By the 1590s the insurgent northern provinces had evolved into a new, independent state thanks to the political stewardship of Holland's land's advocate, Johan van Oldenbarnevelt (1547–1619), and the military talent of Stadholder Maurice of Nassau (1567–1625). Known variously as the United Provinces or the Dutch Republic, this new state would become one of the great European powers of the seventeenth century. In the southern provinces Habsburg dynastic hegemony reasserted itself under a new generation with the Habsburg archdukes Albert (1559–1621) and Isabella (1566–1633), and with it came a recovering economy and a revitalized Catholic Church. The Southern or archducal Netherlands

---

[1] De Schepper, *Belgium Nostrum*, p. 23.
[2] Israel, *Dutch Republic*, pp. 399–420.
[3] Cloet, "De gevolgen," p. 73.

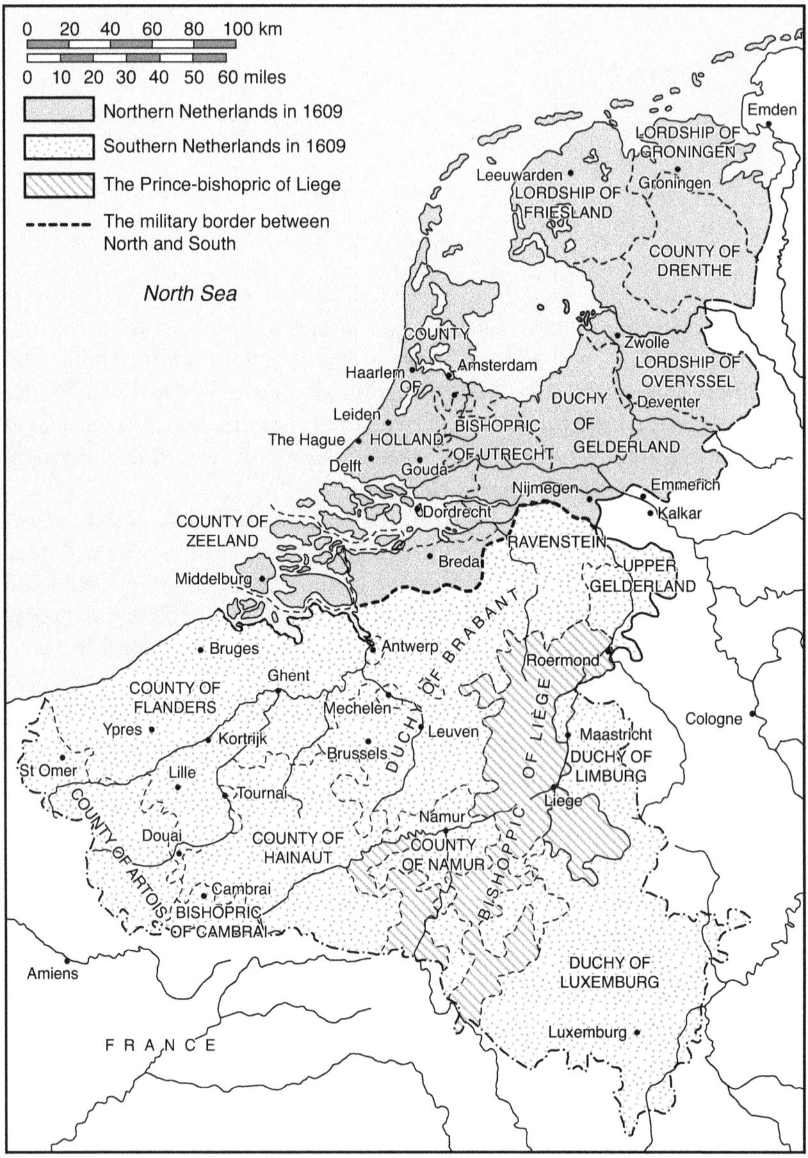

Map 5.1 The Low Countries in 1609

would form the core of what eventually became the modern states of
Belgium and Luxemburg, while the Dutch Republic was the ancestral
state of today's kingdom of the Netherlands.

When the Twelve Years Truce ended in 1621, the Netherlandish wars resumed and would not be finally resolved until the Treaty of Münster in 1648, one of the subsidiary agreements of the Peace of Westphalia that ended the European wars of religion more generally. But already by the time of the Truce the ebb and flow of military campaigns had set more or less permanently the frontiers between the two Netherlandish states. The Dutch Republic comprised the seven insurgent provinces of the north as well as portions of Flanders, Brabant and Limburg. The Southern Netherlands was now a remnant of the original Habsburg territory, comprising the French-speaking Walloon regions of the south as well as the remaining parts of Flanders, Brabant and Limburg.[4]

In both states the process of religious reformation went on, but in vastly different guises. Distinct political circumstances in each state determined the further course of religious change. Catholic reformation continued in the archducal Netherlands while Protestant reform pressed on in the Dutch Republic. The south became a bulwark of Tridentine Catholicism and the north emerged as a society that was at once Reformed and pluralist. State and church labored together in the south to fashion a distinctive Catholic confessional identity, while in the north state and church cooperated at best uneasily, fashioning a society whose religious profile might best be described as multiconfessional. One regime favored religious uniformity while the other opted for religious pluriformity. These different religious trajectories created a considerable cultural gulf between the two states that persisted throughout the early modern era.

The Southern Netherlands: Catholic Reformation

In the Southern Netherlands reformation continued, though entirely within the Catholic fold. The twin goals of this ongoing reformation remained the eradication of heresy and the revitalization of Catholic belief. In this endeavor the Catholic Church became intimately tied to the restored Habsburg government and their conjoined efforts proved quite effective, so much so that, even though in the sixteenth century religious dissent in the Low Countries had been most heavily concentrated in the southern provinces, in the seventeenth century these self-same regions emerged as a center of vigorous and vibrant early modern Catholicism. The principal task facing the archducal regime put in place

---

[4] There is a misleading historiographical tradition, begun in the nineteenth century, of calling these regions the "Spanish" Netherlands; in fact when it came to domestic affairs, including religious ones, the Southern Netherlands enjoyed considerable autonomy from Spain. Vermeir, "How Spanish Were the Spanish Netherlands?"

there in the late 1590s was to restore Habsburg rule after decades of rebellion, an effort that required the dynasty to enlist the moral and cultural support of the Catholic Church. For the church the goal was to eradicate the vestiges of the past century of heresy, restore ecclesiastical authority to its proper place and reinvigorate traditional piety and devotion among the faithful. This alliance between government and church in the Southern Netherlands aimed at establishing a vital and vigorous confessional state – that is, one that was self-consciously and devotedly Catholic.

Archduke Albert, the fifth son of Holy Roman Emperor Maximilian II, was appointed governor-general of the Southern Netherlands by his uncle Philip II in 1596 and married his cousin Isabella, Philip's daughter, two years later. It fell to Albert and Isabella to lead and manage what was left of the "Austro-Burgundian composite state" – that is, the ten (more or less) Netherlandish provinces that had either stayed under or were won back to Habsburg sovereignty.[5] The restoration of the dynasty's authority rested very much on the support of the church. The new regime encouraged the work of a reforming Catholic Church hierarchy dedicated to revitalizing devotion, appointing scores of reform-minded bishops. Archducal religious policy was thus a "classic example of the mixing of genuine religious zeal with clear-eyed political self-interest."[6] So important was this renewal effort, situated as it was so precariously along the borderlands with Protestant heresy, that the papacy also established a special nunciature in the Southern Netherlands in the 1590s so that clerical ambassadors representing the interests of the Holy See could also be involved in the project of ecclesiastical renewal.

The reformation that preoccupied the archducal Netherlands at the turn of the seventeenth century was a continuation of the ongoing measures to reform the Catholic Church that had already been introduced in the mid-1500s, such as the reorganization of the bishoprics, the efforts to apply the canons of the Council of Trent, the establishment of the university at Douai, and the creation of the Jesuit seminary in Leuven.[7] Much of this reforming work had been disrupted by the warfare of the last quarter of the sixteenth century. Only in the later 1590s, as the military situation stabilized along a frontier from northern Flanders, across northern Brabant and through southern Guelders between the two warring states, could the efforts at church renewal in the south proceed more or less unimpeded by the contingencies of war. Tridentine reforms,

[5] Duerloo, *Dynasty and Piety*, p. 6.
[6] Duerloo and Wingens, *Scherpenheuvel*, p. 22.
[7] Dierickx, "Het begin van de Katholieke Reformatie."

intended by Rome to bring uniformity of doctrine and practice to the Catholic world, were reapplied with renewed vigor and resolve.

Catholic reformation was the work of many actors, both clerical and lay. While during the sixteenth century the Netherlandish Catholic clergy had not made much of an intensive effort to encourage lay Catholics to think of themselves in terms of their confessional identity, in this new postwar, counter-reformational environment they were very much spurred to join in the effort of reform and renewal. There was now among the laity "a sense of collective purpose," and the renewal of faith and devotion was seen as a common enterprise, precisely because of the exactions of the wars.[8] Reform in the archducal Netherlands was not a simple top-down affair, but an elaborate and multifaceted collaboration between elite and ordinary Catholics.[9]

The need for church reform was more obvious than ever before. The subject of *reformatio* had of course preoccupied the Netherlandish Catholic Church centuries before the outbreak of the Protestant rebellion, but the unprecedented and destructive success of this latest heretical movement made it alarmingly clear that more urgent measures were needed to rehabilitate and revitalize the church. After the Habsburg reconquest of the 1580s, the Catholic Church in the Southern Netherlands started marshaling its resources and redoubling its efforts to restore and maintain both a healthy institution and a reinvigorated piety, a process that would go on for decades. The project of reformation here comprised at least three major pieces: the rebuilding of the church fabric, the introduction of new religious orders, and the enhancing of popular devotion. All of these efforts would be critical to giving the Southern Netherlands a sharply Catholic confessional identity by the middle of the seventeenth century.

Decades of war had taken their toll on the Catholic Church fabric in the southern provinces. In Flanders and Brabant, where much of the fighting had taken place, churches and monastic houses had been laid waste and many parishes had been abandoned by their clergy.[10] Structurally and institutionally, much of the Catholic church lay in literal ruins. In the diocese of Bruges, a scene of much fighting, all the cloisters outside the city were destroyed or severely damaged.[11] In the deanery of Tielt in Flanders, for example, officials reported in the mid-1610s that of its twenty-two churches only five were usable.[12] Rebel troops and fanatical iconoclasts, especially in those cities where militant Reformed had taken

[8] Pollmann, *Catholic Identity and the Revolt of the Netherlands*, pp. 156–157.
[9] Soen, Vanysacker and François, "Church, Censorship and Reform," p. 1.
[10] Spicer, "After Iconoclasm."
[11] Cloet, *Karel-Filips de Rodoan*, p. 182.
[12] Cloet, *Het bisdom Gent*, p. 138.

power and established the Calvinist republics, had reduced much church decor, from stained glass to paintings to altars to statuary, to dust. Many parishes, particularly in the countryside, had to be effectively rebuilt in terms of structures or personnel. Sometimes this began with the construction of simple side chapels or even outbuildings where the sacraments could be celebrated.[13] Even as late as 1609 many parishes in the bishoprics of Bruges, Ghent and Antwerp were still lacking priests.[14] Attendance at the sacraments, the celebration of high holy days, the catechization of children – much of the normal devotional life of the parishes was uneven, sporadic or even nonexistent, especially in the countryside, in part because of the destruction of churches and in part because of the dearth of priests.[15] Reconstructing the ecclesiastical infrastructure would prove to be the most challenging, costly and slowest part of Catholic reform in the early 1600s.

Rebuilding the church fabric, which was to be the work of decades, fell largely on the shoulders of the church and local governments. The archdukes, eager enthusiasts for this project, also laid out enormous sums for the work of reconstruction. "Never in history had so many churches and cloisters been built and rebuilt as under Albert and Isabella," one scholar has noted.[16] The sovereigns supported this wave of construction through outright subventions, donations or tax privileges; with great ceremony and grandeur they laid the foundation stones for numerous ecclesiastical structures. In Brussels, home of the archducal court, no fewer than twelve new religious houses were established by the time of Isabella's death in 1633. In Lille the number of religious houses doubled. Similar construction took place all across the cities of the Southern Netherlands as a "conventual invasion" of new cloisters and monasteries swept through the country.[17] Catholic piety as expressed in stone and mortar became an ever more noticeable feature of the southern landscape.

Rebuilding also required energetic, reform-minded bishops who had been charged by the Council of Trent with more rigorous supervision of their dioceses than ever before. All manner of problems required episcopal attention. Reconstruction meant not just restoring infrastructure but restoring worship needs as well. Willem van Bergen, bishop of Antwerp between 1596 and 1601, ensured that the parishes in his city were supplied with newly printed liturgical templates prescribed by Trent, such as catechisms, breviaries, missals and martyrologies.[18] His

---

[13] Cloet, *Het bisdom Gent*, p. 174.
[14] Cloet, "De Kerk en haar invloed," p. 15.
[15] Cloet, "La religion populaire," pp. 925–927.
[16] Cloet, "De Kerk en haar invloed," p. 27.
[17] Put, "Les archiducs et la réforme catholique," p. 257.
[18] Marinus, *Contrareformatie*, pp. 54–55.

successor, Joannes Miraeus, devoted himself in particular to pastoral questions, helping launch the bishopric's own seminary, visiting parishes, and attempting to gain greater control over the parish priesthood at the expense of the powerful but hidebound cathedral chapters the members of which resented any loss of their liberties and privileges.[19] One of the first tasks for bishops was simply finding out what shape their dioceses were in. The energetic bishop of Ghent spent a six-week period in the spring of 1611 visiting nearly seventy parishes and a dozen cloisters under his purview, and his even more sedulous successor visited nearly twice that many during his own episcopate.[20] What these episcopal visitors found was not always promising. In his visitations in the countryside in 1610 bishop Karel-Filips de Rodoan of Bruges discovered local farmers storing grain and hay in damaged village churches and livestock grazing in churchyards.[21]

The rich diocesan archives of Belgium have provided scholars with abundant information about these episcopal labors. One of the more well-chronicled members of this new generation of reforming prelates was Mathias Hovius, archbishop of Mechelen during the years 1596 to 1620. With tenacity and dedication Hovius spent his career applying Tridentine standards of devotion, worship and pastoral care to hundreds of parishes in an archbishopric laid waste by decades of war. In 1607 he called a provincial council of clergy to Mechelen to make clear that all priests in his archdiocese were to conform to the standards set by Trent, with the help of episcopal discipline if necessary. This 1607 council was a signal event, the starting point of serious and concentrated Catholic reformation efforts in the Habsburg Netherlands.[22] With the support of the archdukes he secured regular income from the diocese's biggest abbey (not without protest from the Benedictines to whom it belonged) in order to finance the work of reform. He dismissed, again to great resistance, those hidebound, lazy and inadequate clerics he believed were not serving the diocese well. He carefully oversaw the staffing and construction of a new Marian shrine at the village of Scherpenheuvel. He established a seminary in Mechelen under his own control in order to train new generations of zealous and pious priests. He actively encouraged the veneration of saints and their relics, including the Gorinchem priests martyred by Beggar troops at Brielle in 1572. He tirelessly visited the various corners of his far-flung archdiocese, exhorting clergy and laity alike to join in the effort of reform. In doing all this Hovius ran into

---

[19] Marinus, *Contrareformatie*, pp. 56–63.
[20] Cloet, *Het bisdom Gent*, pp. 59, 61.
[21] Cloet, *Karel-Filips de Rodoan*, p. 129.
[22] Vanysacker, "Church Province of Malines," p. 161.

considerable resistance, and the effects of his disciplinary regime on the clergy were uneven at best; like many reformers he died in 1620 perhaps more respected than beloved. Yet without doubt he left the archbishopric in better shape than he found it.[23]

To be sure, none of this happened easily. Such labors required both dedication and patience on the part of clerical leaders. The dean of Torhout, Denijs Christoffels, found himself in the early 1600s dealing with a variety of issues and challenges across his rural Flemish deanery – seven of his seventeen parishes lacked a pastor. He demanded better records and inventories of church goods from parish church wardens, urged village magistracies to combine parish appointments as a way of coping with the shortage of priests, sought the financial means to pay for priestly benefices, and visited the parishes under his supervision as often as he could.[24] The church fabric and the dearth of clergy remained ongoing problems across the archducal Netherlands, at least in part because of the lack of resources to pay for both. The bishop of Bruges brought in both regular and secular priests from bishoprics as far away as Tournai and Cambrai to help with the shortage of pastors in 1609.[25] Only in the 1610s, during the breathing space afforded by the Twelve Years Truce, would clergy be restored to most empty parishes in the Southern Netherlands.

Perhaps the most immediate work of restoring the church fabric was done by the priests in the parishes. On them fell the task of tending to believers, providing them with the salvific instruments of the church and offering prayer and sacraments. In addition to their sacramental duties, parish priests were supposed to function as preachers, comforters of the sick and dying, organizers of processions and feast-day activities, catechizers of children and monitors of lay behavior and belief. The Tridentine canons demanded much of clergy and attentive prelates like Mathias Hovius set high standards for pastoral work. A well-educated clergy was key to this project, so diocesan seminaries were set up across the country, sometimes at considerable cost. This was no guarantee of success, of course. Karel Maes, the bishop of Ghent in 1610–1612, was so dissatisfied with the state of the seminary in his city that he sent all the seminarians home.[26] The bishop of Bruges sternly warned lazy seminarians in the 1610s that "those who fritter away such a privileged opportunity for study are not worthy of the priesthood."[27] In Antwerp the cathedral canons, who appointed parish priests, insisted that their candidates be of

---

[23] Harline and Put, *A Bishop's Tale*.
[24] Cloet, *Karel-Filips de Rodoan*, pp. 161–164.
[25] Cloet, *Karel-Filips de Rodoan*, pp. 170–171.
[26] Cloet, *Het bisdom Gent*, p. 142.
[27] Cloet, *Karel-Filips de Rodoan*, p. 123.

unimpeachable character and belief, that they had some oratorical skills, including mastery of French, and that witnesses had to testify to their capability. The bishops of Antwerp went still further and in some instances set up competitions to select the best priest for the particular job, an interference the canons grumbled against but could do little about.[28] How successfully this ideal priestly image was realized of course varied from diocese to diocese, with some pastors resisting or at least complaining about the demands the new Tridentine standards made on them. Nevertheless their prelates made clear that henceforth more accountability was expected from them.

A second important prong in the reform program of the Catholic Church in the Southern Netherlands involved the deployment of religious orders both old and new in the project of revitalization. This "conventual invasion" brought new religious communities to both town and country; Lille, for example, gained no fewer than six new cloistered communities in the period 1588–1618.[29] Existing orders such as the Franciscans and Dominicans, along with newer orders such as the Society of Jesus and the Capuchins, contributed substantially to the work of restoration. The older monastic orders underwent their own renewal and expansion in the same period. By the middle of the seventeenth century Benedictine, Augustinian and Cistercian houses, male and female, collectively numbered in the hundreds as more and more monasteries dotted the landscape of the archducal Netherlands.[30] Relations between old and new orders, and between secular and regular clergy were sometimes contentious and even competitive as they sought the patronage of powerful officials or the support of ordinary parishioners. Nevertheless regular clergy filled in some of the pastoral and sacramental gap left by the shortage of secular clergy caused by the wars.

The Jesuits in particular responded with zeal to the call for Catholic reformation. The Society of Jesus had been present in the Low Countries since the middle of the sixteenth century, but by 1620 more than a thousand members of the order worked in the Southern Netherlands, nearly 10 percent of them in Antwerp alone.[31] They set up schools, trained members of the secular clergy, preached in the parishes, set up sodalities to mobilize lay devotion, catechized children, offered pastoral care, erected splendid new churches and chapels, and brought considerable devotional and intellectual energy to the work of revitalization. They were financially supported by prominent Antwerp families; in the 1620s

---

[28] Marinus, *Contrareformatie*, p. 131.
[29] Lottin, *Lille*, p. 116.
[30] Cloet, "De Kerk en haar invloed," pp. 20–21.
[31] Cloet, "De Kerk en haar invloed," p. 29; Marinus, *Contrareformatie*, p. 156.

the order built itself, at considerable cost, a splendid Baroque church in the city, lavishly decorated with ceiling paintings by Peter Paul Rubens (Illustration 5.1).[32] Avid exploiters of media technology, the Society produced books and texts for all manner of educational, spiritual and polemical purposes, making themselves "apostles of the printing press."[33] Additionally, from their base in the archducal Netherlands, they formed their own mission to serve beleaguered Catholics in the Dutch Republic.[34]

Sodalities set up by the Jesuits proved particularly effective means to harness the fervor of pious lay Catholics. These confraternities allowed devout Catholic men new avenues of religious expression and sociability, with different sodalities targeting different social groups, such as for students or particular kinds of artisans. Members of sodalities engaged in charitable works, walked in processions, worshiped together and directed their devotions to specific saints or to the Eucharist. They proved quite popular and their membership numbered in the thousands by the 1620s. Established orders, such as the Franciscans, noted the success of these organizations and quickly set up confraternities of their own.[35] Harnessing popular devotion proved to be one of the regular orders' most successful means of engaging the laity in the work of reformation.

Another important new order dedicated to reform that began working in the Southern Netherlands in the 1580s was the Friars Minor Capuchin, an offshoot of the Franciscans that spread throughout Catholic Europe at the turn of the seventeenth century. They first established themselves in Antwerp in 1585 and within a decade had houses in Ghent, Leuven, Douai, Bruges, Arras, Tournai and Lille. By the middle of the 1610s the Capuchins had no fewer than forty houses and nearly seven hundred members in the archducal Netherlands, most of them in the French-speaking regions of the south and east.[36] The Capuchins particularly dedicated themselves to living exemplary lives of piety intended to be visibly inspiring; this was to some extent a continuation of the old medieval observant tradition. It seemed to have some effect; in their reports the bishops of Antwerp regularly noted and commended the admirably strict lives the city's Capuchin friars led.[37] In addition to setting a moral example, the Capuchins furthered the work of reform through preaching. They distinguished themselves in this medium; the bishop of Bruges even gave

[32] Marinus, *Contrareformatie*, pp. 160–161.
[33] Begheyn, "The Jesuits in the Low Countries."
[34] Vanden Bosch, "Saving Souls in the Dutch Vineyard."
[35] Pollmann, *Catholic Identity and the Revolt of the Netherlands*, pp. 145–146.
[36] Hildebrand, *De Kapucijnen in de Nederlanden*, vol. 1, p. 152.
[37] Marinus, *Contrareformatie*, p. 173.

Illustration 5.1 Anton Günter Gheringh, *Jesuit Church in Antwerp*, 1662–1668. Constructed in the 1620s and used by the Society of Jesus until 1773, this splendid Baroque church now serves as the St. Charles Borromeo Church. Courtesy National Trust, United Kingdom

them permission to preach across the entire diocese, so impressed was he by their homiletic effectiveness.[38] Their churches, first built in the 1590s, were eagerly visited by the laity, who perhaps saw in these pious and ascetic regulars a sharp contrast with the sometimes uneven talents of the secular clergy.[39] The Capuchins seem to have made an impact despite their relatively modest numbers. Protestant propagandists were soon lumping them together with the Jesuits as the new shock troops of militant counter-reformation.[40] Such was the success of the order in Antwerp that their convent had to be completely rebuilt and expanded in 1614.[41]

Under the Catholic regime of the archducal Netherlands the religious orders, old and new, enjoyed a golden age. At their highest point in the seventeenth century it was estimated that the total number of men and women in religious orders, along with the diocesan clergy, comprised about 3 percent of the urban population of the Southern Netherlands. The sheer ubiquity and visibility of the clergy, especially the regulars in their distinctive garb, testified to how much church, state and communities invested in the restoration of the church.[42] Without these trained, committed clergy a confessionally Catholic Southern Netherlands would not have been possible.

Diligent and faithful clergy were, however, necessary but not sufficient. A third important part of the Catholic Reformation in the archducal Netherlands was the reinvigoration of lay piety and devotion – that is, part of the confessional project was to rekindle faithful religious observance among the laity. A key component of this was the renaissance of female piety, especially the medieval tradition of Beguines, whose sisters rededicated themselves to the restoration of both their beguinages and their charitable and devotional practices.[43] Likewise the burgeoning, Europe-wide "spiritual daughter" movement (called *kwezels* in the Southern Netherlands) attracted pious women who rejected marriage and embraced celibacy, pursuing the contemplative life in either community or in their families, often engaging in the important work of teaching catechism.[44] Those daughters who came from well-to-do families eagerly supported the work of church reconstruction with substantial gifts to endow chapels.[45] Such women became vital actors in the church's Tridentine project of reformation.

---

[38] Cloet, *Karel-Filips de Rodoan*, p. 185.
[39] Hildebrand, *De Kapucijnen in de Nederlanden*, vol. 1, p. 79.
[40] Hildebrand, *De Kapucijnen in de Nederlanden*, vol. 1, pp. 83–84.
[41] Hildebrand, *De Kapucijnen in de Nederlanden*, vol. 1, p. 88.
[42] Cloet, "De Kerk en haar invloed," p. 26.
[43] Harline, "Actives and Contemplatives."
[44] Nuyttens, *Kwezeltjes dansen niet*, pp. 19–27.
[45] Moran, "Resurrecting the 'Spiritual Daughters.'"

The church specifically encouraged the devotion to Mary and the saints that had been so popular before the reformation. A major project to this end, begun during a period when the war with the Dutch Republic was proving especially dire, was the construction of the shrine at Scherpenheuvel east of Brussels.[46] A Madonna statue hanging in an oak tree on a hill outside the nearby village of Zichem was credited with miraculous cures, and by 1606 the shrine was officially recognized by the pope.[47] Albert and Isabella heavily promoted and subsidized the shrine, laying out an elaborate pilgrimage center along heptagonal lines with a domed church with multiple altars in the center. It was very much a Habsburg project, with the archdukes attempting to build an entirely new city tied directly to their dynasty. The couple reportedly spent hours cozily planning and discussing the shrine's decorative details with each other.[48] Pilgrims swarmed the town a few times each year, and income from this traffic grew steadily.[49] Hundreds of miraculous healings of every ailment, from lameness to infertility to demonic possession, were attributed to the site. It became the most visited Marian pilgrimage center in the southern Low Countries, its "Jerusalem," as scholars have aptly called it. "[God] seems to want to show at this place He ... will make a new covenant with the people of the Netherlands," enthused one observer.[50] Scherpenheuvel was a conspicuous demonstration of the lengths the archducal regime was willing to go in order to yoke confessional identity to political loyalty. This devotional strategy, linked to the larger project of Catholic reformation, proved quite effective. Scherpenheuvel represented the triumph of the Counter-Reformation in the archducal Netherlands; it became in effect the national shrine of a triumphantly Catholic state.[51]

For the vast majority of layfolk in the south, the return to prewar religious normalcy was welcome; the suffering and pain inflicted by decades of war had engendered a renewed zeal for religious activity. Lay devotional practice blossomed to levels of enthusiasm not seen since the early sixteenth century; religious practices and customs that had been so disrupted by reformation and revolt came back to life. Saints, especially Mary, were particular foci of lay veneration; in the second quarter of the seventeenth century the bishop of Ghent reported particularly strong devotion to the mother of God in his parishes.[52] Confraternities dedicated

[46] Harline and Put, *A Bishop's Tale*, pp. 93–108.
[47] Duerloo and Wingens, *Scherpenheuvel*, pp. 23–28, 37–41.
[48] Duerloo, "Archducal Piety," pp. 275, 279.
[49] Thøfner, *Common Art*, pp. 277–297.
[50] Quoted in Pollmann, *Catholic Identity and the Revolt of the Netherlands*, p. 165.
[51] Duerloo and Wingens, *Scherpenheuvel*, p. 51.
[52] Cloet, *Het bisdom Gent*, p. 195.

to the Virgin, the Trinity, the Name of Jesus, the Rosary and the Eucharist flourished in many dioceses in the course of the seventeenth century. The prelates of the archbishopric of Cambrai encouraged the creation of confraternities dedicated to the Eucharist in every parish as a way to refute Protestant doctrine on transubstantiation.[53] Membership in sodalities in Antwerp ballooned from seventy in 1585 to fourteen hundred in 1611.[54] Primary and secondary education were also enlisted in this effort at reigniting devotion; during the course of the seventeenth century schools both urban and rural came almost entirely under church oversight.[55] All of this effort in the first quarter of the seventeenth century seemed to bear fruit in the long term, even if prelates occasionally grumbled that the laity were not conforming to their instruction fast enough.

The revitalization of piety also included the reform of morals. During times of war, church attendance had been widely disrupted and in some parishes had halted completely due to the desertion of war-torn communities, the absence of priests or the destruction of ecclesiastical buildings. Under the Tridentine rules parishioners were expected to attend mass on Sundays and feast days, a challenge not easily met during this period of reconstruction. Ecclesiastical discipline of the laity would come slowly and unevenly. In 1607, for example, the archducal government issued a placard mandating Sabbath observance, including staying out of the taverns during worship times.[56] In an effort to get people out of the taverns and in their homes, the bishop of Ghent and the magistrates of the Flemish town of Deinze agreed in 1620 to an evening curfew bell of 9:00 in winter and 10:00 in summer.[57] Such ordinances were designed to prod parishioners back into the churches.

To what extent local officials enforced these kinds of church decrees is not clear from the sources. Particularism could still get in the way of moral regeneration. More than one bishop locked horns with local magistrates on the issue of prohibitions of work on feast days and Sundays. Many magistracies, anxious to revive their civic economies, tried to negotiate exceptions to the prohibition, much to the annoyance of prelates. Similarly parishioners frequently ignored rules about attending the sacraments only in their own parishes.[58] Disorder among the laity proved a continuing concern. Clergy preached against drunkenness, prostitution, excessive feasting and all manner of sinful behavior, but it is

---

[53] Cloet, "De Kerk en haar invloed," p. 42.
[54] Marinus, *Contrareformatie*, p. 257.
[55] Cloet, "De gevolgen," pp. 60–61.
[56] Cloet, *Het bisdom Gent*, p. 180.
[57] Cloet, *Het bisdom Ghent*, p. 219.
[58] Bauwens, "Restoration and Reform of the Parish after Trent," pp. 173–176.

impossible to know what effect these kinds of admonitions had. The spike in persecutions for witchcraft across the Southern Netherlands between 1590 and 1615 also indicated that church authorities were trying to keep a sharp eye on deviant popular belief.[59] Decreeing moral reform and then enforcing it proved a laborious and not always fruitful exercise.

Many lay Catholics, however, were eager to participate in the work of renewal, much as they had once enthusiastically participated in the practices of late medieval religion. The impetus to reconstruction and reformation therefore came not just from the top down or only from clergy to laity. Ordinary Catholic layfolk also invested in a renewed and reinvigorated church and were very much encouraged to do so by the clergy. They too contributed to the restoration and redecoration of churches, offering their money and labor to provide new altars, new bells, new paintings, new candlesticks and the like. Parish financial records, where they exist, suggest that parishioners donated generously to their congregations after 1590.[60] Not just individuals, but guilds, chambers of rhetoric and confraternities also eagerly committed themselves to rebuilding. In Bruges more than four hundred Mary statues were placed in house gables; devotion could not be too public.[61] Having endured the travails of war and heresy, pious Catholics rejoiced at the reconsecration of churches, believing the salvation of the very land itself was at stake.[62] By the middle of the century popular devotion and lay participation in worship appeared to climb back to levels not seen since the eve of the Protestant Reformation. Catholic reformation, to succeed, needed a large dose of democratization. Lay Catholics in the Southern Netherlands appeared to be willing to do their part.

The other principal goal of Catholic reformation, aside from the revitalization of the church, was of course the extirpation of heresy. The last trial and execution of a person for Protestant heresy in the Low Countries took place in Brussels in 1597; a servant named Anna Utenhove was buried alive for refusing to recant her Anabaptist beliefs. This was to some extent an anomalous event. Since the end of the duke of Alba's regime and its "Council of Blood" and because of the chaos of the ensuing wars, heresy prosecution had dropped sharply. This final case of execution may have been an effort by authorities to use old tactics to scare secret Protestants into embracing the old church, but the government eventually introduced a more pragmatic policy since it was clear that violent judicial persecution of heresy had not worked very well in the past. There were also fears, especially among

---

[59] Vanysacker, *Hekserij in Brugge*, pp. 65–69; Dupont-Bouchat, "La Répression de la sorcellerie," pp. 43–150.
[60] Bauwens, "Restoration and Reform of the Parish after Trent," pp. 179–185.
[61] Cloet, "De Kerk en haar invloed," p. 46.
[62] Pollmann, *Catholic Identity and the Revolt of the Netherlands*, pp. 157.

civic magistrates, that harsh prosecution would provoke still more emigration and bring further economic decline, and the execution of Utenhove incurred much protest. In 1609 the archducal government promulgated a new placard against heresy: no subject was permitted to attend any gathering where doctrines contrary to those of the Catholic Church were espoused. Anyone not professing the Catholic faith would be treated as a disturber of the peace. Recalcitrant heretics would be banned.[63] The placard would be re-promulgated at least five more times over the next ten years, an indication perhaps of the persistence of religious deviance. The enforcement of this edict was largely in the hands of local officials, who would not always be consistent about it. Thus, though the edict itself sounded as severe and as uncompromising as any anti-heresy placard issued in the previous century, the application of it was softer and more supple. There were fears among church officials that too rigid an enforcement might either disturb the common peace or endanger Catholics living under the Protestant regime of the Dutch Republic. Secular magistrates were generally hesitant, as always, to enforce any placard that might threaten municipal order. There was no longer any centralized campaign to root out heresy, as there had been in the sixteenth century.[64]

Still, the official choice given to Netherlandish Protestants now living under Habsburg rule was clear: convert or leave. Considerable social and political pressure was put on them to reconcile. Protestants were purged from the rolls of guilds and other civic organizations. The Catholic Church regained its monopoly on all public worship and all non-Catholic belief was outlawed. Some dissenters, giving in to pragmatism, returned to the old church; about three thousand Antwerpers were reportedly converted by 1590.[65] Much of the work of ridding the southern Netherlands of Protestantism was done by Protestants themselves – of the estimated one hundred southerners who left their homes in this period for the Dutch Republic and other lands, the majority were Protestants of various stripes.[66] This migration led to a dramatic depopulating of many southern cities; the population of Ghent was halved by 1590, for example, as was that of Antwerp.[67] Thus the heretical threat to Catholic reformation in the archducal Netherlands effectively removed itself almost entirely by emigration by the early seventeenth century.

Those Protestants who chose to remain or who were unable to leave the archducal Netherlands lived in a political and cultural environment that

---

[63] Cloet, "La religion populaire," pp. 949–950.
[64] Thomas, "The Treaty of London," p. 295.
[65] Thijs, *Van Geuzenstad tot katholieke bolwerk*, p. 40
[66] Pollmann, *Catholic Identity and the Revolt of the Netherlands*, p. 126.
[67] Briels, *Zuid-Nederlanders in de Republiek*, p. 28; Marinus, *Contrareformatie*, p. 17.

was officially hostile to their beliefs and that expected them to reconcile with the Catholic Church. There is little information to be had about them or their numbers, but underground groups still met in some larger towns. Small Protestant communities gathering in private homes were uncovered by local authorities in cities such as Valenciennes, Arras and Douai in the 1610s.[68] In 1612 authorities in Lille, a staunchly Catholic town, discovered Protestant conventicles gathering in local taverns.[69]

The Twelve Years Truce of 1609–1621 allowed for more traffic between the republican north and the archducal south and many Protestant southerners took advantage of the opportunity to cross the border to worship in Reformed churches (their marginalized Catholic counterparts in the north acted similarly, traveling south to receive the sacraments). In 1609, for example, anywhere from three hundred to six hundred Reformed Antwerpers paid several boatmen to ferry them regularly out to the nearby fort of Lillo, held by the Dutch Republic's troops, to hear the Sunday Reformed preaching in the garrison church there.[70] Scandalized Antwerp Catholics who heard them singing psalms on the barge confronted them on the banks of the river Scheldt when they returned; anti-Protestantism was now becoming a matter of popular sentiment as well as official decree.[71] This opening of frontiers made the prelates in the southern Netherlands distinctly nervous, for they feared that this would allow for more Reformed proselytizing among those secret Protestants still within their dioceses. Bishop Joannes Miraeus of Antwerp complained of Protestants in his city meeting for worship in the home of one of the Republic's truce negotiators.[72] In 1613 the diocese of Ghent required of all schoolmasters an oath of loyalty to the Catholic faith.[73] On the other hand, the Catholic leadership also saw the open frontier as an opportunity to help Catholics living in the Republic; the archdukes in particular were ardent supporters of the Holland Mission created to minister to northern Catholics now living under the "heretical yoke."[74]

The effort to reconcile heretics back to the church required considerable energy and patience on the part of Catholic authorities. The goal was not to drive still more dissenters out of the country but to win back souls, and so anti-heresy placards were enforced at best unevenly. Parish priests approached those suspected of heretical leanings and carefully tried to

---

[68] Thomas, "The Treaty of London," p. 293.
[69] Lottin, *Lille*, pp. 149–151.
[70] Marinus, *Contrareformatie*, p. 62.
[71] Thomas, "The Treaty of London," p. 291.
[72] Marinus, "De protestanten te Antwerpen," p. 329.
[73] Cloet, *Het bisdom Gent*, p. 227.
[74] Arblaster, "The Archdukes and the Northern Counter-Reformation."

persuade and educate them back into the old church but did so with mixed success. Civic officials went to the homes of suspected Protestants to check whether they had been officially reconciled. It was clear, though, that the number of heretics was dwindling; only a handful of stubborn Protestants were banned from the city of Antwerp for their recalcitrance in the period 1585–1615, for example.[75] Church authorities had to be mindful of not treading on the toes of local privilege. There was sometimes disagreement between the city's magistrates and its bishop about how to handle the Protestants in their midst. In 1617 bishop Johannes Malderus of Antwerp tried to impose a twenty-guilder fine on anyone in the city who had not fulfilled the Easter obligation to attend mass. This caused consternation among the city fathers, who preferred a softer hand in religious policy for the sake of civic peace, and they negotiated a compromise with the bishop that allowed for a less drastic imposition of fines.[76] Once again the Netherlandish tradition of assertive local sovereignty, including the reluctance of city governments to obey the dictates of the church, served Protestants well, or at least in this instance gave them a bit of breathing space.

Nevertheless, once the Twelve Years Truce expired in 1621 and hostilities between north and south resumed, official attitudes toward Protestants in the south hardened. In the decade following the end of the Truce the bishop of Antwerp ordered a count of heretics in the city and found there were more than two hundred Protestant families. Evidence suggested that they were served by a shadowy and ambulant network of Protestant schoolmasters, sick visitors and occasional preachers.[77] In the 1620s scores of Protestant families were ordered banned from the city.[78] In the long term, though, Protestantism in the Southern Netherlands remained a small, scattered, largely underground movement. By the second half of the century the number of Protestants in the country diminished markedly. Small islands of dissenters dotted the country, but these were tiny communities that had few opportunities to gather and worship. Protestants in Brussels could sometimes take advantage of the presence of the court and worship in the chapels of the English or Dutch embassies. Still, these dissident communities were small, scattered and effectively marginalized. The bishop of Douai boasted to the pope in 1606 that he no longer knew of anyone who dared openly support Reformed belief.[79] The reduction of Protestant dissent

[75] Marinus, "De protestanten," p. 328.
[76] Marinus, "De protestanten," p. 331.
[77] Marinus, *Contrareformatie*, pp. 236–237.
[78] Marinus, "De protestanten," p. 339.
[79] Cloet, "De Kerk en haar invloed," p. 49.

to a tiny minority may have been one of the greatest successes of Catholic reformation in the Southern Netherlands.[80]

It was not necessarily enough, however, just to remove the heretics from the midst of the faithful. The Southern Netherlands' location on the frontier with Protestantism meant that it was uniquely placed to combat heresy rhetorically and culturally as well. Heresy could be attacked through various media, especially that of print. The south became a center of anti-Protestant printed polemic in the late sixteenth and early seventeenth centuries. Since the Dutch Republic had a lively printing industry of its own, with many of its products directed against Catholic "idolatry," it became vital for the Catholic south to give as good as it got. Presses in Antwerp, Douai and Leuven produced reams of books, tracts and pamphlets intended both to refute heresy and to bolster the faithful. These texts ranged from guides for how to detect heretics to manuals on how to argue with them to accounts of their scandalous errors and gruesome misdeeds.[81] One of the most productive of the southern polemicists was the English Catholic exile Richard Verstegan, who from his base in Antwerp produced scores of tomes, pamphlets, broadsheets, verses and news dedicated to attacking Protestant heresy. He singled out Reformed Protestantism in particular as a dangerous combination of heretical doctrine and Machiavellian politics – the Calvinists "mix gunpowder in their reformation."[82] One of his most important works, *Theater of Cruelties of the Heretics of Our Time*, catalogued the outrages Protestants inflicted on faithful Catholics in a variety of places in northwestern Europe, including the Netherlands. In slightly fewer than one hundred richly illustrated and poem-adorned pages, *Theater of Cruelties* recounted in bloodcurdling detail the sufferings innocent Catholics endured at the hands of impious and inhumane Calvinists during the wars. Most of the stories were about martyred clergy, but one described the plight of the Haarlem beguine Ursula Talesia, dragged to the gallows by Beggar troops who demanded that she renounce her faith and marry one of the soldiers. When she refused they drowned her in the river (see Illustration 5.2).[83] Such merciless atrocities revealed both the demonical theology of the Calvinists and the illegitimacy of their new state, founded as it was on such blasphemous

---

[80] Cloet, "De gevolgen," p. 54; Marinus, "Het verdwijnen van het protestantisme in de Zuidelijke Nederlanden."

[81] Pollmann, *Catholic Identity and the Revolt of the Netherlands*, pp. 147–153; Van der Steen, *Memory Wars in the Low Countries*, pp. 91–94; Van Gennip, *Controversen in context*, pp. 90–174.

[82] Arblaster, *Antwerp and the World*, p. 198.

[83] Verstegan, *Théâtre des Cruautés des hérétiques de notre temps*, p. 122.

67

Barbares cruautez des Gueus
es pays bas.

Le Scythe tant cruel, ny les Barbares fiers,
Qui du mont Caucasin habitent les rochers,
Ny l'Hetrusque tyran, par enuieux venin,
Qui faisoit aux corps morts attacher les viuants,
N'eurent cœurs si felons, si cruels ny sanglants,
Comme a la rauissant canaille de Caluin.

I 2   PLVSIEVRS

Illustration 5.2 Illustration from Richard Verstegan, *Théâtre des cruautez des hérétiques de nostre temps*, 1587. In these two scenes Beggar soldiers inflict horrifying cruelties on innocent Catholics in Holland. No barbarian, the caption notes, is as cruel as the "ravaging mob of Calvin." Courtesy Bibliothèque nationale de France

violence. First printed in 1587, *Theater of Cruelties* would undergo multiple editions and translations well into the seventeenth century. It provided a useful narrative framing the Catholic experience with this newest heresy as yet another chapter in the long history of Christian martyrdom, and it was a pointed rebuttal of Protestant martyrologies printed since the mid-sixteenth century. Such propaganda as Verstegan's was designed to galvanize the Catholic laity in the long war against heresy, strengthening their resolve and dispelling any wavering doubts about the rightness of the true church. Catholic confessional identity demanded constant vigilance at its boundaries against the continuing perils of heresy.

The Dutch Republic: Protestantism and Pluralism

To the north, in the Dutch Republic, religious change in the late sixteenth and early seventeenth centuries was a far more variegated process than it was in the archducal Netherlands. The south experienced a deliberate, state-supported campaign of Catholic (re)confessionalization. In the north, by contrast, continued the inchoate, diversified evolution of reformation that had begun in the Low Countries in the early sixteenth century, with more limited political support for the privileged confession. In the Republic there was one official, privileged public church but also a host of private, tolerated congregations. Virtually all the varieties of Christian sect and belief that had first appeared in the Low Countries in the 1500s would eventually find a home, however constricted, in the Dutch Republic: spiritualist, Mennonite, *Doopsgezinden*, Lutheran, Libertine, plus a substantial remnant of faithful Catholics and an unknown number of unchurched folk. This wide and open diversity of religious allegiance in such a densely populated society was a source of wonderment to visitors to the Republic in the seventeenth century; the British traveler James Howell noticed that in the streets in which he sojourned there were "well near as many religions as there be houses ... the number of conventicles exceeds the number of churches here."[84] In communities of any size one's neighbors could be Reformed, Catholic, Mennonite or Lutheran, to say nothing of one's work associates and even one's relatives.[85]

This array of private confessions coexisted, each uneasily to a greater or lesser degree, with the officially sanctioned public church. Like the Catholic Church in the archducal Netherlands, the Reformed Church in the Republic enjoyed a monopoly on all public religious expression, it

---

[84] Kooi, *Calvinists and Catholics during Holland's Golden Age*, pp. 19–20.
[85] For a microhistorical example of this phenomenon, see Pollmann, *Religious Choice in the Dutch Republic*.

controlled most ecclesiastical buildings, its clergy were paid out of publicly administered funds, and its clergy served as chaplains to the
Republic's navy and army. When the government called for national
days of prayer in times of crisis or thanksgiving, these occasions took
place inside Reformed churches. It became a broadly open church in
that all inhabitants were welcome to worship, be baptized and be married
in it, but at the same time it insisted that membership could only be
granted to professed and committed adult believers.

Consequently the public church's membership comprised at most
a plurality rather than a majority of the Republic's population until well
into the middle of the seventeenth century. In terms of simple demograph-
ics, the public church was thus a privileged minority confession among
many other confessional minorities. Nevertheless by 1600 it had survived
its growing pains and the ecclesiological controversies of the 1570s and
1580s, and it had become a fixed and dominant part of the social and
cultural landscape of the Dutch Republic.[86] Within ten years of the turn of
the new century, however, both church and state would be embroiled in
a theological and political conflict that would shake the young Republic to
its foundations – the Arminian controversy of the 1610s. What began as
a technical point of theological difference between two Leiden University
scholars quickly got entangled in a parallel political dispute about the
continued prosecution of the war against Spain. These twin controversies
polarized the country and threatened to undermine the Republic's fragile
unity. Questions of identity and survival came to the fore, stirred up by
ecclesiastical and political factions that favored either renewed war or
continued peace. Contemporaries viewed the conflict through almost existential lenses: Was the Republic a Reformed state? Did it have both
a religious and political obligation to continue fighting the war against
Catholic Spain? Was the conflict with Spain in fact a political war rather
than a religious one? What had reformation been all about? These kinds of
issues swirled in the air in the 1610s, fanned by partisan print media and
dividing public opinion, exacerbating political antagonism, sparking political violence and, in the end, prompting a coup that would permanently
change the complexion of the Republic's polity and public church.

The internal disputes that plagued the Reformed Church the 1570s
and 1580s had been largely quieted but never really settled. Disagreement
on points of church autonomy, doctrine and the authority of creedal
statements such as the Belgic Confession and Heidelberg Catechism
still simmered, and by the early 1600s there was some interest among
both church and political elites in calling for another national synod to

---

[86] Parker, "Reformed Protestantism," pp. 191–194.

resolve them. To this mix was added broader theological debates in Reformed Europe about the nature of salvation. Theodore Beza, who led the Reformed Church in Geneva after John Calvin's death, stressed much more than his predecessor the centrality of the doctrine of predestination to Reformed teaching. He espoused a supralapsarian understanding of predestination, which argued that God had chosen some to be saved and others to be damned even before the fall of Adam. This decree revealed both God's omnipotence and his consoling grace. Critics countered that this caused needless anxiety among believers as they wondered whether they were among the elect or the reprobate; this interpretation, they argued, effectively turned God into a tyrant. Worse still, by logical extension it suggested that God was the author of human sin.[87] Still, Beza's interpretation had considerable currency and authority, and it predominated in Reformed Church in the Dutch Republic. In their soteriology, their theology of salvation, most Dutch divines followed the Genevan interpretation, which led their opponents to deride them as Calvinists, but not all: the classes and synods of the Reformed Church found themselves dealing increasingly with cases of ministers disagreeing on the question of predestination in the course of the 1580s and 1590s.[88]

One Dutch Reformed preacher in particular would be most closely associated with this dissent: Jacobus Arminius (1560–1609), who already in the 1590s, as a minister in Amsterdam, had grown increasingly skeptical of Beza's high predestinarian views, doubts he expressed more boldly after joining the theology faculty at the University of Leiden in 1603. Arminius had studied in Geneva under Beza, so his Reformed credentials were not in doubt, but he had serious reservations about Beza's understanding of predestination. God's decree of election, Arminius instead argued, was not supralapsarian (before the fall) but in fact infralapsarian – it happened after the fall of Adam and Eve into sin. God instead predestined to eternal life those whom he foresaw would be faithful believers. In effect Arminius placed a degree of human agency into the process of salvation. One's election was preconditioned by one's faith. Human souls exercised their free will by accepting or rejecting God's grace.[89]

Some of Arminius's faculty colleagues, most notably theologian Franciscus Gomarus (1563–1641), took issue with what they saw as a dangerously heterodox challenge to the doctrine of unconditional election, one smacking suspiciously of Catholic notions of salvation by human works. Gomarus and Arminius held a number of formal disputes on the subject, but

---

[87] Benedict, *Christ's Churches Purely Reformed*, pp. 302–303.
[88] Van Lieburg, "Gisbertus Samuels."
[89] Van Deursen, *Bavianen en slijkgeuzen*, pp. 228–229; Bangs, *Arminius*, pp. 186–221.

nothing resolved their disagreement. Before long the Leiden theologians, professors and students alike, grew divided on the issue, and word about the dispute spread beyond the academy into wider ecclesiastical circles across the country. A significant minority of Reformed ministers, mostly in the provinces of Holland and Utrecht, supported Arminius's position. Unrest within the church spread and Arminius found himself under attack.

Because of their minority status, Arminius and his clerical allies appealed for political protection. Among the urban patricians who sat in the States of Holland, the Republic's politically and economically dominant province, there was considerable sympathy for the position of Arminius, whose chief political supporter was none other than land's advocate and anticlerical *politique* Johan van Oldenbarnevelt, the Republic's most powerful politician. Oldenbarnevelt and most of Holland's urban oligarchs preferred a public church that was both more inclusive in membership and more subordinate to state authority, as they had since its establishment in 1572. He had tried to convince Reformed divines to agree to a national synod, but while they wanted a synod, they had balked at his condition that the Belgic Confession come under review at such a gathering; they refused to consider revising what they saw as foundational creedal statements. Arminius's explicit solicitation of political support was congenial to Oldenbarnevelt and his allies; it appealed to their Erastian notions of the proper place of the church in the political hierarchy.[90]

Added to this widening theological controversy was a burning political issue. Oldenbarnevelt noted with alarm the financial cost of the war to the young Republic and labored hard to bring about a cessation of hostilities with Spain; the war was dragging into its fourth decade and exhausting the treasury. In 1609 he successfully brought this goal to fruition with the signing of the Twelve Years' Truce.[91] There was, however, loud opposition to the ceasefire from various quarters, such as the province of Zeeland and the powerful city of Amsterdam, both of which had benefited economically from the ongoing war. Opposition also included the formidable figure of Oldenbarnevelt's rival the Stadholder Maurice of Nassau, son of William of Orange and commander of the Dutch military, who feared a truce might drain him of political influence. The provincial synods of the Reformed Church, whose militants, many of them southern refugees, viewed the conflict with Spain through a religious lens, also opposed the Truce; for them the war was being fought not just for independence but for true religion. They also looked on with great dismay at the tolerationist policies of Holland's patrician regime, especially

---

[90] Bangs, *Arminius*, pp. 222–227.
[91] Israel, *Dutch Republic*, pp. 399–410.

toward Catholics. The pro-Truce party, embodied by Oldenbarnevelt and most of the cities represented in the States of Holland, saw their political goals against Spain as largely achieved: independence had been secured and the Truce included an implicit recognition by the Habsburgs of the Republic's sovereignty. The anti-Truce faction, coalescing increasingly around the figure of Maurice, dreamed of liberating the whole of Low Countries from Habsburg (i.e., Catholic) control and bringing reformation to the whole region. In this respect this dispute over the Truce was a reprise or continuation of the same tensions between political and religious insurgents that had plagued the rebel coalition in the late 1570s. The old division between *libertatis ergo* and *religionis ergo* as the principal motive for fighting Spain seemed to have resurrected itself. This fraught political atmosphere was further enflamed by the Arminian controversy. Arminius and his supporters continued to seek political protection, much to the outrage of their opponents, who saw the dispute as purely ecclesiastical. An angry Franciscus Gomarus predicted that his opponent's opinions would set the whole country ablaze in civil conflict.[92]

Gomarus was not far wrong, in part because his like-minded supporters within the public church continued to fan the flames, insisting that Arminian students within the theology schools should not be allowed pulpits (Arminius himself died in 1609). Responding to this pressure, a group of Arminian preachers, desperate for political protection, petitioned the States of Holland in a "Remonstrance" calling for a revision of the Belgic Confession, insisting on the government's authority over the public church and reasserting Arminius's views on predestination. Not to be outdone, their opponents presented a "Counter-Remonstrance" arguing exactly the opposite, insisting that church bodies and not the state should settle all questions of religion and reasserting the supralapsarian soteriology of Beza. The two sides, Remonstrant (Arminian) and Counter-Remonstrant (Calvinist), were now clearly drawn. Churches, classes, synods, university faculties and civic governments, primarily in Holland but also in other provinces, became sharply divided over the controversy, with some congregations erupting into schism. In the ensuing decade the controversy grew wider and more vehement, polarizing the entire country, just as Gomarus had predicted. The Arminians or Remonstrants were a clear minority, but because of the political support in Holland they enjoyed they were able to foment considerable acrimony in the wider church. The war with Spain had temporarily come to an end, but in its place came equally harrowing civil strife. Across the Republic lay and clerical Reformed Christians discussed, argued and confronted each other vehemently on the issue.

---

[92] Bangs, *Arminius*, p. 299.

Popular violence erupted on a few occasions here and there, sometimes literally around the pulpit. Remonstrants and Counter-Remonstrants called each other names like "baboon" and "mud-beggar."[93] The controversy was stoked by the flames of print. Nearly five hundred pamphlets supporting (or attacking) one camp or the other were printed in the period 1615–1619, approximately 75 percent of the total number of pamphlets published in that period.[94] These ranged from high theological treatises to lampooning satires. So, for example, in an Arminian pamphlet, "The Predestined Thief," a convicted robber assures a Counter-Remonstrant minister on the eve of his execution that "I now know for certain that everything I have done was God's secret will, intention and resolution," and thus his salvation was assured.[95] Not to be outdone, a 1618 Counter-Remonstrant pasquil imagined the leading Remonstrant preachers in a dung-cart on their way to Rome; up front sat Arminius, "who introduces heresy, who destroys God's word, and calls the pope a brother, son and member of the church."[96] Dutch literary culture in this period became positively obsessed with the controversies.[97] The patricians of Holland, led by Oldenbarnevelt, tried to use political solutions to quell the controversy, but the Counter-Remonstrant majority would have none of it. Ministerial candidates with suspected Remonstrant views were being rejected by the Counter-Remonstrant classes who examined them, and the appointment of Remonstrants to university theology faculties sparked fierce opposition. So in 1614 Oldenbarnevelt had a placard passed by the States of Holland, after much discussion, called (perhaps wishfully) "For the Peace of the Church."

The placard banned the public discussion of certain Reformed doctrines, including predestination, whether in print or from the pulpit. In practice towns with Remonstrant-leaning governments used the placard to silence Counter-Remonstrant ministers, while in Counter-Remonstrant towns it was not even enforced. In the second half of the 1610s the economy took a downturn, which sparked incidents of popular violence in such towns as The Hague, Amsterdam, Delft and Brielle. By the summer of 1617 the atmosphere in Holland's towns was so tense that the States of Holland empowered civic governments to mobilize special mercenary troops to keep order because the traditional civic militias were mostly full of Counter-Remonstrants; this move provoked the Counter-Remonstrants into still greater outrage. Oldenbarnevelt's support shrank while Maurice

---

[93] Van Deursen, *Bavianen en slijkgeuzen*, pp. 320–321.
[94] Harms, *Pamfletten en publieke opinie*, p. 39.
[95] Slatius, *De Gepredestineerde Dief*, p. 17.
[96] *Den Arminiaenschen Dreck-waghen*, p. Aii recto.
[97] Sierhuis, *Literature of the Arminian Controversy*.

of Nassau gained public popularity, particularly after he pointedly attended Counter-Remonstrant church services in The Hague around the same time. After a year of cautiously biding his time Maurice made his move in July 1618, toppling Oldenbarnevelt in a coup d'état with the help of his political allies outside Holland. He purged town councils of Remonstrant sympathizers and had Oldenbarnevelt himself executed the following year. The Stadholder became the unquestioned leader of the United Provinces and remained so until his death in 1625.[98]

As a companion to this political purge came a parallel purging of the public church. Once the political patrons of the Remonstrants were removed from power by Maurice, the Counter-Remonstrants saw an opportunity to remove Arminian ministers from the public church. With the full support of the Orangist, anti-Holland faction now in power in the States-General they set about the work of further internal confessionalization – that is, of clarifying precisely what the doctrines of the Reformed church were. To this end they organized the long-awaited national synod to settle once and for all the urgent theological questions that had been plaguing the church, especially on the issue of predestination. In November 1618 the National Synod gathered in the South Holland city of Dordrecht, a Counter-Remonstrant bulwark, under the observation of representatives from the States-General. The Synod comprised delegates from all the provincial synods, the Walloon (or French-speaking) Reformed church and the Leiden theological faculty, as well as dignitaries from several parts of Reformed Europe (Illustration 5.3).[99]

Although the Remonstrant preachers were allowed to make their theological case to the assembly, the outcome was never in doubt. The Synod reaffirmed the majority theological opinion on predestination and then convicted the Remonstrants of heresy and of disturbing the political and ecclesiastical order.[100] Remonstrant theologians were dismissed from the Leiden theological faculty. Remonstrant preachers were ordered to subscribe to a statement of reconciliation and submission; they had to conform to the Belgic Confession, the Heidelberg Catechism and the acts of the National Synod or else lose their position as ministers in the public church. Most of the two hundred or so Remonstrant preachers refused to sign and were stripped of their pulpits; some retired quietly into private life, others went into exile, still others met and worked in small, underground Remonstrant gatherings in the Republic. These scattered clandestine groups would suffer occasional judicial persecution, but by the

---

[98] Israel, *Dutch Republic*, pp. 421–449.
[99] For a detailed account of the Synod, see Van Lieburg, *Synodestad*.
[100] Van Lieburg, *Synodestad*, pp. 131–143.

Illustration 5.3 Anonymous, *The Synod of Dordrecht*, 1618. Roughly one hundred delegates, including more than two dozen from outside the Republic, attended the Synod for a seven-month period in 1618–1619. Courtesy Rijksmuseum Amsterdam

1630s they constituted themselves into a tolerated minority confession known as the Remonstrant Brotherhood.[101]

The National Synod of Dordrecht, which adjourned in May 1619, seven months after it began, signaled the formal triumph of one precisian Reformed school of opinion, popularly known as Calvinism, within the Dutch Republic's public church, including its supralapsarian interpretation of predestination coming from Theodore Beza's Geneva.[102] The hopes of the Arminians to revise the official creeds to allow for more theological nuance on the subject of predestination came to naught. Dordrecht officially established the majority theological opinion as the formal orthodoxy of the public church, an orthodoxy that would not change during the lifetime of the Republic. Schism would not afflict the Dutch Reformed Church again until 1816, and the States-General allowed no more national synods to take place. The variety of theological opinion that had both characterized and troubled the first fifty years of the public church's existence – on doctrine, on practice, on ecclesiology – was effectively neutralized. With the issuance of the Dordrecht Synod's official canons on doctrine the Dutch Reformed Church had accomplished its own internal confessionalization.[103] The Calvinists had won, at least on paper. In fact after 1619 the enforcement of Dordrecht's prescriptions within the public church proved at best uneven and locally inconsistent.[104] And some more pietistically inclined Calvinists even concluded the Synod had not done enough and in the ensuing decades demanded still "further reformation," principally of public morals.[105] Despite the canons of Dordrecht, theological disputes would still occasionally roil the public church in the course of the next two centuries.

The other major accomplishment of the Synod was to set into motion the production of a new and authorized translation of the Bible into Dutch from the original Hebrew and Greek to replace the unsatisfactory Deux-Aes Bible used by the Reformed movement since the mid-sixteenth century. A team of translators was commissioned to fashion a new vernacular edition of the Bible to be used in the public church. In 1637 they completed their work, and the States General and the Reformed Church formally accepted the "States" Bible (*Statenbijbel*) as the definitive translation of scripture for the privileged church. Henceforth this was the normative version of scripture that would be preached from in all the pulpits of the public church.[106]

---

[101] Israel, *Dutch Republic*, pp. 460–465.
[102] Van Veen, *Een nieuwe tijd, een nieuwe kerk*, p. 63.
[103] Sinnema, "Canons of Dordt."
[104] Van Veen, "Tegen 'papen' en 'slaverny,'" p. 38.
[105] Van Lieburg, "From Pure Church to Pious Culture."
[106] De Bruin and Broeyer, *De Statenbijbel en zijn voorgangers*, pp. 233–332.

The National Synod of Dordrecht was a signal event in the history of the Reformation in the Netherlands. It ensured that the Dutch Reformed Church, which had arisen out of disparate movements and impulses for church reform in the Netherlands in the mid-sixteenth century, became, at least formally, a settled institution with an established Calvinist orthodoxy. It was in effect the latest pivot in the Netherlandish Reformed movement's long process of self-fashioning that had started with the confessional turn in the mid-sixteenth century. The Reformed movement, at least formally and institutionally, had reached the culmination of its reformation by turning itself into a church of confessional Calvinism. The official doctrinal identity and boundaries of the public church were now fixed and would remain so for the next two hundred years. To be sure, the Reformed Church would continue to have its dissenters and outliers, but they tended not to stay within the fold. Those who refused to subscribe to the public church's orthodoxies would have to seek spiritual sustenance elsewhere, and thanks to the peculiarities of the Dutch Republic's religious settlement, they had many other places to look.

The National Synod of Dordrecht was a watershed moment, but only for the portion of the Republic's population, roughly 20–30 percent by the best estimates, that worshiped in the public, Reformed Church. It had little effect on or meaning to the many others who adhered to other confessions or to no confession at all. Thanks to the vagueness of the Republic's religious settlement as described in the 1579 Union of Utrecht, these non-Reformed Christians' legal, political and social status within the young state was at best ambiguous. Two conditions were clear: freedom of conscience was guaranteed, but public worship by any but Reformed Christians was illegal. In keeping with the Low Countries' decentralized political tradition, there was no central political authority in place to force confessional uniformity; instead each of the seven provinces was tasked with managing its own religious affairs. Thus enforcement of those two rules was left entirely in local hands, so the situation and safety of confessional minorities varied considerably from place to place. What emerged from this state affairs was a privileged public church and a host of tolerated private confessions.[107]

The Dutch Republic's multiconfessional society was decidedly a work in progress through the first quarter of the seventeenth century. What slowly emerged over the first half-century or so of the Republic's existence might be termed a regime of toleration where political authorities sanctioned one official church but allowed religious minorities to gather and

[107] Kaplan, *Divided by Faith*, pp. 177–183.

worship privately within certain legal and social parameters.[108] To the local magistracies that enforced this regime, the paramount social virtue was peace and order, and so in effect non-Reformed minorities were tolerated, for the most part, as long as they did not trouble the social fabric.[109] Toleration was a political tool used by state authorities to manage religious coexistence. It arose not out of ideology but out of a combination of "sentiment, tradition and expediency."[110] The degree of toleration varied widely according to time and place and was sensitive to lobbying and pressure from the public church. Nevertheless the regime of toleration's basic features were in place by the 1620s; like the Republic's polity, its religious policy gave the distinct impression of being made up as it went along. It was situational, localized and protean.

By 1620 the principal religious minorities in the Dutch Republic were, in roughly descending numerical order, Catholics, Mennonites/*Doopsgezinden*, Lutherans and Jews. Although absolute numbers are impossible to come by, the best estimates of historians suggest that in the early 1620s Catholics made up anywhere from roughly 12–25 percent of the population in the cities of Holland and Utrecht, while in the other provinces they made up a much lower proportion of civic populations, on the order of 10 percent or less (except for those portions of Brabant, Flanders and Limburg under the Republic's military control; they remained overwhelmingly Catholic).[111] They were most numerous in the provinces of Holland, Utrecht, Gelderland and Overijssel.[112] In 1656 the Catholic Church through its Holland Mission claimed to serve about four hundred and fifty thousand Catholics, one-third of the Republic's total adult population.[113] Estimates put the various Mennonite/*Doopsgezinden* congregations at about 3 percent of the Republic's population in 1665, again with considerable variation from province to province; Friesland, for example, counted at least 12 percent of its population as Mennonite.[114] By mid-century the communities of Lutherans and Jews in the Republic each numbered roughly in the mid-thousands.[115] Aside from those who were confessionally committed, there were also tens of thousands of inhabitants of the Republic who

[108] Walzer, *On Toleration*, pp. 14–36; Kooi, "Religious Toleration," pp. 213–215.

[109] Spohnholz, "Confessional Coexistence in the Early Modern Netherlands," p. 49.

[110] Van Rooden, "Jews and Religious Toleration in the Dutch Republic," p. 132.

[111] Israel, *Dutch Republic*, pp. 380–381. On the circumstances of Catholics in the conquered areas, see Lenarduzzi, *Katholiek in de republiek*, pp. 247–292.

[112] Frijhoff and Spies, *1650*, p. 352.

[113] Parker, *Faith on the Margins*, p. 17.

[114] Zijlstra, *Om de ware gemeente en de oude gronden*, p. 431.

[115] Hiebsch, "The Coming of Age of the Lutheran Congregation," p. 19; Israel, *Dutch Republic*, pp. 657–658.

apparently affiliated with no religious community at all, at least formally. They may have attended worship services, including those in the public church, but they did not officially join any particular confession.

The religious minority that perhaps flourished the most under the Republic's regime of toleration was, ironically enough, the confession the new regime was most officially hostile to, the Catholics. Or perhaps this was not so ironic: the movement for reformation that swept through the Low Countries and elsewhere in Europe had prompted vigorous spiritual renewal within the church of Rome as well as without. By the late sixteenth century the post-Tridentine church was aggressively pushing back against the advance of the various Protestant heresies and was setting up missions to tend to the needs of Catholics under the heretical yoke. The Catholic Church was busily revitalizing itself in the southern Netherlands in this period, and it did so likewise, as best it could, for the dispossessed and beleaguered Catholics of the Dutch Republic.[116]

The disestablishment of the Catholic Church in the Republic meant that since the 1570s Dutch Catholics had been deprived of churches, priests and prelates. Many Catholics had fled into exile in the southern Netherlands and Catholic imperial territories such as Cologne.[117] Those who remained were not allowed to worship openly and gathered privately, ministered to by those few priests still available. In the 1590s, however, Rome created the *Missio Hollandica* under the leadership of an apostolic vicar to minister to faithful Dutch Catholics. The Holland Mission, through an ambulant, semi-clandestine network of priests, provided Catholics in the Dutch Republic with pastoral and sacramental care. By mid-century the Mission maintained some five hundred secular priests to minister to the faithful, while at the same time in a separate effort the Jesuit, Franciscan and Carmelite orders also fielded scores of clerics in the Republic. The relationship between the Mission and these orders was occasionally fractious and competitive, particularly with the Society of Jesus. In the later seventeenth century this fractiousness between secular and regular clergy would, in an interesting parallel to the Arminian controversy in the Reformed Church, evolve into serious doctrinal disputes over questions of salvation and free will.[118] Nevertheless the totality of this missionary effort, directed out of the archducal Netherlands, ensured that the Catholic population in the Republic not only survived but thrived.

Lay Catholics were also active agents in this work, providing worship spaces, material support for priests and financial outlays. Like their

---

[116] Parker, *Faith on the Margins*, pp. 14–20.
[117] Janssen, *Dutch Revolt and Catholic Exile*, pp. 33–57.
[118] Lenarduzzi, *Katholiek in de republiek*, pp. 311–316; Parker, *Faith on the Margins*, pp. 98–99.

coreligionists to the south, they were eager for some restoration of ecclesiastical normalcy, though under very different circumstances. Catholic nobles in Utrecht and Guelders, for example, tapped into their extensive familial and social networks to support the missionary effort.[119] Spiritual maidens, known popularly as *klopjes* or *kloppen*, were devout Catholic laywomen who, like their southern counterparts, the *kwezels*, lived celibate lives in community and supported the work of priests through such activities as catechizing children and maintaining worship spaces.[120] Once again female devotion was critical to the work of revitalization. It proved an enormously successful collective effort. "The Catholic religion in Holland flourishes even more in secret than if it were in public," observed one astonished papal nuncio.[121] Indeed, between vigorous missionary travail and uneven enforcement of the anti-Catholic placards, Dutch Catholics were able to rebuild their faith communities, worshiping in permanent private spaces and creating a fixed place for themselves in the social landscape of the seventeenth-century Republic. In this respect they continued the prewar tradition of vigorous and enthusiastic lay devotion.

Despite this success, the regime of toleration affected Catholics the most repressively.[122] This was due mostly to the unremitting confessional hostility of the Reformed Church, which wished to see the complete eradication of "popish superstition" from its newly won state. The wars, for the Reformed, had been about religion after all. The public church persistently lobbied local, provincial and national governments to enforce the placards and suppress Catholic worship through the end of the seventeenth century. Reformed polemic complained of "popish impudence" and "idolatry."[123] Nor was there just confessional antagonism. The ongoing war with Catholic Spain at times made Catholic activity at home suspect in the eyes of political leaders, especially after the end of the Twelve Years Truce. Some politicians feared Catholics in the north might well act as a kind of fifth column within the Republic. During the first half of the seventeenth century (the war ended in 1648), the Republic's political and confessional environment was most hostile to Catholics among all of its tolerated confessions.

For Catholics in the Republic this meant that the regime of toleration was characterized principally by uncertainty. Judicial harassment of Catholics occurred, haphazardly and unpredictably, all across the

---

[119] Geraerts, *Patrons of the Old Faith*, pp. 190–249.
[120] Monteiro, *Geestelijke maagden*; Spaans, *De "Levens der Maechden."*
[121] Kooi, *Calvinists and Catholics during Holland's Golden Age*, p. 47.
[122] Parker, *Faith on the Margins*, p. 47.
[123] Kooi, "'A Serpent in the Bosom of Our Dear Fatherland.'"

Republic, especially in the first half of the seventeenth century. The security of Catholic congregations depended very much on the disposition of local law enforcement authorities. Their attitudes toward Catholic activity in their communities could run the gamut from indifferent to hostile, and the risk of harassment was always present. Clergy were the particular target in most cases. In virtually every province priests were on occasion hunted down, apprehended, jailed and ransomed for sometimes thousands of florins. Sometimes they were banned from a locality, a province or the entire country. Especially zealous sheriffs would raid Catholic homes in hopes of finding conventicles there. Early on in the seventeenth century Catholic congregations got into the habit of paying out "recognition money" to local sheriffs and bailiffs. This was an unofficial combination of fine and bribe paid in order to shield congregations from judicial harassment. It could be exorbitant and presented a considerable financial constraint on congregations; it was also subject entirely to the whims of the sheriffs and local governments and was therefore no absolute guarantee of protection.[124] The sheriff of Delft, for example, extracted a thousand florins from that city's Catholic congregation in a single nine-month period in 1612, but four years later was back to harassing Catholic priests again.[125] The parishioners of one Utrecht priest, desperate to get their consecrated host back, offered the sheriff a gold coin for each wafer he had confiscated.[126] Some civic magistracies, such as those of Utrecht, Arnhem, Nijmegen and Deventer, took further legal measures and under popular pressure barred Catholics from obtaining citizenship.[127] This kind of sporadic harassment served to reinforce the regime of toleration, signaling to Catholics that they were entirely subject to magisterial sufferance.[128] They remained a subaltern minority.[129] They were not free but merely tolerated. Local governments managed religious diversity within their populations by reminding Catholics through occasional legal persecution of their lower rank in the confessional pecking order.[130] Dutch Catholics seem to have indeed gotten the message, and within the limits imposed by the regime of toleration they survived and even, over the long term, flourished.

As we have seen, Anabaptists and their successors the Mennonites and *Doopsgezinden* had been active in the Low Countries since at least 1530

[124] Parker, *Faith on the Margins*, p. 50.
[125] Abels, *Nieuw en ongezien*, vol. 2, pp. 133–135.
[126] Lenarduzzi, *Katholiek in de republiek*, pp. 149–150.
[127] Prak, "Politics of Intolerance," pp. 162–163.
[128] Spaans, "Religious Policies in the Seventeenth-Century Dutch Republic."
[129] Lenarduzzi, *Katholiek in de republiek*, pp. 15–49.
[130] Parker, *Faith on the Margins*, pp. 57–58.

and had borne the brunt of particularly harsh Habsburg persecution until the outbreak of the wars in the 1570s. In addition, their disputes over church discipline had splintered them by 1570 into at least four different streams: Waterlanders, Hoogduitsers (High Germans), Friezen (Frisians) and Vlamingen (Flemings); schisms arose again in the 1580s and persisted through the next several decades. Fractiousness seemed to have become a Mennonite habit; "and they built church after church, each choosing their own worship and work," lamented one Harlingen elder in the 1620s.[131] Each time the divisive point centered on the relationship of the congregation to the society beyond it. They all varied in the degree of strictness of their self-segregation of the larger community, as well as how rigidly to enforce church discipline. By the early seventeenth century these various communities, including substantial numbers of refugees from the south, found a settled and largely secure place in the Dutch Republic. Placards against Mennonite worship were issued by the various provincial estates, but these were not rigorously enforced.[132] The Mennonites proved to be important contributors to the young Republic's economic expansion and occupied a respected place in the commercial sector.[133] On the whole the political authorities who superintended the regime of toleration looked upon them benignly, legally accommodating their various theological reservations about serving in civic militias, swearing oaths and serving in public office. In return for this connivance the Mennonites made very little trouble for the social order; under the regime of toleration they went from being radical dissenters to model citizens.[134]

While political authorities did not interfere much with the various Mennonite congregations, the Reformed Church looked upon them with suspicion and hostility (though perhaps not as viscerally as they did Catholics), seeing them not only as lost in doctrinal error but also as potential rivals for souls. The Mennonites had developed a reputation for both piety and communal discipline, practices that could certainly attract those longing for spiritual and ecclesiastical reform. In the mid-1500s the Reformed felt the threat of competition from these groups who seemed even more zealous and admirable in their search for *reformatio*.[135] Once the Reformed gained their privileged status as the public church, they still directed a fair amount of rhetorical ire against the Mennonite congregations, lobbying the government to suppress their activities, especially in North Holland, Groningen and

---

[131] Quoted in Zijlstra, *Om de ware gemeente en de oude gronden*, p. 270.
[132] Zijlstra, *Om de ware gemeente en de oude gronden*, pp. 357–362.
[133] Visser, "Mennonites and Doopsgezinden in the Netherlands," pp. 329–331.
[134] Zijlstra, "Anabaptism and Tolerance," pp. 113–114.
[135] Duke, "Ambivalent Face of Calvinism," in *Reformation and Revolt*, pp. 275–276.

Friesland, where they were most numerous.[136] In the province of Friesland, where Mennonites formed a large minority, the Reformed synod did its best to make them uncomfortable, persistently urging the provincial government to take legal action against such practices as refusing to take up arms or to swear oaths, yet local officials more often than not accommodated such beliefs for the sake of communal harmony.[137] Reformed divines insisted on public disputations with Mennonite leaders and excoriated their teachings in print, accusing them of doctrinal confusion, error and even heresy. Despite all of this confessional hostility, the regime of toleration did very little to constrain the various Mennonite communities, and they became largely assimilated into early modern Dutch society and did much to shape its economic and cultural life.[138]

Among the religious refugees who fled the Habsburg reconquest for the Republic were also Lutherans, many of whom had been members of the large Antwerp congregation. By 1605 there were some fourteen Lutheran congregations in the Republic, with Amsterdam's being the largest by far.[139] The Lutherans' relationship to the regime of toleration was initially bumpy; Lutheran congregations suffered some restriction and constraint in the Republic. The Reformed Church saw the followers of the Augsburg Confession as potential competitors for souls and lobbied loudly against them.[140] In the 1580s, for example, Amsterdam preachers even briefly persuaded the city regents to not allow Lutherans to meet there by claiming that the differences in the Reformed and Lutheran confessions were too minimal to allow for a second Protestant congregation in the city. The Lutherans had to petition the States of Holland for the right to gather.[141] Civic authorities in a number of the Republic's towns in the 1580s and 1590s were reluctant to accommodate Lutheran worship within their walls, mostly for reasons of public order. In the 1590s, when the Amsterdam Lutherans got embroiled in a bitter internal dispute about the nature of original sin, the controversy sent ripple effects into other towns; in Leiden, for example, the dispute led to angry confrontations in the city streets between disputing Lutherans. The magistrates of Leiden used this opportunity to suppress Lutheran worship within the city limits in 1594 and again in 1596.[142] Similar bans on Lutheran worship were imposed during the same decade in Utrecht, Middelburg,

---

[136] Zijlstra, *Om de ware gemeente en de oude gronden*, pp. 340–343.
[137] Zijlstra, *Om de ware gemeente en de oude gronden*, pp. 362–363.
[138] Waite, "A Reappraisal of the Contributions of Anabaptists."
[139] Hiebsch, "De geschiedenis van de lutheranen," *De Reformatie*, p. 57.
[140] Van Manen, *Lutheranen in de Lage Landen*, pp. 109–115.
[141] Hiebsch, "Coming of Age," pp. 9–10.
[142] Kooi, *Liberty and Religion*, pp. 171–174.

Amsterdam and Haarlem.[143] By the 1610s, however, strictures against Lutherans had largely disappeared. As the Arminian conflict embroiled the public church and focused its attention on internal concerns, the Lutherans were able to negotiate the regime of toleration more successfully. The Leiden and Haarlem Lutherans, congregations of a few hundred each, were allowed to build their own house-churches in 1613 and 1615, respectively. The initial decades of suspicion and dislocation of the Republic's Lutherans gradually gave way to a settled existence in the broader multiconfessional landscape, with their connections to the Holy Roman Empire and Scandinavia aiding in the growth of the Republic's commercial economy. It was primarily German and Scandinavian money, for example, that funded the Amsterdam Lutherans' brand new church in the heart of the city in 1630; by that time there was no longer any pretense that this structure was in any way a private house-church.

The regime of toleration also made room, haltingly at first, for the most despised and persecuted religious minority in Christendom, the Jewish diaspora. Sephardic Jews, *conversos* or New Christians whose ancestors had been forcibly baptized, began leaving Iberia for other parts of Europe in substantial numbers in the 1590s and early 1600s. Some settled in Amsterdam in the 1590s after the towns of Middelburg and Haarlem refused them admittance. Christian Europe had a long history of blaming the Jews for the killing of Christ; the Reformed Church was no different in this regard and viewed the newcomers with suspicion. Initially the Amsterdam Reformed consistory and city council put some stumbling blocks in the way of Sephardic settlement in the city, but by the mid-1610s Jews in Amsterdam were meeting privately and mostly unhindered in a house-synagogue.[144] Very early on the Jews of Amsterdam began contributing significantly to the young state's explosive commercial economy thanks to their links to Portugal, and outside the economic sphere they kept largely to themselves. They also would prove to be model subjects of the regime of toleration.[145] With the migration of Ashkenazi Jews from the east as the century progressed, their numbers grew, their communities spread to other towns, and they were allowed to live and worship largely unmolested, although certain legal provisos were unique to them: they were prohibited from certain occupations, from attempts at conversion and from marriage with Christians, and they had to ask local permission before settling into a new town or city.[146] Alongside the Ottoman Empire and a few Italian states, the Dutch Republic offered

[143] Israel, *Dutch Republic*, pp. 375–376.
[144] Bodian, *Hebrews of the Portuguese Nation*, pp. 56–60.
[145] Van Rooden, "Jews and Religious Toleration in the Dutch Republic," pp. 142–144.
[146] Swetschinski, *Reluctant Cosmopolitans*, pp. 10–21.

one of the few havens of relative security in early modern Europe for Jews dispersed by a hostile Christianity.

By the 1620s, most of the Dutch Republic's non-Reformed minorities found a more or less viable home within the evolving regime of toleration, though Catholics remained under suspicion as long as the war with Spain persisted. Virtually every non-Reformed confession within the Dutch Republic indirectly benefited from the Arminian controversy that consumed the public church in the 1610s. As the Reformed Church's attention focused on almost entirely on its own internal divisions and local political authorities managed those divisions as best they could, far less attention was paid to those who worshiped outside the public church.

Confessional minorities found themselves the object of far less political and sectarian scrutiny and were able to function more easily within their private worlds. The Arminian controversy, in the end, did have an effect on the Republic's non-Reformed population after all: it gave in effect a jump start to the regime of toleration. It facilitated the religious diversity that outsiders found so astonishing about the Dutch Republic. There could be a great deal of rhetorical hostility among the various confessions, but that seldom translated into judicial suppression, popular violence or social disturbance. The state applied constraints on tolerated congregations when it felt it necessary, but the notion of freedom of conscience still held sway. Across the crowded towns of the Republic a peaceful if sometimes wary religious coexistence largely prevailed.

This did not mean that the Republic was a paradise of interconfessional harmony during the seventeenth century. As we have seen, the Reformed Church, when it did pay attention to other confessional minorities, could be quite hostile to them, lobbying governments to curtail or constrain their activities. Local governments would indeed do so when they thought public order was being threatened, to say nothing of greedy local sheriffs wanting income from fines. In the 1620s, for example, Catholics found themselves subject to increased judicial harassment, as the war with Spain resumed and Reformed fears of international Catholicism resurfaced. In this confessionally hierarchical polity, the public church gave the Republic its formal religious identity while minority faiths remained marginalized legally and socially. Non-Reformed religious groups in the Dutch Republic were not free but merely tolerated; legal emancipation would not come for them until French revolutionary armies invaded the Republic in 1795. The goal of the regime of toleration was to ensure religious coexistence rather than religious freedom, and in this it succeeded. It regulated, through the selected exercise of political and judicial power, the religious diversity that had arisen out of the maelstrom of reformation and revolt. Thus the inchoate reformation of the early sixteenth century helped create, in the long term, a new state and society that was both Reformed and multiconfessional.

By the time of the expiration of the Twelve Years Truce in 1621, the separation of Netherlandish identities became permanent. The schism into two distinct confessional states, Catholic and Protestant, was by the 1620s established fact. There were, to be sure, militants on both sides of the border who dreamed of and called for reconquest, but it became increasingly clear that this was an unrealistic prospect. War between the two states would rage fitfully on for another two decades, but the story of reformation in the Low Countries would from now on be a tale of two countries. One would be self-consciously Catholic, the other nominally Reformed but socially pluralist. What had been an eclectic, wildly varie-gated deluge of religious change in the sixteenth century divided into two streams, one confessional and the other multiconfessional, by the early seventeenth century. The cessation of war brought about by the Twelve Years Truce allowed for the creation of discrete religious identities. The Truce, a dry diplomatic document whose text had virtually nothing to say on the subject of religion, brought about a permanent Netherlandish schism.[147] Nevertheless, as the Dutch painter Adriaen van de Venne depicted in his 1614 allegorical painting of the Twelve Years Truce, churches in both Netherlandish states would continue to "fish for souls" (Illustration 5.4).

Religious change in either state did not stop in 1621, of course. The reinvigoration of the Catholic Church continued unabated in the archdu-cal Netherlands – church, state and laity continued to cooperate to forge a highly successful Counter-Reformation that made Catholic piety, wor-ship and sensibility an integral if not omnipresent part of the social and cultural landscape.[148] And in the Dutch Republic all the confessions, the privileged and the tolerated, jostled and elbowed each other under a watchful regime into a grudging coexistence that allowed each one to evolve and change internally. In the south religious dissenters were reduced, mostly through political and ecclesiastical constraint, to a tiny, marginalized and harmless minority. In the north political authority neutralized religious dissenters by managing them carefully, and the privileged church, not without protest, went along. Thus in both states confessionalization continued: in the south along the model of German lands where church and governments worked in close cooperation to establish a Catholic identity, while in the north the state propped up one privileged church and allowed the others to confessionalize internally

---

[147] Brake, *Religious War and Religious Peace*, pp. 172–178.
[148] Cloet, "De Kerk en haar invloed," p. 62.

Illustration 5.4 Adriaen Pietersz van de Venne, *Fishing for Souls*, 1614. Politics and religion conjoined: on the left, Maurice of Nassau and black-clad Reformed ministers personify the Dutch Republic, while on the right bank stand the archdukes and Catholic clergy, representing the Southern Netherlands. The two Netherlandish states are linked by a rainbow while in the water clergy of various confessions fish for souls. Courtesy Rijksmuseum Amsterdam

without much interference.[149] The archducal Netherlands' Catholic regime and the Dutch Republic's regime of toleration were both outcomes of the Reformation in the Low Countries. Schism, as the Belgian historian Michel Cloet put it, made the south more Catholic and the north more Protestant.[150] Religious change continued in both states, but henceforth on very separate paths.

---

[149] Mörke, "'Konfessionaliserung' als politisch-soziales Prinzip?"
[150] Cloet, "De gevolgen," p. 53.

Conclusion

On October 18, 1618, the proud Habsburg capital of Brussels was once again scene to a spectacular display centered on themes of faith and martyrdom. On this occasion the relics of nineteen priests and Franciscan friars from the Holland city of Gorinchem, who had been brutally murdered in Brielle by sectarian Beggar soldiers in 1572, were translated with great pomp and fervor to the city's Franciscan convent. At the command of archduke Albert and his consort Isabella, her Franciscan confessor Andrés de Soto had orchestrated a grand religious tableau that carried the martyrs' remains through the city with resplendent luster and ceremony.[1] Starting from Saint Gudula, the city's principal church, a long procession of clergy and laity followed in solemn step behind the martyrs, whose bones were ensconced in ornate reliquaries covered in gold and studded with jewels. Portraits of the murdered men, of Saint Francis and of the Virgin Mary, queen of martyrs, followed. Prominent in the procession were the archdukes themselves, along with the papal nuncio, court nobles, high prelates, civic magistrates and leading guildsmen splendidly arrayed in their most formal finery. Once inside the church, the reliquaries were reverently placed on the altar dedicated to Saint Anne amidst the singing of the *Te Deum*. For eleven days afterward the relics of the Gorinchem martyrs remained there on glorious display, visited and venerated, sometimes tearfully, by thousands.[2] As if to signal divine favor, miracles attended the event: rainstorms that had drenched the city continuously for days suddenly stopped during the procession itself and then resumed immediately afterward. An epidemic of plague that had struck the city suddenly subsided, and an ailing six-year-old boy whose father was present at the translation of the relics was completely healed of a malady in his intestines.[3] High ceremonial united prince, city, church and people in a powerful act of veneration and devotion; the

---

[1] Duerloo, "Pietas Albertina," p. 10; Van Wyhe, "Court and Convent."
[2] *Historia beatorum martyrum Gorcumiensium*, pp. 283–284.
[3] *Historia beatorum martyrum Gorcumiensium*, p. 284; Claessens, *Geschiedenis der martelaren van Gorkum*, pp. 120–121.

Habsburg regime's talent for impressive display once again served both to express and to reinforce religious solidarity.[4]

The 1618 translation ceremony of the relics of the Gorinchem martyrs took place in Brussels's Franciscan conventual church, just over a block away from the Grand Place, where, not quite one hundred years earlier in an equally impressive display, Hendrik Vos and Johannes van den Esschen had been executed for their evangelical beliefs. Like their Franciscan confreres, those two Augustinian monks had also died for their faith. In Catholic eyes, of course, Vos and Van den Esschen were heretics, but in the Protestant imagination they too were heroic believers who had been killed for their convictions. One of the principal results of the Reformation in the Low Countries was that all sides could justifiably claim their martyrs.

Despite the ninety-five years that separated these two events, on the surface some things seemed quite the same: Brussels was still the capital of the Habsburg Netherlands and that storied dynasty remained as ever vigorous princely supporters of the Catholic Church who enlisted the help of its clerical hierarchy in their state-building ambitions. As had been the case in 1523, in 1618 there was barely any religious dissent in the Habsburg Netherlands at all. Popular devotion, so widespread and robust in the early 1500s, seemed equally vital and heartfelt in the early seventeenth century as well. An observer could be well forgiven for believing that *reformatio*, the continuous tradition of spiritual improvement and renewal that had long characterized Latin Christendom, had served the Netherlands well.

But of course everything had changed. The Habsburg Netherlands, no longer the proud and prosperous composite state so laboriously and precariously forged by Charles V and his ancestors, had in the intervening decades lost its northern territories to rebellion and heresy. That heresy that had seemed so marginal in 1523 had grown much more powerful, dangerous and formidable, eventually backed by armies and supported by an entirely new state. That new state, composed of seven breakaway provinces, was an anomaly whose polity was neither fish nor fowl, not quite a republic but not a monarchy either, officially Reformed but bewilderingly pluralist. This outcome, the consequence of reformation and war, was not foreseen by anyone, not by the most wild-eyed zealot and not by the shrewdest prelate. In the space of a little over a century religious dissent and political discontent brought an end to the Habsburg effort to strengthen dynastic power in the entire Low Countries. And, as

---

[4] Thøfner, *Common Art*, pp. 255–331.

was the case elsewhere in Europe, in this small corner of the continent Christendom splintered permanently into multiple Christianities.

This account of the Reformation in the Low Countries ends around the year 1620 because after then it becomes two narratives. Like all narratives it has sought to impose some coherent order on a complicated and messy historical phenomenon and is therefore to that degree constructed and artificial. In fact, the Reformation in the Low Countries was a congeries of thousands of local stories and circumstances with variations as numerous and localized as the region itself. The duchy of Luxemburg was virtually untouched by Protestant agitation, while the county of Flanders fairly seethed with it. Lille remained relatively placid through all the upheavals, while Amsterdam often found itself in the thick of them all. Most farmers in rural Namur appeared unmoved by the ranting of unruly heretics, while many of their counterparts in Friesland embraced preaching evangelicals as divinely guided prophets. Iconoclastic fury ravaged the churches of Ghent but left nearby Bruges untouched. For every generalization that can be made about the Reformation in the Netherlands, exceptions can be found. The decentralized nature of authority in the Low Countries, which the Habsburg dynasty tried to counteract, meant for fissiparous reformation.

Nevertheless, for all the region's particularism, a larger trajectory of religious change can be traced precisely because of that Habsburg effort to increase dynastic power; politics and religion were inextricably intertwined. This meant that reformation affected virtually all Netherlanders, including the majority who remained loyal to the traditional church, at one point or another in the course of the sixteenth century. That impact may have been as mundane as a priest or preacher exhorting them from the pulpit to live more godly lives, or as dramatic as armed assaults on their churches, their communities or even their lives. For many Netherlanders reformation of all kinds brought displacement, catastrophe, confusion or terror; for others it brought answers, liberation, solace or newfound devotion. For virtually everyone, even those indifferent to the profound existential and spiritual questions that reformation in all its guises provoked, it brought war, political change and ecclesiastical transformation.

Reformation in the Low Countries arose out of the rich and venerable traditions, practices and teachings of late medieval Latin Christendom. As scholars have noted, Christianity in the Low Countries at the beginning of the sixteenth century was not moribund or in decay; on the contrary, it was vital and multifaceted or, put another way, "modern."[5]

---

[5] Pollmann, *Catholic Identity and the Revolt of the Netherlands*, pp. 42–43.

The splendor, the devotion, the popular fervor, the materially rich fabric of the late medieval Christian church fully saturated the cultural and social landscape of the Netherlands. The church was truly catholic in that it comprised all baptized Christians and framed their understanding of the supernatural order of the universe; through its sacerdotal and sacramental power it provided everyone with a conduit between the living and the dead. It was also catholic in its supple embrace of a wide array of unofficial beliefs and practices that could vary considerably according to local needs and circumstances.

It was precisely this richness that caused some Christians, those who took their faith very seriously, to question and to criticize. In the fourteenth and fifteenth centuries there were already in the Low Countries stirrings of dissatisfaction among those who sought a truer, deeper piety. Movements such as the Beguines and the Modern Devotion were symptomatic of a spiritual hunger among some Netherlandish Christians, a small number to be sure, for more than what traditional quotidian religion could offer them. These Christians, engaging in practices of self-segregation, study, service and practical devotion rooted in the monastic tradition, did not so much dissent from traditional religion as supplement it with their own habits of devotion. The Beguines and the Modern Devout, in their collective efforts at imitating the life of Christ, formed a distinctly Netherlandish religious sensibility that both augmented traditional everyday religion and also, at least implicitly, criticized it.

Other Netherlandish Christians were much more open in their criticism of some contemporary religious practices. Serious-minded scholars and churchmen questioned customs and ideas that seemed at variance with what scripture taught. Marshaling their scholarship and erudition in the service of *reformatio*, they advocated for a Christianity based on what they saw as biblical norms, norms supposed to apply to everyone, from the ordinary parishioner to the pope himself. Thanks in part to the fame of its native son Erasmus, the Netherlands proved especially receptive to this learned critique; the region was culturally more urban and literate than most in Europe and its commercial economy traded in new ideas as well as new goods.

By 1520 some of the ideas circulating along those Netherlandish trade routes were the evangelical dissents coming out of the German lands. Lutheran and Zwinglian messages about salvation, the sacraments, the Bible and the authority of the clergy found a hearing among those Netherlandish Christians who were growing spiritually dissatisfied with traditional religion. In the power and wealth of the church there was much to criticize, and the evangelical message attracted those discontented with its doctrinal and cultural claims. These Netherlandish evangelicals read their Bibles, questioned the sacraments, and wondered if the grand, centuries-old ecclesiastical intermediary between them and God was truly necessary.

They picked and chose from among the reforming programs coming from the east and did not espouse a uniform set of ideas or beliefs. By the 1530s other discontented Netherlanders were coming to even more radical conclusions, heeding prophets whose extreme biblical literalism led them to foresee the imminent coming of the day of judgment. The Anabaptists' protest became social as well as religious and a handful of them indulged in extreme theocratic experiments that sparked horror among most Christians and led to their undoing. The Habsburg dynasty that ruled over the Low Countries responded to the evangelical and Anabaptist challenge by branding both groups heretical and actively working at their extermination. The judicial machinery used to suppress heresy sparked much outcry for both its severity and its indifference to local judicial sensibilities; for the Netherlands' regional political elites it became one more grievance against an aggrandizing central government that seemed indifferent to local rights.

By the middle of the sixteenth century, partly in response to the harshness of the legal measures taken against heresy, the nature of religious change in the Low Countries evolved into more organized and well-defined streams. The various groupings calling for the reformation of souls and churches began to establish programs, creeds, structures and procedures in order to realize their particular visions of how to restore Christianity. These new movements would try to set careful doctrinal boundaries among each other so as to distinguish themselves as the true church from all other false sects, heresies and idolatries. Mennonite or *Doopsgezind* Christianity foreswore its revolutionary antecedents and instead turned inward, focusing intensely on personal and communal piety and eschewing engagement with a sinful world, an impulse it shared with such pre-Reformation lay movements as the Modern Devotion and the Beguines. Reformed Christianity, coming out of the Swiss cities, preached a biblically centered message and offered an alternative vision of a simplified yet adaptable ecclesiology designed to make believers godlier. And Tridentine Catholicism, now equipped with a solid and specific program of ecclesiastical improvement and renewed devotion, set about restoring the vigor and vitality of the traditional church. All three of these broad confessional strains would dominate Netherlandish religious life through the second half of the century.

This confessionalization of multiple Christianities, with its attendant hardening of stances, boundaries and polarizations, would contribute to the most far-reaching effect of reformation on the Netherlands – war.

When they erupted in the late 1560s, the Netherlandish wars were initially about the relationship between central power and local rights – that is, they were a contest between the Habsburgs and regional political elites over dominance of the region.[6] The Habsburg composite state built up in the course of the 1500s had seriously threatened the customary privileges and dominance enjoyed by the native aristocracy and urban patriciate. Reformation became an integral part of the conflict, however, when local elites protested the unrelenting nature of the central government's anti-heresy edicts and the high-handed way it reformed the region's episcopal structures. Confessional polarization, the gradual formation of boundaries and attitudes, fed antagonisms still further. The destructive violence that broke out in 1566 was the result of a burgeoning Reformed zealotry that sought to replace "idolatry" with "true" religion. Philip II responded by imposing a draconian regime that sought to quash rebellion and heresy once and for all. Instead heresy and rebellion went into exile, stiffened their resolve and a general armed revolt against his rule broke out, led by grandees in uneasy alliance with Reformed militants. Within a few years that alliance fell apart under the pressure of confessional animosities and the revolt turned into a civil war. The political rebels, with the indispensable help of their Reformed allies, gained control of a substantial part of the Low Countries for about a decade or so. In the provinces under insurgent control revolutionary reformation was instituted, disestablishing the Catholic church and imposing in its place Reformed Christianity. Then in the mid-1580s a reinvigorated Spanish military reasserted royal control over most of the southern provinces, and the rebellion was limited to seven northern provinces.

Across this military frontier arose what became by the dawn of the seventeenth century two states, an independent republic in the north and a restored Habsburg regime in the south. It was also a schism that resulted in the permanent religious division of the Low Countries. Yet even with schism there were continuities. In the Southern Netherlands state and church recommenced the program of vigorous Catholic reformation that had begun long before conflict broke out; the Catholic church there eventually emerged from reformation and war as a vastly reinvigorated institution. Lay piety reached levels of enthusiasm not seen since the later Middle Ages. In the Dutch Republic reformation was a much more variegated affair, producing by 1600 one official Reformed public church and a host of tolerated confessions; it was in many respects a continuation of the Netherlands' eclectic reformation of the previous century. It took fifty years of internal wrangling before the public church fully established

---

[6] De Schepper, "The Burgundian–Habsburg Netherlands," pp. 526–527.

its confessional orthodoxy, and not without nearly tearing the new state apart in the process. If the success of reformation can be defined in terms of the creation of a spiritually unified population under the aegis of a revitalized church, then arguably the Southern Netherlands enjoyed a much more successful reformation than the Dutch Republic ever did.

The Reformation in the Low Countries was many things at once. Sometimes it was a matter of devout individual or group Bible lecture or heartfelt veneration of a saint, sometimes it was an affair of high politics in the councils of court, occasionally it was a matter of state or mob violence. It might have been a renewed fervor for the mysteries of the Eucharist or an insight that came from an evangelical sermon on a biblical passage. Here, as everywhere else, it was heresy and war and revelation and liberation. Indeed in the story of reformation we see much of the contours and features of the sixteenth-century Netherlands. It was a region that was open, geographically and economically, to outside influences; from the German and French hinterlands all manner of ideas flowed in, including notions of religious reform. It was a society that was unusually urban and literate. In the teeming cities of the Low Countries words, ideas and proposals were read about, talked about, exchanged and circulated with dizzying speed. It was a culture where ordinary folk clearly felt a strong sense of agency, so that a reformation from below erupted from significant popular sympathy for evangelical ideas and demands to participate more in the life of the church. It was a region where power was traditionally decentralized and shared; when the Habsburg dynasty tried to impose its political will, which included religious uniformity, on the population local authorities and religious dissidents rebelled in the most violent possible way. These qualities made the Reformation in the Low Countries extremely divisive, so much so that it began in one polity and ended in two.

Over the longer term, the influence of the Netherlandish Reformation would be felt well beyond the borders of the Low Countries. The 1618–1619 Synod of Dordrecht, for example, for all its immediate relevance to the Republic's own internal ecclesiastical settlement, was an occasion of international interest and importance across Protestant Europe. Theologians from England, the Empire and Switzerland gathered there in a tense political atmosphere as armed confessional conflict had broken out in Bohemia, skirmishes that turned out to be the beginning of the destructive Thirty Years' War.[7] The vast majority of Reformed clergy in the rest of Europe accepted the canons of Dordrecht as normative and rejected Arminian theology, relegating its adherents to a marginalized

[7] Van Lieburg, *Synodestad*, pp. 51–74.

minority. Within the Church of England, however, a party its opponents labeled "Arminian" gained influence in the 1620s, pitting itself against a Puritan faction that wanted further reformation. The English Arminians had little in common with their Dutch namesakes aside from a shared antipathy toward high predestinarian theology; their disputes focused on internal Anglican matters of worship and clerical status rather than soteriology.[8]

Mennonitism, perhaps the most native if not the largest of all the Netherlandish reform movements, proved to be a particularly enduring and even globally successful form of Netherlandish Protestantism. Its spiritual descendants founded communities as they migrated first across Europe and then around the world, especially in the Americas. Likewise the Dutch Reformed church was one of the direct heirs of the Netherlandish Reformation, and like Mennonitism its eventual reach would extend worldwide. The public church followed the Dutch Republic as the latter traversed the globe as a colonial power in the seventeenth century, from Asia to Africa to the Americas. Under the auspices of the East and West India Companies, commercial enterprises that also took seriously the challenge of Christian mission, outposts of Dutch Reformed Protestantism would be planted during the seventeenth century in such far-flung regions as New Netherland, the Cape of Good Hope and Java, the first sustained Protestant effort to evangelize outside of Europe. These churches were principally intended to serve company personnel, but spreading the gospel was also an important aim. Missionaries booked some modest success at converting indigenous peoples, at least nominally, to Reformed Christianity, especially in the Asian colonies.[9] Nevertheless, the global reach of Reformed Protestantism never matched that of the early modern Catholic Church in either depth or breadth.

The Wider Context

The Reformation in the Netherlands was, of course, not purely Netherlandish. Precisely because of their geographic, economic and cultural openness, the Low Countries' experience of reformation in the sixteenth century was very much influenced by currents of religious change in the rest of Latin Christendom. In many respects its reformation was quite typical of religious transformation elsewhere in Europe, and in a few respects it was distinctive from it. The characteristics and

[8] Benedict, *Christ's Churches*, p. 324; Platt, *Britain and the Bestandstwisten*, pp. 204–216.
[9] Parker, "Reformed Protestantism," pp. 203–206; Noorlander, *Heaven's Wrath*.

consequences that attended religious upheaval in the Netherlands could also be found in other places. Reformation was a shared experience that ignored boundaries and polities.

The religious enthusiasm that characterized late medieval Netherlandish society and culture, for example, was part of a much wider European phenomenon. Layfolk everywhere eagerly participated in the sacramental and salvific tools and mechanisms that the Catholic Church and its clergy offered them. All over Latin Christendom stretched "an intricate industry of prayer," built up and expanded upon over the course of centuries, that offered to believers an impressive array of devotional customs and opportunities that could be at once spiritual and practical, individual and social.[10] The late medieval church provided an arena ample and flexible enough to address the religious desires and needs of baptized Christians everywhere, and Netherlanders were no different from other Europeans in taking eager advantage of this. The concomitant call for *reformatio*, for the moral regeneration of both souls and institutions, that was ringing through the Catholic ecclesiastical landscape echoed through the Low Countries as well. Christian humanism, which found a home all over Europe, received a warm reception here. Its most famous sixteenth-century embodiment, the humanist Erasmus, may have been born a Netherlander, but his fame and career were decidedly European.

Another characteristic of the Netherlandish Reformation, the significant degree of popular support reforming ideas received, can also be found in other places. Unlike in England, where vernacular Bible translations were banned, Dutch and French versions of sacred scripture were available to literate urban classes, and that custom of Bible lecture may have primed Netherlanders to be more receptive to evangelical ideas.[11] This was reformation from below, the enthusiasm for religious reform coming from an active minority within municipal populations who hoped for change. In this regard the highly urbanized Low Countries mirrored the experiences of many of the cities of the Holy Roman Empire and Switzerland. In towns such as Strasbourg, Nuremberg or Zurich evangelical ideas gained enough traction and popularity to convince magistracies to adopt policies of church reform in the 1520s and 1530s. A similar social dynamic could be found in Netherlandish towns, where calls for reform proved attractive to a significant minority. Unlike their imperial coreligionists, however, the best Netherlandish evangelicals could hope for

---

[10] MacCulloch, *Reformation*, p. 13; Cameron, *European Reformation*, pp. 9–19.
[11] Marshall, *Heretics and Believers*, p. 117.

from their civic magistracies was protection from the worst exactions of anti-heresy laws, as was the case in Antwerp, and not outright adoption of church reform. Imperial free cities, by contrast, had the power to choose their own courses of religious reform. In the Netherlands the "reformation in the cities" was never divorced from the larger political and constitutional context. No city could legislate its own religious identity, though arguably the Calvinist republics of the 1570s and 1580s in Flanders and Brabant were an attempt at autonomous civic reformation. In those cities Reformed militants succeeded in pushing their agenda of church reform as long as they had backing from municipal governments, an experiment that would end with Parma's reconquest of Flanders and Brabant in 1585 and the region's subsequent recatholicization.[12]

Thanks to its proximity to the Empire the Netherlands also shared in the *Wildwuchs* or "wild growth" of evangelical ideas spread by preaching and print in the early decades of the Reformation. This was especially true of the more radically biblicist beliefs espoused by the various Anabaptist movements; some scholars of Anabaptism have argued that one regional variant, Melchiorite apocalypticism, can be said to have the Low Countries, in addition to northern Germany, as its birthing grounds.[13] With the rise of Mennonite and *Doopsgezind* groups starting in the 1540s the Netherlands found its own variation of the kinds of gathered, self-segregating religious communities reminiscent of the Hutterites of central Europe, who de-radicalized and turned inward, concentrating on reforming themselves rather than the world.[14]

Reformed Protestantism first spread across Europe, including the Low Countries, in the middle of the sixteenth century. In each of the places where it took root, from Scotland to Poland, it developed its own localized characteristics. This was never a monolithic confession, to be sure, but across regions some similarities can be traced. Historians have particularly have been struck by parallels between the Netherlandish and French Reformations.[15] In very rough outline the two regions did indeed have comparable trajectories of religious change: evangelical ideas first gaining a following among intellectuals and urban populations, a crackdown on heresy by royal authority that forced many evangelicals to flee abroad, the rise of a militant Reformed movement by the 1550s, religious and political dissent against the crown coalescing into armed opposition and rebellion, destructive and bloody religious and civil war, and eventually a tenuous

[12] Marnef, "Dynamics of Reformed Religious Militancy," pp. 65–68.
[13] Depperman, Packull and Stayer, "From Monogenesis to Polygenesis," pp. 111–121.
[14] Driedger, "Anabaptism and Religious Radicalism," pp. 223–226.
[15] See, for example, the conference volume *Reformation, Revolt and Civil War in France and the Low Countries*.

peace that allowed for some degree of religious coexistence.[16] Judith Pollmann has noted an important difference between the two reformations, however: while the French civil wars often saw eruptions of bloody popular violence against the Huguenots, most confessional violence in the Netherlands was committed by soldiers rather than civilians. The difference, she argues, was in the attitudes of the Catholic clergy. While French prelates and priests were inclined to incite their parishioners into attacks on heretics, their Netherlandish counterparts enjoined their flocks instead to penitence as a response to heresy. This difference in pastoral strategies led to strikingly different levels of popular sectarian violence among ordinary Christians in each country.[17] The French "rites of violence" first so perceptively observed by Natalie Zemon Davis did not have a widespread counterpart in the Netherlands.[18]

When Reformed Protestantism first arose in a small clutch of territories in the Holy Roman Empire, principally the Palatinate and lower Rhenish lands, its dynamics were starkly different than those of Netherlandish Reformed Protestantism. Whereas in the Low Countries, Reformed Protestantism was a popular movement that arose from below, this "Second Reformation" in the Empire was primarily a princely one, as rulers newly converted from Lutheranism attempted to impose their new faith on subject populations.[19] Church elites and political elites in these lands cooperated closely to establish Reformed models of creeds, catechisms, church discipline and schools. This was a degree of political backing and collaboration of which Reformed divines in the Dutch Republic could only have been envious. Still, in both cases success was mixed: there was a fair amount of popular indifference, even resistance, to efforts at instilling moral reform and radical changes to church liturgy and practice.[20]

Another realm where Reformed Protestantism provoked substantial religious and political change was the kingdom of Scotland. Here also, as was the case in France and the Netherlands, the desire for religious reform was thoroughly entwined with aristocratic rivalries and court politics. In the Scottish case, however, political revolution was much more successful in toppling the Catholic Church throughout the entire kingdom. A weak monarchy in the second half of the sixteenth century allowed for the official introduction of Reformed Protestantism there in

---

[16] Roberts, "France," pp. 102–123; Holt, *French Wars of Religion*.
[17] Pollmann, "Countering the Reformation in France and the Netherlands."
[18] Davis, "Rites of Violence."
[19] Benedict, *Christ's Churches Purely Reformed*, pp. 202–229; Cohn, "Territorial Princes in Germany's Second Reformation."
[20] Schilling, "Second Reformation."

1560. A halting but determined process of official reformation ensued, attended by noble factions, civil war and dynastic intrigue, but by the end of the century the Scottish kirk, with its distinctive episcopal-presbyterian hybrid polity, had effectively replaced the Catholic Church at the heart of the kingdom's religious culture.[21] Jane Dawson has plausibly argued, however, that Protestant reformation in Scotland came at the cost of ecclesiastical autonomy; the new, reformed polity that emerged by the 1580s, though loudly committed to the formation of a godly common-wealth, was not the independent counterbalance to the monarchy that the medieval church had been. The Stewart king James VI labored hard and successfully to mold and subordinate the kirk according to his own theological preferences and political interests (although under his succes-sor the Scots eventually rebelled this royal domination in the 1630s).[22] The Dutch Republic's political elites, by contrast, were less successful than the Stewart dynasty in imposing their own ecclesiastical vision on the Reformed church, which in many respects remained a cultural counter-weight to the ruling oligarchy, especially in Holland.

When it came to Catholic Reformation, the Low Countries certainly shared in the full panoply of efforts across Europe to reform the tradi-tional church, starting in the 1560s with local efforts to implement the canons of the Council of Trent.[23] After the split of the Netherlands into two states, Catholic reformation in the archducal southern Netherlands followed along lines parallel to those of other states in Catholic Europe, as a collaboration among rulers, clergy and laity. Like the Catholic terri-tories in the Empire such as Würzburg and Bavaria, the revitalization of the church here was accomplished through the superintending of clergy, the introduction of new church orders (especially the Society of Jesus), the reform of morals and the encouragement of lay piety.[24] Catholic confessionalization aimed at creating a religiously unified population, though even in imperial Catholic states there were likewise small Protestant minorities. Like their confreres all over Catholic Europe, most Netherlandish bishops applied themselves conscientiously to the work of rejuvenation. An industrious archbishop like Mathias Hovius of Mechelen could certainly be compared to his Milanese counterpart Carlo Borromeo, who pursued an assiduous and ambitious program of reform in his own archdiocese.[25] In the Dutch Republic, by contrast, Catholics were a subaltern minority unable to enjoy the institutional support of the

[21] Graham, "Scotland."
[22] Dawson, *Scotland Re-formed*, pp. 332–335, 338–341.
[23] Bireley, *Refashioning of Catholicism*, pp. 25–69, 96–120.
[24] Forster, *Catholic Germany*, pp. 38–84.
[25] De Boer, *Conquest of the Soul*.

Counter-Reformation church except through more attenuated channels such as the religious orders and the Holland Mission. Nevertheless, despite obstacles, the orders and the Mission successfully reinvigorated Dutch Catholic life along Tridentine precepts with the substantial help of the laity, even though it was a faith community driven to the margins of the Republic's society.[26] Notwithstanding their depredations, Catholics in the Dutch Republic found ways to exercise their beliefs and rituals in ways that very much conformed, at least spiritually if not quite materially, to the broader Baroque Catholicism of early modern Europe.[27]

While the Southern Netherlands took the more traditional route of trying to root out and remove religious minorities from its society and impose confessional uniformity on its population, the Dutch Republic by contrast opted to manage its religious pluralism rather than erase it. Multiconfessionalism was not unique to the Republic; it was but one of many European states in the late sixteenth and early seventeenth centuries grappling with the novel problem of confessional coexistence within its borders. Across the northern parts of Europe many early modern states, even those that adopted a formal confessional identity, found themselves confronted with religious minorities. Although spiritual uniformity was the stated goal of virtually all polities, sometimes forcing conformity was simply not practicable. Some European rulers, like the regents of the Republic, opted for accommodation and management of religious diversity rather than suppression. These could range from church-sharing to private house chapels to *Auslauf*, allowing religious minorities to travel, sometimes across borders, to worship according to their conscience.[28] The Republic's polite fiction that belief was a matter of individual conscience, which allowed it to look the other way when religious minorities worshiped in private spaces, was an arrangement that could also be found in a variety of iterations in societies ranging from Ireland to Poland.[29] In managing religious pluralism this way the Republic was thus not unusual, but what struck outside observers perhaps most forcefully was how open the Republic's society was about these arrangements.[30] The tolerationist policies that characterized the Dutch Republic indicated that the new state's ruling elites were not interested in the creation of a confessional regime in cooperation with the privileged church. Unlike in the Southern Netherlands, here state-building was not

---

[26] Parker, *Faith on the Margins*, pp. 24–46.
[27] Lenarduzzi, *Katholiek in de Republiek*, pp. 143–244.
[28] Kaplan, *Divided by Faith*, pp. 127–234. For an interesting taxonomy of these multi-confessional arrangements, see Te Brake, *Religious War and Religious Police*, pp. 179–214.
[29] Kaplan, *Divided by Faith*, pp. 183–197.
[30] Bots, "Tolerantie of gecultiveerde tweedracht."

tied to the public church and there was little effort to impose social discipline, the reform of morals, on the population as a whole. Instead at most internal confessionalization within the Republic's different religious communities obtained. Historians have generally concluded that the confessionalization model of church–state collaboration to discipline and unify populations, as developed by historians of the Holy Roman Empire, has little applicability to the Dutch case.[31]

In many respects, therefore, the Reformation in the Low Countries paralleled religious developments elsewhere in sixteenth-century Europe; its broad contours, disruptions and outcomes found echoes in other European societies. What perhaps set the Netherlandish case apart from reformation elsewhere were two characteristics: the high degree of government persecution of religious dissidents, and the creation of a new state as a result of the region's religious wars. State judicial violence against religious dissidents was more extensive and rigorous in the Low Countries than anywhere else in Europe, though it ultimately failed in suppressing that dissent, at least in part. The Habsburg central government executed far more heretics in the Netherlands than its French or English counterparts; estimates place two-fifths of all the Protestant executions in Europe from the 1520s to the 1560s in the Netherlands; the Duke of Alba's Council of Troubles killed another thousand in the period 1567–1572.[32] The campaign against heresy was a part of Habsburg state-building in the Netherlands; the chief objection of the gentry in their "Compromise" petition of 1566 was the exactions of what it called "the inquisition." Arguably the very severity of that persecution, and its associations with tyranny and the deprivation of liberty, was what led to the tolerationist attitudes of the Dutch Republic. Likewise in the archducal Netherlands, where Habsburg rule continued, the official approach to dealing with heresy became more supple and less bloodthirsty after the exactions of the sixteenth century.

The Dutch Republic itself was the other peculiarity of the Reformation in the Low Countries. All over northern Europe states changed their religious complexion as a result of the Reformation. Only in the Netherlands, however, did the bloody civil wars, fueled in part by religion, result in the creation of a completely new state, thereby permanently altering the political map of early modern Europe. The stalemating of the military frontier between the insurgent provinces and the Habsburg government by the late 1580s effectively created a new polity in the

---

[31] Mörke, "'Konfessionaliserung' als politisch-soziales Prinzip?"; Pettegree, "Confessionalization in North Western Europe."

[32] Monter, "Heresy Executions in Reformation Europe"; Duke, "The 'Inquisition' and the Repression of Religious Dissent in the Habsburg Netherlands 1521–1566," in *Dissident Identities*, pp. 100–102.

independent north, a development that was solidified and confirmed by the Twelve Years Truce in 1609. In retrospect the Dutch Republic, because of its official Protestantism, has been come to be seen as the principal heir of the Netherlandish Reformation, but the revitalized Catholicism of the Southern Netherlands was an equally important legacy of that Reformation. As this study has been at pains to point out, reformation, understood as sixteenth-century religious change more broadly, engulfed and shaped the whole of the Low Countries. By 1620, because of religion and the questions it engendered, the political landscape of this small corner of Europe looked vastly different than it had just a century earlier. Two states, one Catholic and the other Protestant, would enter the modern era each with its own distinct cultural identity. Those separate identities, formed in the cauldron of reformation and war, have persisted, down even to this more secular and less sectarian age.

Bibliography

Abels, P. H. A. M. *Nieuw en ongezien: Kerk en samenleving in de classis Delft en Delfland 1572–1621*. Vol. 2. Delft: Eburon, 1994.

Akerboom, Dirk, and Marcel Gielis, "'A New Song Shall Begin Here … ': The Martyrdom of Luther's Followers among Antwerp's Augustinians on July 1, 1523 and Luther's Response." *More Than a Memory: The Discourse of Martyrdom and the Construction of Christian Identity in the History of Christianity*. Ed. Johan Leemans. Leuven: Peeters, 2005, pp. 243–270.

Allen, P. S., ed. *Opus Epistolarum Des: Erasmi Roterodami*. Vol. 8. Oxford: Oxford University Press, 1934.

Arblaster, Paul. *Antwerp and the World: Richard Verstegan and the International Culture of Catholic Reformation*. Leuven: Leuven University Press, 2004.

——— "The Archdukes and the Northern Counter-Reformation." *Albert and Isabella 1598–1621: Essays*. Ed. Werner Thomas and Luc Duerloo. Turnhout: Brepols, 1998, pp. 87–92.

——— *A History of the Low Countries*. Basingstoke: Palgrave Macmillan, 2006.

Den Arminiaenschen Dreck-waghen. Amsterdam, 1619.

Arnade, Peter. *Beggars, Iconoclasts and Civic Patriots: The Political Culture of the Dutch Revolt*. Ithaca, NY: Cornell University Press, 2008.

Arndt, Johannes. *Das Heilige Römische Reich und die Niederlande 1566 bis 1648: Politisch- konfessionelle Verflechtung und Publizistik in Achtzigjährigen Krieg*. Köln: Böhlau, 1998.

Augustijn, Cornelis. "Anabaptism in the Netherlands: Another Look." *Mennonite Quarterly Review* 62 (1988): 197–210.

——— *Erasmus: His Life, Works, and Influence*. Toronto: University of Toronto Press, 1991.

——— "Niederlande." *Theologische Realenzyklopädie* 24 (1994): 474–502.

——— "De opmars van de calvinistische beweging in de Nederlanden." *Theoretische geschiedenis* 20 (1993): 424–438.

Backhouse, Marcel. *Beeldenstorm en bosgeuzen in het Westkwartier (1566–1568)*. Kortrijk: Koninklijke Geschied- en Oudheidkundige Kring, 1971.

——— *The Flemish and Walloon Congregations at Sandwich during the Reign of Elizabeth I (1561–1503)*. Brussels: Paleis der Academiën, 1995.

Bakhuizen van den Brink, J. N., ed. *De nederlandse belijdenisgescrhiften*. Amsterdam: Ton Bolland, 1976.

Bangs, Carl. *Arminius: A Study in the Dutch Reformation*. Eugene: Wipf and Stock, 1998.

Bauwens, Marcel. "Restoration and Reform of the Parish after Trent: The Case of Saint James in Ghent (1561–1630)." *Church, Censorship and Reform in the Early Modern Habsburg Netherlands.* Ed. Violet Soen, Dries Vanysacker and Wim François. Turnhout: Brepols, 2017, pp. 167–185.

Beatis, Antonio de. *The Travel Journal of Antonio de Beatis: Germany, Switzerland, the Low Countries, France and Italy, 1517–1518.* Ed. J. R. Hale. London: Hakluyt Society, 1979.

Begheyn, Paul. "The Jesuits in the Low Countries 1540–1773: Apostles of the Printing Press." *The Jesuits of the Low Countries: Identity and Impact (1540–1773).* Ed. Rob Faesen and Leo Kenis. Leuven: Peeters, 2012, pp. 129–138.

Benedict, Philip. *Christ's Churches Purely Reformed: A Social History of Calvinism.* New Haven, CT: Yale University Press, 2002.

Benedict, Philip, Guido Marnef, Henk van Nierop and Marc Venard, eds. *Reformation, Revolt and Civil War in France and the Netherlands 1555–1585.* Amsterdam: Koninklijke Akademie van Wetenschappen, 1999.

Bergsma, W. "The Low Countries." *The Reformation in National Context.* Ed. Bob Scriber, Roy Porter and Mikuláš Teich. Cambridge: Cambridge University Press, 1994, pp. 67–79.

Tussen Gideonsbende en publieke kerk: Een studie over het gereformeerd protestantisme in Friesland, 1580–1650. Hilversum: Verloren, 1999.

Beyen, Marnix, Judith Pollmann and Henk te Velde. *De Lage Landen: Een geschiedenis voor vandaag.* Rekkem: Ons Erfdeel, 2021.

Bijsterveld, A. J. A. *Laveren tussen kerk en wereld: De pastoors van Noord-Brabant 1400–1570.* Amsterdam: VU Uitgeverij, 1993.

Bireley, Robert. *The Refashioning of Catholicism, 1450–1700.* Washington, DC: Catholic University Press, 1999.

Blockmans, Wim. *Emperor Charles V: 1500–1558.* London: Arnold, 2002.

Blockmans, Wim, and Walter Prevenier. *The Burgundian Netherlands.* Cambridge: Cambridge University Press, 1986.

Blom, J. C. H., and E. Lamberts, eds. *History of the Low Countries.* New York: Berghahn, 1999.

Blondé, Bruno, Mark Boone and Anne-Laure van Bruaene, eds. *City and Society in the Low Countries.* Cambridge: Cambridge University Press, 2018.

Bodian, Miriam. *Hebrews of the Portuguese Nation: Conversos and Community in Early Modern Amsterdam.* Bloomington: Indiana University Press, 1999.

Boer, Wietse de. *The Conquest of the Soul: Confession, Discipline, and Public Order in Counter-Reformation Milan.* Leiden: Brill, 2001.

Bogaers, Llewellyn. *Aards, betrokken en zelfbewust: De verwervenheid van cultuur en religie in katholieke Utrecht, 1300–1600.* Vol. 1. Utrecht: Levend Verleden, 2008.

Boogman, J. C. "The Union of Utrecht: Its Genesis and Consequences." *BMGN* 91 (1974): 377–407.

Bosch, Gerrit vanden. "Saving Souls in the Dutch Vineyard: The Missio Hollandica of the Jesuits (1592–1773)." *Jesuits of the Low Countries: Identity and Impact (1540–1773).* Ed. Rob Faesen and Leo Kenis. Leuven: Peeters, 2012, pp. 139–151.

Bots, Hans. "Tolerantie of gecultiveerde tweedracht: Het beeld van de Nederlandse tolerantie bij buitenlanders in de zeventiende en achttiende eeuw." *BMGN* 107 (1992): 657–669.

Braekman, E. M. *Guy de Brès : Un Réformateur en Belgique et dans le nord de la France (1522–1567)*. Mons: Cercle Archéologique, 2014.

Brake, Wayne P. te. *Religious War and Religious Peace in Early Modern Europe*. Cambridge: Cambridge University Press, 2017.

Brall, Carsten. *Konfessionelle Theologie und Migration: Die Antwerpener Gemeinde Augsburger Konfession im 16. Jahrhundert*. Göttingen: Vandenhoeck & Ruprecht, 2017.

Bremmer, R. H. "De nationale betekenis van de Synode van Dordrecht (1578)." *Nationale Synode van Dordrecht (1578)*. Ed. D. Nauta and J. P. van Dooren. Amsterdam: Buijten & Schipperheijn, 1978, pp. 68–117.

Briels, J. *Zuid-Nederlanders in de Republiek 1572–1630: Een demografische en cultuurhistorische studie*. Sint-Niklaas: Dante, 1985.

Bromley, J. S. "The Rise and Fall of the Dutch Republic." *Historical Journal* 22 (1979): 985–995.

Bruaene, Anne-Laure van. "The Habsburg Theatre State, Court, City and the Performance of Identity in the Early Modern Southern Low Countries." *Networks, Region and Nations: Shaping Identities in the Low Countries, 1300–1650*. Ed. Robert Stein and Judith Pollmann. Leiden: Brill, 2010, pp. 131–149.

Om beters wille: Rederijkerskamers en de stedelijke cultuur in de Zuidelijke Nederlanden (1400–1650). Amsterdam: Amsterdam University Press, 2008.

Bruin, C. C. de, and F. G. M. Broeyer. *De Statenbijbel en zijn voorgangers*. Haarlem: Nederlands Bijbelgenootschap, 1993.

Cameron, Euan. *The European Reformation*. Oxford: Clarendon, 1991.

Cameron, James K. "Humanism in the Low Countries." *The Impact of Humanism on Western Europe*. Ed. Anthony Goodman and Angus MacKay. London: Longman, 1990, pp. 137–163.

Caspers, Charles M. A. *De eucharistische vroomheid en het feest van Sacramentsdag in de Nederlanden tijdens de late middeleeuwen*. Leuven: Peeters, 1992.

"Indulgences in the Low Countries, c. 1300–c.1500." *Promissory Notes on the Treasury of Merits: Indulgences in Late Medieval Europe*. Ed. R. N. Swanson. Leiden: Brill, 2006, pp. 65–99.

Christman, Robert. "Early Modern German Historians Confront the Reformation's First Executions." *Archaeologies of Confession: Writing the German Reformation 1517–2017*. Ed. Carina L. Johnson, David M. Luebke, Marjorie Elizabeth Plummer and Jesse Spohnholz. New York: Berghahn, 2017, pp. 242–261.

Christman, Victoria. *Pragmatic Toleration: The Politics of Religious Heterodoxy in Early Reformation Antwerp 1515–1555*. Rochester: University of Rochester Press, 2015.

Claessens, P. *Geschiedenis der martelaren van Gorkum, die in 1572 voor het Rooms-Katholieke geloof gestorven zijn*. Mechelen: Ryckmans-Van Deuren, 1867.

Clark, Geoffrey. "An Urban Study during the Revolt of the Netherlands: Valenciennes 1540–1570." PhD dissertation, Columbia University, 1972.

Cloet, Michel. *Het bisdom Gent (1559–1991): Vier eeuwen geschiedenis.* Gent: Vanmelle, 1992.

"De gevolgen van de scheiding der Nederlanden op religieus, cultureel en mentaal gebied, van circa 1600 tot 1650." *1585: op gescheiden wegen ... Handelingen van het colloquium over de scheiding der Nederlanden, gehouden op 22–23 november 1985 te Brussel.* Ed. J. Craeybeckx. Leuven: Peeters, 1988, pp. 53–78.

Karel-Filips de Rodoan en het bisdom Brugge tijdens zijn episcopaat (1602–1616). Brussels: Paleis der Academiën, 1970.

"De Kerk en haar invloed." *België in de 17de Eeuw: De Spaanse Nederlanden en het prinsbisdom Luik.* Vol. 2. Ed. Paul Janssens. Ghent: Snoeck, 2006, pp. 11–62.

"Een kwarteeuw historische produktie in België betreffende de religieuze geschiedenis van de Nieuwe Tijd." *Trajecta* 5 (1995): 198–223.

"La religion populaire dans les Pays-Bas méridionaux au xviiᵉ siècle." *Revue du Nord* 67 (1985): 923–954.

Cohn, Henry J. "The Territorial Princes in Germany's Second Reformation, 1559–1622." *International Calvinism, 1541–1715.* Ed. Menna Prestwich. Oxford: Clarendon, 1985, pp. 135–165.

Cools, Hans. "De Beeldenstorm." *De Reformatie: Breuk in de Europese geschiedenis en cultuur.* Ed. Huib Leeuwenberg, Henk Slechte and Theo van Staalduine. Zutphen: Walburg, 2017, pp. 160–169.

"Bishops in the Habsburg Netherlands on the Eve of Catholic Renewal, 1515–59." *Episcopal Reform and Politics in Early Modern Europe.* Ed. Jennifer Mara DeSilva. Kirksville: Truman State University Press, 2012, pp. 46–62.

Cramer, Samuel, and Frederik Pijper, eds. *Bibliotheca Reformatoria Neerlandica: Geschriften uit den tijd der Hervorming in de Nederlanden.* Vol. 8. Den Haag: Martinus Nijhoff, 1911.

Crespin, Jean. *Histoire des martyrs persecutez et mis a mort pour la vérité de l'Évangile, depuis le temps des apostres jusques à present.* Toulouse: Chauvin, 1889.

Crew, Phyllis Mack. *Calvinist Preaching and Iconoclasm in the Netherlands 1544–1569.* Cambridge: Cambridge University Press, 1978.

Dagboek van Broeder Wouter Jacobsz (Gualtherus Jacobi Masius) Prior van Stein. Ed. I. H. van Eeghen. 2 vols. Groningen: Wolters, 1959.

Darby, Graham, ed. *The Origins and Development of the Dutch Revolt.* London: Routledge, 2001.

Davis, Natalie Zemon. "The Rites of Violence: Religious Riot in Sixteenth-Century France." *Past & Present* 59 (1973): 51–91.

Dawson, Jane. *Scotland Re-formed, 1488–1587.* Edinburgh: Edinburgh University Press, 2007.

Decavele, Johan. *De dageraad van de Reformatie in Vlaanderen (1520–1565).* Brussels: Paleis der Academiën, 1975.

"Historiografie van het zestiende-eeuws Protestantisme in Belgie." *NAKG* 62 (1982): 1–27.

"Kerk en geloofsbeleving onder druk aan de vooravond van de Reformatietijd." *Handelingen voor het genootschap voor geschiedenis* 140 (2009): 3–92.

"Vroege reformatorische bedrijvigheid in de grote Nederlandse steden: Claes van der Elst te Brussel, Antwerpen, Amsterdam en Leiden (1524–1528)." *NAKG* 70 (1990): 13–29.

Deppermann, Klaus. *Melchior Hoffman: Social Unrest and Apocalyptic Visions in the Age of Reformation.* Edinburgh: Clark, 1987.

Deppermann, Klaus, Werner Packull and James Stayer. "From Monogenesis to Polygenesis: The Historical Discussion of Anabaptist Origins." *Mennonite Quarterly Review* 49 (1975): 83–121.

Despretz, André. "De instauratie der Gentse Calvinistische Republiek (1577–1579)." *Handelingen van de maatschappij voor geschiedenis en oudheidkunde te Gent* 17 (1963): 119–229.

Deursen, A. Th. van. *Bavianen en slijkgeuzen: Kerk en kerkvolk ten tijde van Maurits en Oldenbarnevelt.* Franeker: Van Wijnen, 1998.

Deyon, Solange, and Alain Lottin. *Les "Casseurs" de l'Été 1566: L'iconoclasme dans le Nord.* Paris: Hachette, 1981.

Dickens, A. G., and John Tonkin. *The Reformation in Historical Thought.* Cambridge, MA: Harvard University Press, 1985.

Dierickx, M. "Het begin van de Katholieke Reformatie." *Algemene Geschiedenis der Nederlanden.* Vol. 4. Ed. J. A. van Houtte, F. Niermeyer, J. Presser, J. Romein, and H. van Werveke. Utrecht: De Haan, 1962, pp. 350–368.

L'Erection des Nouveaux Diocèses aux Pay-Bas, 1559–1570. Brussels: Renaissance du Livre, 1967.

De oprichting der nieuwe bisdommen in de Nederlanden onder Filips II 1559–1570. Utrecht: Het Spectrum, 1950.

Dieterich, D. Henry. "Confraternities and Lay Leadership in Sixteenth-Century Liège." *Renaissance and Reformation* 13 (1989): 15–34.

Dirkse, P., ed. *Ketters en papen onder Filips II.* N.p.: Staatsuitgeverij, 1986.

Doedens, Anne, and Jan Houter. *De Watergeuzen: Een vergeten geschiedenis, 1568–1575.* Zutphen: Walburg, 2018.

Donaldson, B. C. *Dutch: A Linguistic History of Holland and Belgium.* The Hague: Martinus Nijhoff, 1983.

Driedger, Michael. "Against the 'Radical Reformation': On the Continuity between Early Modern Heresy-Making and Modern Historiography." *Radicalism and Dissent in the World of Protestant Reform.* Ed. Bridget Heal and Anorthe Kremers. Göttingen: Vandenhoeck & Ruprecht, 2017, pp. 139–161.

"Anabaptism and Religious Radicalism." *The European Reformations.* Ed. Alec Ryrie. Basingstoke: Palgrave, 2006, pp. 212–231.

Duerloo, Luc. "Archducal Piety and Habsburg Power." *Albert and Isabella 1598–1621: Essays.* Ed. Werner Thomas and Luc Duerloo. Turnhout: Brepols, 1998, pp. 267–284.

Dynasty and Piety: Archduke Albert (1598–1621) and Habsburg Political Culture in an Age of Religious Wars. Farnham: Ashgate, 2012.

"Pietas Albertina: Dynastieke vroomheid en herbouw van het vorstelijke gezag." *BMGN* 112 (1997): 1–18.

Duerloo, Luc, and Marc Wingens. *Scherpenheuvel: Het Jeruzalem van de Lage Landen*. Leuven: Davidsfonds, 2002.

Duke, Alastair. *Dissident Identities in the Early Modern Low Countries*. Ed. Judith Pollmann and Andrew Spicer. Aldershot: Ashgate, 2009.

Reformation and Revolt in the Low Countries. London: Hambledon, 1990.

Duke, Alastair, Gillian Lewis and Andrew Pettegree, eds. *Calvinism in Europe 1540–1610: A Collection of Documents*. Manchester: Manchester University Press, 1992.

Dunthorne, Hugh. *Britain and the Dutch Revolt 1560–1700*. Cambridge: Cambridge University Press, 2013.

DuPlessis, Robert S. *Lille and the Dutch Revolt: Urban Stability in an Era of Revolution, 1500–1582*. Cambridge: Cambridge University Press, 1991.

Dupont-Bouchat, Marie-Sylvie. "La Repression de l'hérésie dans le Namurois au XVIe siècle." *Annales de la Société archéologique de Namur* 56 (1972): 179–230.

"La Répression de la sorcellerie dans le Duché de Luxembourg aux XVIe et XVIIe Siècles." *Prophètes et Sorciers dans les Pays Bas aux XVIe et XVIIe Siècle*. Ed. Marie-Sylvie Dupont-Bouchat et al. Paris: Hachette, 1978, pp. 41–154.

Dürer, Albrecht. *Diary of His Journey to the Netherlands 1520–1521*. Ed. J.-A. Goris and G. Marlier. Greenwich: New York Graphic Society, 1971.

Eijnatten, J. van, and F. A. van Lieburg. *Nederlandse religiegeschiedenis*. Hilversum: Verloren, 2005.

Eire, Carlos M. N. *War against the Idols: The Reformation of Worship from Erasmus to Calvin*. Cambridge: Cambridge University Press, 1986.

Engen, John van. "Late Medieval Anticlericalism: The Case of the New Devout." *Anticlericalism in Late Medieval and Early Modern Europe*. Ed. Peter Dykema. Leiden: Brill, 1993, pp. 19–52.

Sisters and Brothers of the Common Life: The Devotio Moderna and the World of the Later Middle Ages. Philadelphia: University of Pennsylvania Press, 2008.

Enno van Gelder, H. A. *Revolutionnaire Reformatie: De vestiging van de Gereformeerde Kerk in de Nederlandse gewesten, gedurende de eerste jaren van de Opstand tegen Filips II, 1575–1585*. Amsterdam: P. N. van Kampen en Zoon, 1943.

Erasmus, Desiderius. "The Praise of Folly." *The Praise of Folly and Other Writings*. Ed. Robert M. Adams. New York: Norton, 1989, pp. 3–87.

Esser, Raingard. *Niederländische Exulanten in England des 16. und frühen 17. Jahrhunderts*. Bonn: Duncker & Humblot, 1996.

Estes, James M., ed. *The Correspondence of Erasmus*. Vol. 10. Toronto: University of Toronto Press, 1992.

Fagel, Raymond. "The Origins of the Spanish Fury at Antwerp (1576): A Battle within City Walls." *Early Modern Low Countries* 4 (2020): 102–123.

Fagel, Raymond, and Joke Spaans. *Nonnen verdreven door Geuzen: Cathalina del Spiritu Sancto's verhaal over de vlucht van Nederlandse clarissen naar Lissabon*. Hilversum: Verloren, 2019.

Forster, Marc R. *Catholic Germany from the Reformation to the Enlightenment.* Basingstoke: Palgrave, 2007.

François, Wim. "De doopsgezinde Biestkensbijbel (1560) en de gereformeerde Deux-Aesbijbel (1562): Bijbelvertalingen voor de protestanten." *De Bijbel in de Lage Landen: Elf eeuwen van vertalen.* Ed. Paul Gillaerts. Heerenveen: Royal Jongbloed, 2015, pp. 304–341.

Frijhoff, Willem, and Marijke Spies. *1650: Hard-Won Unity: Dutch Culture in a European Perspective.* Assen: Van Gorcum, 2004.

Fudge, Thomas A. "Heresy and the Question of Hussites in the Southern Netherlands." *Campin in Context: Peinture et société dans la vallée de l'Escaut à l'époque de Robert Campin 1375–1445.* Ed. L. Nys and D. Vanwijnsberghe. Valenciennes: Presses universitaires de Valenciennes, 2007, pp. 73–88.

Führer, Jochen. *Die Kirchen- und antireformatorische Religionspolitik Kaiser Karls V. in den siebzehn Provinzen der Niederlande 1515–1555.* Leiden: Brill, 2014.

Gelderen, Martin van. *The Political Thought of the Dutch Revolt.* Cambridge: Cambridge University Press, 1992.

Gennip, Joep van. *Controversen in context: Een comparatief onderzoek naar de Nederlandstalige controversepublicaties van de jezuïeten in de zeventiende-eeuwse Republiek.* Hilversum: Verloren, 2014.

Geraerts, Jaap. *Patrons of the Old Faith: The Catholic Nobility in Utrecht and Guelders, c. 1580–1702.* Leiden: Brill, 2019.

"The Prosecution of Anabaptists in Holland, 1530–1566." *Mennonite Quarterly Review* 86 (2012): 5–47.

Gielis, Gert. "Een pleidooi voor klerikale herbronning: Ruard Tapper (1487–1559) en zijn ideën over kerkhervorming." *Religie, hervorming en controverse in de zestiende-eeuwse Nederlanden.* Ed. Violet Soen and Paul Knevel. Herzogenrath: Shaker, 2012, pp. 21–36.

"'Post exactam et diligentiam examinationem': How the Louvain Theologians Condemned Luther in 1519." *Annali di Storia della Università Italiane* 21 (2017): 121–134.

Gielis, Gert, and Violet Soen, "The Inquisitorial Office in the Sixteenth-Century Habsburg Netherlands: A Dynamic Perspective." *Journal of Ecclesiastical History* 66 (2015): 47–66.

Goosens, Aline. *Les Inquisitions modernes aux Pays-Bas méridionaux 1520–1633.* 2 vols. Brussels: Editions de l'Université de Bruxelles, 1997.

Gootjes, Nicolaas H. *The Belgic Confession: Its History and Sources.* Grand Rapids, MI: Baker, 2008.

Gorter, Peter. *Gereformeerde migranten: De religieuze identiteit van Nederlandse gereformeerde migrantengemeenten in de rijkssteden Frankfurt am Main, Aken en Keulen (1555–1600).* Hilversum: Verloren, 2021.

Gottschalk, Linda Stuckrath. *Pleading for Diversity: The Church Caspar Coolhaes Wanted.* Göttingen: Vandenhoeck & Ruprecht, 2017.

Graham, Michael. "Scotland." *The Reformation World.* Ed. Andrew Pettegree. London: Routledge, 2000, pp. 410–430.

Gregory, Brad S. *Salvation at Stake: Christian Martyrdom in Early Modern Europe.* Cambridge, MA: Harvard University Press, 1999.

Groenveld, S. "Mislukte matiging, 1575–1581." *De Tachtigjarige Oorlog.* Ed. S. Groenveld et al. Zutphen: Walburg, 2008, pp. 102–116.

Grochowina, Nicole. "Confessional Indifference in East Frisia." *Renaissance and Reformation Review* 7 (2005): 111–124.

Groenveld, S., and G. J. Schutte. *Delta 2: Nederlands verleden in vogelvlucht: De nieuwe tijd: 1500 tot 1830.* Groningen: Martinus Nijhoff, 1992.

Guicciardini, Lodovico. *The Description of the Low Countreys and the Provinces Thereof, Gathered into an Epitome out of the Historie of Lodouico Guicchardini.* Trans. Thomas Danett. London, 1593.

Gurp, Gerard van. *Reformatie in Brabant: Protestanten en katholieken in de Meierij van 's- Hertogenbosch, 1523–1634.* Hilversum: Verloren, 2013.

Haemstede, Adriaen van. *Geschiedenis der martelaren, die om de getuigenis der evangelische waarheid hun bloed gestort hebben.* Arnhem: Swaen, 1868.

Halkin, Léon-E. "Protestants des Pays-Bas et de la Principauté de Liège réfugiés à Strasbourg." *Strasbourg au coeur religieux du XVIe siècle.* Ed. Georges Livet et al. Strasbourg: Istra, 1977, pp. 297–307.

La Réforme en Belgique sous Charles-Quint. Brussels: La Renaissance du Livre, 1957.

Hamilton, Alastair. *The Family of Love.* Cambridge: J. Clarke, 1981.

Harline, Craig. "Actives and Contemplatives: The Female Religious of the Low Countries before and after Trent." *Catholic Historical Review* 81 (1994): 541–567.

Harline, Craig, and Eddy Put. *A Bishop's Tale: Mathias Hovius among His Flock in Seventeenth-Century Flanders.* New Haven, CT: Yale University Press, 2000.

Harms, Roeland. *Pamfletten en publieke opinie: Massamedia in de zeventiende eeuw.* Amsterdam: Amsterdam University Press, 2011.

Herwaarden, J. van and R. de Keyser. "Het gelovige volk in de late middeleeuwen." *AGN.* Vol. 4. Ed. D. P. Blok et al. Haarlem: Fibula-van Dishoeck, 1980, pp. 405–420.

Hibben, C. C. *Gouda in Revolt: Particularism and Pacifism in the Revolt of the Netherlands 1572–1588.* Utrecht: HES, 1983.

Hiebsch, Sabine. "The Coming of Age of the Lutheran Congregation in Early Modern Amsterdam." *Journal of Early Modern Christianity* 3 (2016): 1–29.

Hildebrand, P. *De Kapucijnen in de Nederlanden en het prinsbisdom Luik.* Antwerp: Archief der Kapucijnen, 1945.

Hollander, August den. "Edition History of the Deux Aes Bible." *Religious Minorities and Cultural Diversity in the Dutch Republic.* Ed. August den Hollander et al. Leiden: Brill, 2014, pp. 41–72.

De Nederlandse Bijbelvertaling 1522–1545. Nieuwkoop: De Graaf, 1997.

Holt, Mack P. *The French Wars of Religion, 1562–1629.* Cambridge: Cambridge University Press, 2005.

Hooijer, C. ed. *Oude kerkordeningen der Nederlandsche Hervormde Gemeente (1563–1638).* Zaltbommel: Joh. Noman, 1865.

Horst, Daniel R. *De Opstand in zwart-wit: Propagandaprenten uit de Nederlandse Opstand [1566–1584].* Zutphen: Walburg, 2003.

Houtte, J. A. van. *An Economic History of the Low Countries 800–1800.* New York: St. Martin's Press, 1977.

Huizinga, Johan. "How Holland Became a Nation." *Verzamelde werken.* Vol. 2. Ed. L. Brummel et al. Haarlem: Tjeenk Willink, 1948, pp. 266–283.

Ijsewijn, Josef. "The Coming of Humanism to the Low Countries." *Itinerarium Italicum: The Profile of the Italian Renaissance in the Mirror of Its European Translations.* Ed. Heiko A. Oberman and Thomas A. Brady Jr. Leiden: Brill, 1975, pp. 193–301.

"Humanism in the Low Countries." *Humanism in the Low Countries.* Ed. Josef Ijsewijn. Leuven: Leuven University Press, 2015, pp. 391–453.

Israel, Jonathan I. *The Dutch Republic: Its Rise, Greatness and Fall, 1477–1806.* Oxford: Clarendon, 1995.

Janse, Wim. "The Protestant Reformation in the Low Countries: Developments in Twentieth-Century Historiography." *Reformation and Renaissance Review* 6 (2004): 179–202.

Janssen, Geert H. *The Dutch Revolt and Catholic Exile in Reformation Europe.* Cambridge: Cambridge University Press, 2014.

Jelsma, A. J. *Adriaan van Haemstede en zijn martelaarsboek.* The Hague: Boekencentrum, 1970.

Jong, Otto de. *Nederlandse Kerkgeschiedenis.* Nijkerk: Callenbach, 1972.

Johnston, Andrew. "The Eclectic Reformation: Vernacular Evangelical Pamphlet Literature in the Dutch-Speaking Low Countries, 1520–1565." PhD dissertation, University of Southampton, 1986.

Jürgens, Henning P. *Johannes a Lasco in Ostfriesland: Das Werdegang eines europäischen Reformators.* Tübingen: Mohr Siebeck, 2002.

Kamen, Henry. *The Duke of Alba.* New Haven, CT: Yale University Press, 2004.

Kaplan, Benjamin J. *Calvinists and Libertines: Confession and Community in Utrecht, 1578–1620.* Oxford: Clarendon, 1995.

Divided by Faith: Religious Conflict and the Practice of Toleration in Early Modern Europe. Cambridge, MA: Harvard University Press, 2007.

Reformation and the Practice of Religious Toleration: Dutch Religious History in the Early Modern Era. Leiden: Brill, 2019.

Kaptein, Herman. *De beeldenstorm.* Hilversum: Verloren, 2002.

Kennedy, James C. *A Concise History of the Netherlands.* Cambridge: Cambridge University Press, 2017.

Klink, H. *Opstand, politiek en religie bij Willem van Oranje 1559–1568: Een thematische biografie.* Heerenveen: J. J. Groen en Zoon, 1998.

Knetsch, F. R. J. "Church Ordinances and Regulations of the Dutch Synods 'Under the Cross' (1563–1566) Compared with the French (1559–1563)." *Studies in Church History* 8 (1991): 187–205.

Knevel, Paul. *Burgers in het geweer: De schutterijen in Holland, 1550–1700.* Hilversum: Verloren, 1994.

Koenigsberger, H. G. *Monarchies, States Generals and Parliaments: The Netherlands in the Fifteenth and Sixteenth Centuries.* Cambridge: Cambridge University Press, 2001.

"Prince and States-General: Charles V and the Netherlands (1500–1555)." *Transactions of the Royal Historical Society* 4 (1994): 127–151.

Kooi, Christine. *Calvinists and Catholics during Holland's Golden Age: Heretics and Idolaters*. Cambridge: Cambridge University Press, 2012.

Liberty and Religion: Church and State in Leiden's Reformation, 1572–1620. Leiden: Brill, 2000.

"The Netherlands." *Reformation and Early Modern Europe: A Guide to Research.* Ed. David M. Whitford. Kirksville: Truman State University Press, 2008, pp. 273–289.

"Religious Toleration." *Cambridge Companion to the Dutch Golden Age.* Ed. Helmer J. Helmers and Geert H. Janssen. Cambridge: Cambridge University Press, 2018, pp. 208–224.

"'A Serpent in the Bosom of Our Dear Fatherland': Reformed Reaction to the Holland Mission in the Seventeenth Century." *The Low Countries As a Crossroads of Religious Beliefs.* Ed. Arie-Jan Gelderblom et al. Leiden: Brill, 2003, pp. 165–176.

Koopmans, J. W. *De Staten van Holland en de Opstand: De ontwikkeling van hun functies en organisatie in de periode 1544–1588.* 's-Gravenhage: Hollandse Historische Reeks, 1990.

Kossmann, E. H., and A. F. Mellink, eds. *Texts concerning the Revolt of the Netherlands.* Cambridge: Cambridge University Press, 1974.

Krahn, Cornelius. *Dutch Anabaptism: Origin, Spread, Life and Thought (1450–1600.* The Hague: Martinus Nijhoff, 1968.

Lau, Franz, and Ernst Bizer. *Reformationsgeschichte Deutschlands bis 1555.* Göttingen: Vandenhoeck & Ruprecht, 1969.

Leeuwenberg, H. L. Ph. "De religie omstreeks 1559." *De Tachtigjarige Oorlog.* Ed. S. Groenveld et al. Zutphen: Walburg Pers, 2008, pp. 52–71.

Leeuwenberg, Huib van et al., eds. *De Reformatie.* Zutphen: Walburg Pers, 2017.

Lem, Anton van der. *Revolt in the Netherlands: The Eighty Years War, 1568–1648.* London: Reaktion, 2018.

Lenarduzzi, Carolina. *Katholiek in de republiek: De belevingswereld van een religieuze minderheid.* Nijmegen: Van Tilt, 2019.

Lieburg, Fred van. "Gisbertus Samuels, a Reformed Minister Sentenced by the Synod of Zeeland in 1591 for His Opinions on Predestination." *Revisiting the Synod of Dordt (1618–1619).* Ed. Aza Goudriaan and Fred van Lieburg. Leiden: Brill, 2011, pp. 1–22.

"From Pure Church to Pious Culture: The Further Reformation in the Seventeenth-Century Dutch Republic." *Later Calvinism: International Perspectives.* Ed. W. Fred Graham. Kirksville: Northeast Missouri State University Press, 1994, pp. 409–429.

Synodestad: Dordrecht 1618–1619. Amsterdam: Prometheus, 2019.

Limberger, Michael. "'No Town in the World Provides More Advantages': Economies of Agglomeration and the Golden Age of Antwerp." *Urban Achievement in Early Modern Europe: Golden Ages in Antwerp, Amsterdam and London.* Ed. Patrick O'Brien et al. Cambridge: Cambridge University Press, 2001, pp. 39–62.

Limm, Peter. *The Dutch Revolt.* London: Longman, 1989.

Lottin, Allain. *Lille: Citadelle de la Contre-Réforme? (1598–1668).* Dunkerque: Westhoek, 1984.

Lotz-Heumann, Ute. "Confessionalization." *Reformation and Early Modern Europe: A Guide to Research*. Ed. David M. Whitford. Kirksville: Truman State University Press, 2008, pp. 136–157.

Löwe, Andreas. "Richard Smyth and the Founding of the University of Douai." *Nederlands Archief for Kerkgeschiedenis* 79 (1999): 142–169.

Luria, Keith P. *Sacred Boundaries: Religious Coexistence and Conflict in Early Modern France*. Washington, DC: Catholic University Press, 2005.

MacCulloch, Diarmaid. *The Reformation: A History*. New York: Viking, 2003.

Maltby, William S. *Alba: A Biography of Fernando Alvarez de Toledo, Third Duke of Alba, 1507–1582*. Berkeley: University of California Press, 1983.

Mancusi-Ungaro, Harold. *Michelangelo: The Bruges Madonna and the Piccolomini Altar*. New Haven, CT: Yale University Press, 1971.

Manen, K. G. van. *Lutheranen in de Lage Landen: Geschiedenis van een godsdienstige minderheid 1520–2004*. Zoetermeer: Boekencentrum, 2011.

Marinus, Marie Juliette. *De Contrareformatie te Antwerpen*. Brussels: Paleis der Academiën, 1995.

"De protestanten te Antwerpen, 1585–1700." *Trajecta* 2 (1993): 327–343.

"Het verdwijnen van het protestantisme in de Zuidelijke Nederlanden." *De zeventiende eeuw* 13 (1997): 261–271.

Marnef, Guido. *Antwerp in the Age of Reformation: Underground Protestantism in a Commercial Metropolis 1550–1577*. Baltimore, MD: Johns Hopkins University Press, 1996.

"Belgian and Dutch Postwar Historiography on the Protestant and Catholic Reformation in the Netherlands." *ARG* 100 (2009): 270–292.

"Brabants calvinisme in opmars: De weg naar de calvinistische republieken te Antwerpen, Brussel en Mechelen, 1577–1580." *Bijdragen tot de geschiedenis* 70 (1987): 7–21.

"Chambers of Rhetoric and the Transmission of Religious Ideas in the Low Countries." *Cultural Exchange in Early Modern Europe*. Vol. 1. Ed. Heinz Schilling and István György Tóth. Cambridge: Cambridge University Press, 2006, pp. 274–293.

"The Dynamics of Reformed Religious Militancy: The Netherlands, 1566–1585." *Reformation, Revolt and Civil War in France and the Low Countries*. Ed. Philip Benedict et al. Amsterdam: KNAW, 1999, pp. 65–68.

"Erasmus of Rotterdam and His Influence on the Development of the Protestant Reformation in the Southern Netherlands." *Erasmus Studies* 36 (2016): 35–52.

"The Netherlands." *The Reformation World*. Ed. Andrew Pettegree. London: Routledge, 2000, pp. 344 364.

"From Prosecuted Minority to Dominance: The Changing Face of the Calvinist Church in the Cities of Flanders and Brabant (1577–1584)." *Reformed Majorities in Early Modern Europe*. Ed. Herman Selderhuis and J. Marius J. Lange van Ravenswaay. Göttingen: Vandenhoeck & Ruprecht, 2015, pp. 227–244.

Marshall, Peter. *Heretics and Believers: A History of the English Reformation*. New Haven, CT: Yale University Press, 2017.

Mellink, Albert F. *Amsterdam en de wederdopers in de zestiende eeuw.* Nijmegen: SUN, 1978.

"Preformatie en vroege reformatie." *AGN.* Vol. 6. Ed. D. P. Blok et al. Haarlem: Fibula-van Dishoeck, 1979, pp. 146–165.

De wederdopers in de noordelijke Nederlanden. Leeuwarden: Gerben Dykstra, 1981.

Meulebroucke,Aurelie van de, Violet Soen and Wim François, "Robrecht van Croÿ, bisschop van Kamerijk (1519–1556), tussen adellijke traditie, Leuvense theologie en tridentijnse kerkhervorming." *Trajecta* 27 (2018): 27–56.

Monteiro, Marit. *Geestelijke maagden: Leven tussen klooster en wereld in Noord-Nederland gedurende de zeventiende eeuw.* Hilversum: Verloren, 1994.

Monter, William. "Heresy Executions in Reformation Europe." *Tolerance and Intolerance in the European Reformation.* Ed. Ole Peter Grell and Bob Scribner. Cambridge: Cambridge University Press, 1996, pp. 48–63.

Moran, Sarah Joan. "Resurrecting the 'Spiritual Daughters': The Houtappel Chapel and Women's Patronage of Jesuit Rebuilding Programs in the Spanish Netherlands." *Women and Gender in the Early Modern Low Countries.* Ed. Sarah Joan Moran and Amanda Pipkin. Leiden: Brill, 2019, pp. 267–322.

Moreau, Gérard. *Histoire du Protestantisme à Tournai jusqu'à la veille de la Révolution des Pays-Bas.*Paris: Les Belles Lettres, 1962.

Mörke, Olaf. "'Konfessionaliserung' als politisch-soziales Prinzip? Das Verhältnis von Religion und Staatsbildung in der Republik der Vereinigten Niederlande im 16. und 17. Jahrhundert." *Tijdschrift voor Sociale Geschiedenis* 16 (1990): 31–60.

Mout, N. E. H. M. "The Family of Love (Huis der Liefde) and the Dutch Revolt." *Britain and the Netherlands.* Ed. A. C. Duke and C. A. Tamse. Den Haag: Martinus Nijhoff, 1981, pp. 76–93.

Muylaert, Silke. *Shaping the Stranger Churches: Migrants in England and the Troubles in the Netherlands, 1547–1585.* Leiden: Brill, 2021.

Nauta, D. "De reformatie in Nederland in de historiografie." *Geschiedschrijving in Nederland.* Vol. 2. Ed. P. A. M. Geurts and A. E. M. Janssen. Den Haag: Martinus Nijhoff, 1981, pp. 206–227.

"De Nationale Synode van Dordrecht (1578)." *De Nationale Synode van Dordrecht 1578.* Ed. D. Nauta and J. P. van Doren. Amsterdam: Buijten & Schipperheijn, 1978, pp. 9–52.

Nierop,Henk van. "The Beggars' Banquet: The Compromise of the Nobility and the Politics of Inversion." *European History Quarterly* 21 (1991): 419–443.

Treason in the Northern Quarter: War, Terror, and the Rule of Law in the Dutch Revolt. Princeton, NJ: Princeton University Press, 2009.

Nijenhuis, W. "Variants within Dutch Calvinism in the Sixteenth Century." *AHN* 12 (1979): 54–64.

Nissen, Peter. "De gevolgen van de Reformatie voor de kloosters in Nederland." *De middeleeuwse kloostergeschiedenis van de Nederlanden.* Vol. 1. Ed. Pauline de Nijs and Hans Kroeze. Zwolle: Waanders, 2008, pp. 179–197.

Noordzij, Aart. "Against Burgundy: The Appeal of Germany in the Duchy of Guelders." *Networks, Regions and Nations: Shaping Identities in the Low Countries*. Ed. Robert Stein and Judith Pollmann. Leiden: Brill, 2010, pp. 111–129.

Noordzij, Huib. *Handboek van de Reformatie: De Nederlandse kerkhervorming in de zestiende en zeventiende eeuw*. Kampen: Kok, 2012.

Noorlander, D. L. *Heaven's Wrath: The Protestant Reformation and the Dutch West India Company*. Ithaca, NY: Cornell University Press, 2019.

Noreña, Carlos. *Juan Luis Vives*. The Hague: Martinus Nijhoff, 1970.

Nuyttens, Michel. *Kwezeltjes dansen niet: Kwezels en devote gemeenschappen in Vlaanderen in de 17de–18de eeuw*. Leuven: Davidsfonds, 2013.

Panhuysen, Luc. *De beloofde stad: Opkomst en ondergang van het koninkrijk der wederdopers*. Amsterdam: Atlas, 2008.

Parker, Charles H. *Faith on the Margins: Catholics and Catholicism in the Dutch Republic*. Cambridge, MA: Harvard University Press, 2008.

The Reformation of Community: Social Welfare and Calvinist Charity in Holland, 1572–1620. Cambridge: Cambridge University Press, 1998.

"Reformed Protestantism." *The Cambridge Companion to the Dutch Golden Age*. Ed. Helmer J. Helmers and Geert J. Janssen. Cambridge: Cambridge University Press, 2018, pp. 189–207.

Parker, Geoffrey. *The Dutch Revolt*. London: Penguin, 1985.

The Grand Strategy of Philip II. New Haven, CT: Yale University Press, 1998.

Parsons, Ben and Bas Jongenelen, eds. *Comic Drama in the Low Countries, c. 1450–1560*. Cambridge: D. S. Brewer, 2012.

Pettegree, Andrew. "Adriaan van Haemstede: The Heretic As Historian." *Protestant History and Identity in Sixteenth-Century Europe*. Vol. 2. Ed. Bruce Gordon. Aldershot: Ashgate, 1996, pp. 59–76.

"Confessionalization in North Western Europe." *Konfessionalisierung in Ostmitteleuropa: Wirkungen des religiösen Wandels im 16. und 17: Jahrhundert in Staat, Gesellschaft und Kultur*. Ed. Joachim Balcke and Arno Strohmeyer. Stuttgart: Franz Steiner, 1999, pp. 105–120.

Emden and the Dutch Revolt: Exile and the Development of Reformed Protestantism. Oxford: Clarendon, 1992.

Foreign Protestant Communities in Sixteenth-Century London. Oxford: Clarendon, 1986.

Platt, Eric. *Britain and the Best andstwisten: The Causes, Course and Consequence of British Involvement in the Dutch Religious and Political Disputes of the Early Seventeenth Century*. Göttingen: Vandenhoeck & Ruprecht, 2015.

Plcij, Herman. *Het gilde van de Blauwe Schuit: Literatuur, volksfeest, en burgermoraal in de late middeleeuwen*. Amsterdam: Meulenhoff, 1983.

Poelhekke, J. J. "The Nameless Homeland of Erasmus." *AHN* 7 (1974): 54–87.

Pol, F. van der. *De reformatie te Kampen in de zestiende eeuw*. Kampen: Kok, 1990.

Pollmann, Judith. *Catholic Identity and the Revolt of the Netherlands 1520–1635*. Oxford: Oxford University Press, 2011.

"Countering the Reformation in France and the Netherlands: Clerical Leadership and Catholic Violence, 1560–1585." *Past & Present* 190 (2006): 83–120.

"'Hey ho, let the cup go round!' Singing for Reformation in the Sixteenth Century." *Cultural Exchange in Early Modern Europe*. Vol. 1. Ed. Heinz Schilling and István György Tóth Cambridge: Cambridge University Press, 2006, pp. 294–316.

"The Low Countries." *The European Reformations*. Ed. Alec Ryrie. Basingstoke: Palgrave Macmillan, 2006, pp. 80–101.

Religious Choice in the Dutch Republic: The Reformation of Arnoldus Buchelius. Manchester: Manchester University Press, 1999.

Post, R. R. *Kerkelijke Verhoudingen in Nederland vóór de Reformatie van 1500 tot 1580*. Utrecht: Spectrum, 1954.

Postma, Folkert. "Nieuw licht op een oude zaak: De oprichting van de nieuwe bisdommen in 1559." *TvG* 103 (1990): 10–27.

Viglius van Aytta: De jaren met Granvelle 1549–1564. Zutphen: Walburg, 2000.

Prak, Maarten. "The Politics of Intolerance: Citizenship and Religion and the Dutch Republic (Seventeenth to Eighteenth Centuries)." *Calvinism and Religious Toleration in the Dutch Golden Age*. Ed. R. Po-Chia Hsia and H. F. K. van Nierop. Cambridge: Cambridge University Press, 2002, pp. 159–175.

Prestwich, Menna, ed. *International Calvinism 1541–1715*. Oxford: Clarendon, 1985.

Put, Eddy. "Les archiducs et la réforme catholique: Champs d'action et limites politiques." *Albert and Isabella 1598–1621: Essays*. Ed. Werner Thomas and Luc Duerloo. Turnhout: Brepols, 1998, pp. 255–265.

Reusens, E. H. J., ed. *Historia beatorum martyrum Gorcumiensium a Guilielmo Estio Hesselio conscripta*. Leuven: Peeters, 1867.

Ridder-Symoens, Hilde de. "Education and Literacy in the Burgundian–Habsburg Netherlands." *Canadian Journal of Netherlandic Studies* 16 (1995): 16–21.

Roberts, Penny. "France." *The European Reformations*. Ed. Alec Ryrie. Basingstoke: Palgrave, 2006, pp. 102–119.

Roegiers, J. "Awkward Neighbours: The Leuven Faculty of Theology and the Jesuit College (1542–1773)." *The Jesuits of the Low Countries: Identity and Impact (1540–1773)*. Ed. Rob Faesen and Leo Kenis. Leuven: Peeters, 2012, pp. 153–176.

Roobol, Marianne. *Disputation by Decree: The Public Disputations between Reformed Ministers and Dirck Volckertzoon Coornhert As Instruments of Religious Policy during the Dutch Revolt (1577–1583)*. Leiden: Brill, 2010.

Rooden, Peter van. "Jews and Religious Toleration in the Dutch Republic." *Calvinism and Religious Toleration in the Dutch Golden Age*. Ed. R. Po-Chia Hsia and Henk van Nierop. Cambridge: Cambridge University Press, 2002, pp. 132–147.

Religieuze Regimes: Over godsdienst en maatschappij in Nederland, 1570–1990. Amsterdam: Bert Bakker, 1996.

Roosbroeck, R. van. *Het Wonderjaar te Antwerpen (1555–1567)*. Antwerp: De Sikkel, 1930.

Rooze-Stouthamer, C. *Hervorming in Zeeland (ca. 1520–1572)*. Goes: De Koperen Tuin, 1996.

De opmaat tot de Opstand: Zeeland en het centrale gezag (1566–1572). Hilversum: Verloren, 2009.

Rowen, Herbert, ed. *The Low Countries in Early Modern Times*. New York: Walker, 1972.

Rubin, Miri. *Corpus Christi: The Eucharist in Late Medieval Culture*. Cambridge: Cambridge University Press, 1991.

Rummel, Erika. "Voices of Reform from Hus to Erasmus." *Handbook of European History, 1400–1600*. Vol. 2. Ed. Thomas A. Brady et al. Leiden: Brill, 1994, pp. 61–86.

Schepper, Hugo de. *"Belgium Nostrum": 1500–1650: Over integratie en desintegratie van het Nederland*. Antwerp: De Orde van den Prince, 1998.

"The Burgundian–Habsburg Netherlands." *Handbook of European History 1400–1600*. Vol. 1. Ed. Thomas A. Brady et al. Leiden: Brill, 1994, pp. 499–533.

"De mentale rekonversie van de Zuidnederlandse hoge adel naar de Pacifikatie van Gent." *TvG* 89 (1976): 420–428.

Schilling, Heinz. "Confessional Europe." *Handbook of European History, 1400–1600*. Vol. 2. Ed. Thomas A. Brady Jr. et al. Leiden: Brill, 1995, pp. 641–675.

Niederländishe Exulanten im 16: Jahrhundert. Gütersloh: Mohn, 1972.

"The Second Reformation: Problems and Issues." *Religion, Political Culture and the Emergence of Early Modern Society*. Ed. Heinz Schilling. Leiden: Brill, 1992, pp. 247–301.

Secretan, Catherine. *Les privileges, berceau de la liberté: La révolte des Pays-Bas*. Paris: Vrin, 1990.

Selderhuis, H. J., ed. *Handboek Nederlandse kerkgeschiedenis*. Kampen: Kok, 2006.

Sierhuis, Freya. *The Literature of the Arminian Controversy: Religion, Politics and the Stage in the Dutch Republic*. Oxford: Oxford University Press, 2016.

Simon, Nicholas. "The Council of Trent and Its Impact on Philip II's Legislation in the Habsburg Netherlands (1580–98)." *Church, Censorship and Reform in the Early Modern Habsburg Netherlands*. Ed. Violet Soen et al. Turnhout: Brepols, 2017, pp. 201–216.

Simons, Walter. *Cities of Ladies: Beguine Communities in the Medieval Low Countries, 1200–1565*. Philadelphia: University of Pennsylvania Press, 2001.

Sinnema, Donald. "The Canons of Dordt: From Judgment on Arminianism to Confessional Standard." *Revisiting the Synod of Dordt (1618–1619)*. Ed. Aza Goudriaan and Fred van Lieburg. Leiden: Brill, 2011, pp. 313–333.

Slatius, Henricus. *De Gepredestineerde Dief, ofte Een't Samensprekinghe/gehouden tusschen een Predicant der Calvinusgesinde ende een Dief, die verwesen was om te sterven*. N.p., 1619.

Smit, J. W. "The Present Position of Studies regarding the Revolt of the Netherlands." *Geschiedschrijving in Nederland*. Ed. P. A. M. Geurts and A. E. M. Janssen. The Hague: Martinus Nijhoff, 1981, pp. 42–54.

Soen, Violet. "The *Beeldenstorm* and the Spanish Habsburg Response." *BMGN-Low Countries Historical Review* 131 (2016): 99–120.

"Between Dissent and Peacemaking: The Dutch Nobility on the Eve of the Revolt (1564–1567)." *Revue Belge de Philologie et d'Histoire* 86 (2008): 735–758.

"De reconciliatie van 'ketters' in de zestiende-eeuws Nederlanden." *Trajecta* 14 (2005): 337–362.

"Reconquista and Reconciliation in the Dutch Revolt: The Campaign of Governor-General Alexander Farnese (1578–1592)." *Journal of Early Modern History* 16 (2012): 1–22.

"Which Religious History for the (Two) Early Modern Netherlands before 1648?" *Revue d'Histoire Ecclésiastique* 112 (2017): 758–788.

Soen, Violet, and Laura Hollevoet. "Le 'Borromée' des anciens Pays-bas? Maximilien de Berghes, archevêque de Cambrai et l'application du Concile de Trente (1564–1567)." *Revue du Nord* 99 (2017): 41–65.

Soen, Violet, Dries Vanysacker and Wim François. "Church, Censorship and Reform: Questions and Answers regarding the Early Modern Habsburg Netherlands." *Church, Censorship and Reform in the Early Modern Habsburg Netherlands.* Ed. Violet Soen et al. Turnhout: Brepols, 2017, pp. 1–9.

Soen, Violet, Dries Vanysacker, Wim François and Paul Knevel, "Slingerbewegingen: Controverse en geschiedschrijving over religie in de zestiende-eeuwse Nederlanden." *Religie, hervorming en controverse in de zestiende-eeuwse Nederlanden.* Ed. Violet Soen and Paul Knevel. Hertogenrath: Shaker, 2012, pp. 3–19.

Soetaert, Alexander. *De katholieke drukpers in de kerkprovincie Kamerijk: Contact, mobiliteit en transfers in een grensgebied.* Leuven: Peeters, 2019.

Soly, H., and A. K. L. Thys. "Nijverheid in de Zuidelijke Nederlanden." *Algemene Geschiedenis der Nederlanden.* Vol. 6. Ed. D. P. Blok et al. Haarlem: Fibula-van Dishoeck, 1979, pp. 27–57.

Spaans, Joke. *Haarlem na de Reformatie: Stedelijke cultuur en kerkelijk leven.* 's-Gravenhage: Hollandse Historische Reeks, 1989.

De "Levens der Maechden": Het verhaal van een religieuze vrouwengemeenschap in de eerste helft van de zeventiende eeuw. Hilversum: Verloren, 2012.

"Reform in the Low Countries." *A Companion to the Reformation World.* Ed. R. Po-chia Hsia. Oxford: Blackwell, 2004, pp. 118–134.

"Religious Policies in the Seventeenth-Century Dutch Republic." *Calvinism and Religious Toleration in the Dutch Golden Age.* Ed. R. Po-Chia Hsia and Henk van Nierop. Cambridge: Cambridge University Press, 2002, pp. 77–85

Spicer, Andrew. "After Iconoclasm: Reconciliation and Resacralization in the Southern Netherlands, ca. 1566–1585." *SCJ* 44 (2013): 411–433.

Spiertz, M. G. "Succes en falen van de katholieke reformatie." *Ketters en papen onder Filips II.* Ed. P. Dirkse. N.p.: Staatsuitgeverij, 1986.

Spohnholz, Jesse. "Confessional Coexistence in the Early Modern Netherlands." *A Companion to Multiconfessionalism in the Early Modern World.* Ed. Thomas Max Safley. Leiden: Brill, 2011, pp. 47–73.

The Convent of Wesel: The Event That Never Was and the Invention of Tradition. Cambridge: Cambridge University Press, 2017.

The Tactics of Toleration: A Refugee Community in the Age of Religious Wars. Newark: University of Delaware Press, 2011.

Spohnholz, Jesse, and Mirjam G. K. van Veen. "The Disputed Origins of Dutch Calvinism: Religious Refugees in the Historiography of the Dutch Reformation." *Church History* 86 (2017): 398–426.

Spruyt, Bart Jan. *Cornelius Henrici Hoen (Honius) and His Epistle on the Eucharist (1525): Medieval Heresy, Erasmian Humanism, and Reform in the Early Sixteenth-Century Low Countries.* Leiden: Brill, 2006.

Steen, Jasper van der. *Memory Wars in the Low Countries, 1550–1700.* Leiden: Brill, 2015.

Stein, Robert. "Seventeen: The Multiplicity of a Unity in the Low Countries." *The Ideology of Burgundy: The Promotion of National Consciousness.* Ed. D'Arcy Jonathan Dacre Boulton and Jan Veenstra. Leiden: Brill, 2006, pp. 223–285.

Sterk, J. *Philips van Bourgondië (1465 1524), bisschop van Utrecht, als protagonist van de Renaissance: Zijn leven en maecenaat.* Zutphen: Walburg, 1980.

Strauss, Gerald. "Ideas of *Reformatio* and *Renovatio* from the Middle Ages to the Reformation." *Handbook of European History 1400–1600.* Vol. 2. Ed. Thomas A. Brady et al. Leiden: Brill, 1994, pp. 1–11.

Strietman, Elsa. "The Low Countries." *The Renaissance in National Context.* Ed. Roy Porter and Mikuláš Teich. Cambridge: Cambridge University Press, 1992, pp. 68–91.

Swart, K. W. *William of Orange and the Revolt of the Netherlands, 1572–84.* Aldershot: Ashgate, 2003.

Swetschinski, Daniel M. *Reluctant Cosmopolitans: The Portuguese Jews of Seventeenth- Century Amsterdam.* London: Littman Library, 2000.

Tappert, Theodore G., ed. *Luther: Letters of Spiritual Counsel.* Philadelphia: Westminster Press, 1960.

Thelen, Emily S. *The Seven Sorrows Confraternity of Brussels: Drama, Ceremony, and Art Patronage (16th–17th Centuries).* Turnhout: Brepols, 2015.

Thijs, Alfons K. L. *Van Geuzenstad tot katholieke bolwerk: Maatschapelijke betekenis van der Kerk in contrareformatorisch Antwerpen.* Turnhout: Brepols, 1990.

Thøfner, Margit. *A Common Art: Urban Ceremonial in Antwerp and Brussels during and after the Dutch Revolt.* Zwolle: Waanders, 2007.

Thomas, Werner. "The Treaty of London, the Twelve Years Truce and Religious Toleration in Spain and the Netherlands." *The Twelve Years Truce (1609): Peace, Truce War and Law in the Low Countries at the Run of the 17th Century.* Ed. Randall Lesaffer. Leiden: Brill Nijhoff, 2014, pp. 277–297.

Tollebeek, Jo. "Enthousiasme en evidentie: De negentiende-eeuwse Belgisch-nationale geschiedschrijving." *De ijkmeesters: Opstellen over de geschiedschrijving in Nederland en België.* Ed. Jo Tollebeek. Amsterdam: Bert Bakker, 1994, pp. 57–74.

Tracy, James D. "Elements of Anticlerical Sentiment in the Province of Holland under Charles V." *Anticlericalism in Late Medieval and Early Modern Europe.* Ed. Peter Dykema and Heiko Oberman. Leiden: Brill, 1993, pp. 257–269.

Erasmus of the Low Countries. Berkeley: University of California Press, 1996.

"Heresy Law and Centralization under Mary of Hungary: Conflict between the Council of Holland and the Central Government over the Enforcement of Charles V's Placards." *Archiv für Reformationsgeschichte* 73 (1982): 284–308.

Holland under Habsburg Rule, 1506–1566: The Formation of a Body Politic. Berkeley: University of California Press, 1990.

The Low Countries in the Sixteenth Century: Erasmus, Religion and Politics, Trade and Finance. Aldershot: Ashgate, 2005.

Trapman, J. "'Erasmianism' in the Early Reformation in the Netherlands." *Erasmianism: Idea and Reality.* Ed. M. E. H. N. Mout et al. Amsterdam: KNAW, 1997, pp. 169–176.

"Le role des 'sacramentaires' des origines de la Réforme jusqu'en 1530 aux Pays-Bas." *NAKG* 61 (1983): 1–24.

. ed. *De Summa der godliker scrifturen.* Leiden: Elve/Labor Vincit, 1978.

Trio, Paul. *Volksreligie als spiegel van een stedelijke samenleving: De broederschappen te Gent in de late middeleeuwen.* Leuven: Universitaire Pers, 1993.

Ubachs, P. J. H. "De Nederlandse religievrede van 1578." *NAKG* 77 (1997): 41–61.

Vanysacker, Dries. "The Church Province of Malines and Its Official Printings (1559/1607–13): A State of the Art on the Implementation of the Council of Trent in the Netherlands." *Church, Censorship and Reform in the Early Modern Habsburg Netherlands.* Ed. Violet Soen et al. Turnhout: Brepols, 2017, pp. 145–165.

Hekserij in Brugge: De magische leefwereld van een stadsbevolking, 16de–17de eeuw. Brugge: Genootschap voor Geschiedenis, 1988.

Veen, Mirjam van. "Dirck Volckertz Coornhert: Exile and Religious Coexistence." *Exile and Religious Identity.* Ed. Jesse Spohnholz and Gary K. Waite. London: Pickering & Chatto, 2014, pp. 67–80.

Een nieuwe tijd, een nieuwe kerk: De opkomst van het "calvinisme" in de Lage Landen. Zoetermeer: Meinema, 2009.

"Tegen 'papery en slaverny': Gereformeerde geschiedschrijvers over de Nederlandse reformatie." *Pietas Reformata: Religieuze vernieuwing onder gereformeerden in de vroegmoderne tijd.* Ed. J. van de Kamp et al. Zoetermeer: Boekencentrum, 2015, pp. 37–46.

Vercauteren, Fernand. *Cent ans d'histoire nationale en Belgique.* Brussels: La Renaissance du Livre, 1959.

Vercruysse, Jos E. "De Antwerpse augustijnen en de lutherse Reformatie, 1513–1523." *Trajecta* 16 (2003): 193–216.

Verheyden, A. L. E. *Anabaptism in Flanders, 1530–1630: A Century of Struggle.* Scottsdale: Herald Press, 1961.

Le Conseil des Troubles. Florennes: Editions le Phare, 1981.

Le Martyrologe Protestant des Pays-Bas du Sud au XVIme Siècle. Brussels: Librairie des eclaireurs unionistes, 1960.

Verhoeven, G. *Devotie en negotie: Delft als bedevaartplaats in de late middeleeuwen.* Amsterdam: VU Uitgeverij, 1992.

Vermeir, René. "How Spanish Were the Spanish Netherlands?" *Dutch Crossing* 36 (2012): 3–18.

Verstegan, Richard. *Théâtre des Cruautés des hérétiques de notre temps*. Ed. Frank Lestringant. Paris: Editions Chandeigne, 1995.

Verweij, Michiel. *Adrianus VI (1459–1523): De tragische paus uit de Nederlanden*. Antwerp: Garant, 2011.

Visser, C. Ch. G. *Luther's Geschriften in de Nederlanden tot 1546*. Assen: Van Gorcum, 1969.

Visser, Piet. "Mennonites and Doopsgezinden in the Netherlands, 1535–1700." *A Companion to Anabaptism and Spiritualism, 1521–1700*. Ed. John D. Roth and James L. Stayer. Leiden: Brill, 2007, pp. 299–345.

Waardt, Hans de. "I Beg Your Pardon: I Am a Heretic! A Countryside Conventicle in Holland in the 1520s." *Religious Minorities and Cultural Diversity in the Dutch Republic*. Ed. Michael Driedger and Gary Waite. Leiden: Brill, 2015, pp. 329–339.

Waite, Gary K. *David Joris and Dutch Anabaptism 1524–1543*. Waterloo: Wilfred Laurier University Press, 1990.

"A Reappraisal of the Contributions of Anabaptists to the Religious Culture and Intellectual Climate of the Dutch Republic." *Religious Minorities and Cultural Diversity in the Dutch Republic*. Ed. Michael Driedger and Gary Waite. Leiden: Brill, 2015, pp. 6–28.

Reformers on Stage: Popular Drama and Religious Propaganda in the Low Countries of Charles V, 1515–1556. Toronto: University of Toronto Press, 2000.

Walzer, Michael. *On Toleration*. New Haven, CT: Yale University Press, 1997.

Wee, H. van der. "Handel in de Zuidelijke Nederlanden." *Algemene Geschiedenis der Nederlanden*. Vol. 6. Ed. D. P. Blok et al. Haarlem: Fibula-van Dishoeck, 1979, pp. 75–97.

Weiler, A. G. "Recent Historiography on the Modern Devotion: Some Debated Questions." *AGKKN* 26 (1984): 161–179.

Wenger, John Christian, ed. *The Complete Writings of Menno Simons c. 1496–1561*. Scottdale, PA: Herald Press, 1956.

Wiele, Johan van der. "De inquisitierechtbank van Pieter Titelmans in de zestiende eeuw in Vlaanderen." *BMGN-Low Countries Historical Review* 97 (1982): 19–63.

Williams, George Hunston. *The Radical Reformation*. 3rd ed. Kirksville: Truman State University Press, 2000.

Woltjer, J. J. "Het beeld vergruisd?" *Holland* 4 (1972): 131–142.

"Dutch Privileges, Real and Imaginary." *Britain and the Netherlands: Some Political Mythologies*. Ed. J. S. Bromley and E. H. Kossmann. The Hague: Martinus Nijhoff, 1975, pp. 19–35.

Friesland in Hervormingstijd. Leiden: Universitaire Pers, 1962.

Op weg naar tachtig jaar oorlog. Het verhaal van de eeuw waarin ons land ontstond. Amsterdam: Balans, 2011.

Woltjer, J. J., and M. E. H. N. Mout. "Settlements: The Netherlands." *Handbook of European History 1400–1600*. Vol. 2. Ed. Thomas A. Brady Jr. et al. Grand Rapids, MI: Eerdmans, 1995, pp. 385–415.

Wyhe, Cordula van. "Court and Convent: The Infanta Isabella and Her Franciscan Confessor Andrés de Soto." *SCJ* 35 (2004): 411–445.

Zeeden, Ernst Walter. "Grundlage und Wege der Konfessionsbildung im Zeitalter der Glaubenskämpfe." *Historische Zeitschrift* 185 (1958): 249–299.

Zijlstra, S. "Anabaptism and Tolerance: Possibilities and Limitations." *Calvinism and Religious Toleration in the Dutch Golden Age*. Ed. R. Po-Chia Hsia and Henk van Nierop. Cambridge: Cambridge University Press, 2002, pp. 112–131.

Om de ware gemeente en de oude gronden: Geschiedenis van de dopersen in de Nederlanden 1531–1675. Hilversum: Verloren, 2000.

Index

Lightning Source UK Ltd.
Milton Keynes UK
UKHW050656171022
410399UK00021B/98

9 781316 513521